To Carmella and Benjamin Quinones, my parents

Published in the United States by Potter Craft, an imprint of the Crown
Publishing Group, a division of Random House, Inc., New York.
www.crownpublishing.com
www.pottercraft.com

POTTER CRAFT and colophon is a registered trademark
of Random House, Inc.

Library of Congress Cataloging-in-Publication Data
Epstein, Nicky.
  Knitting block by block / Nicky Epstein. -- 1st ed.
    p. cm.
  Includes bibliographical references and index.
  ISBN 978-0-307-58652-0
  1. Knitting--Patterns. I. Title.
  TT825.E49 2010
  746.43'2--dc22
                      2010022303
Printed in China

Design by Chi Ling Moy
Fashion photography by Rose Callahan
Swatch photography by Heather Weston
Technical illlustrations by Jeannie Chin
Colorwork charts by Frances Soohoo
Knitting Technique illustrations by Kara Gott Warner
Crochet Technique illustrations by Lana Le
Embroidery illustrations by Chi Ling Moy

10 9 8 7 6 5 4 3 2 1

First Edition

table of contents

introduction

*E*gyptians; Eskimos; Mayans; Aztecs—for centuries civilizations have used blocks to build magnificent and functional structures, from igloos to pyramids. I've always been fascinated by how people created bricks, tiles, and shingles, and cut marble, granite and concrete into blocks to make so many different and wonderful shapes and designs.

In this book we'll use yarn for our blocks, and I'll teach you not only how to create blocks but also how to magically transform them into beautiful afghans, bags, sweaters, and more. You'll learn a variety of knitting techniques to form these blocks, discover how to combine and construct them in new and unusual ways that go beyond tradition. You'll be inspired to push your creativity.

Knitting with blocks is a joy. Because blocks are small, they make it easier to learn a technique that you may not have tried before. They are also "travel friendly"—you don't have to carry an entire garment with you. They're fantastic to work on with others; lots of friends can knit different sections that can be used to build a wonderful piece for charity or a special loved one.

By using mix-and-match blocks together with the design diagrams, you will see how to assemble these squares and turn them into exciting pieces, without using increases or decreases, but letting the positioning of the blocks do all the shaping. It's easy, exciting, unique, and fun! I had so much fun designing this way, and I'm happy to share the process and make block designing an option for all knitters.

My father, Benjamin, was a mason for awhile and created many impressive structures. It was fascinating to see stone and bricks become fireplaces and homes, so it may seem natural that I love creating projects by knitting block by block, and watching the blocks blossom into new designs. Become a knitting "blockhead" and join the block party!

Nicky Epstein

gauge

The yarn you choose to use plays an important part in the size of your block and finished piece. Here you see the same basketweave pattern, but by using a variety of yarn weights and corresponding needles, the blocks all vary in sizes. When you're making or designing a piece, use this to your advantage to get the size, fit, and drape that you want. Note that texture is also important in the look of your design. (Clockwise from top left) Lace, Baby, DK, Bulky, Worsted.

designing with blocks

Designing with blocks is easy, fun, instructive, and exciting for all knitters. You can easily design your own "blockbusters!"

With this book you have 150 blocks at your fingertips, along with diagrams to design with. You can simply make printed copies of the blocks of your choice, cut them out, and arrange them in the block layout diagrams. See page 230 for methods you can use to join your blocks, and page 228 for special edgings you can use.

The size of your piece will depend upon the size of your blocks. Choose the yarn you want to use and work a gauge swatch. This will allow you to determine the size of your block. Example: If your gauge is 5 stitches per 1" (2.5cm) and you want to use 10" (25cm) blocks, you would cast on 50 stitches.

Here are a few more examples:

10" blocks
at 4 stitches per 1" (2.5cm) cast on 40 stitches.
at 3 stitches per 1" (2.5cm) cast on 30 stitches.

6" blocks
at 6 stitches per 1" (2.5cm) cast on 36 stitches.
at 8 stitches per 1" (2.5cm) cast on 48 stitches.

Rows are easily determined by working the pattern until your length is the same as the width of your stitches.

Many of the motifs I have given you throughout the book may be placed wherever on the block you wish.

As a knitter and designer, writing this book has been beyond fun for me and I'm so excited to share block knitting with my fellow knitters. You'll love the visual and tactile experience of actually moving the blocks around in different configurations to design your piece.

Choose the design shape you want—to make an afghan, bag, sweater, or scarf, for example—and either select one block to repeat, or several blocks to mix and match. The design combinations are endless! Designing with blocks is a rewarding, creative experience that will help you become more confident in designing your own projects, and add to your wardrobe or gift giving.

Happy block knitting and designing!

gallery of block projects

MÉLANGE COUNTERPANE AFGHAN
page 208

WINTER SOLSTICE
HOODED SCARF
page 210

SCARFOSAURUS
page 211

FAIRY LEAVES SHRUG DUO
page 212

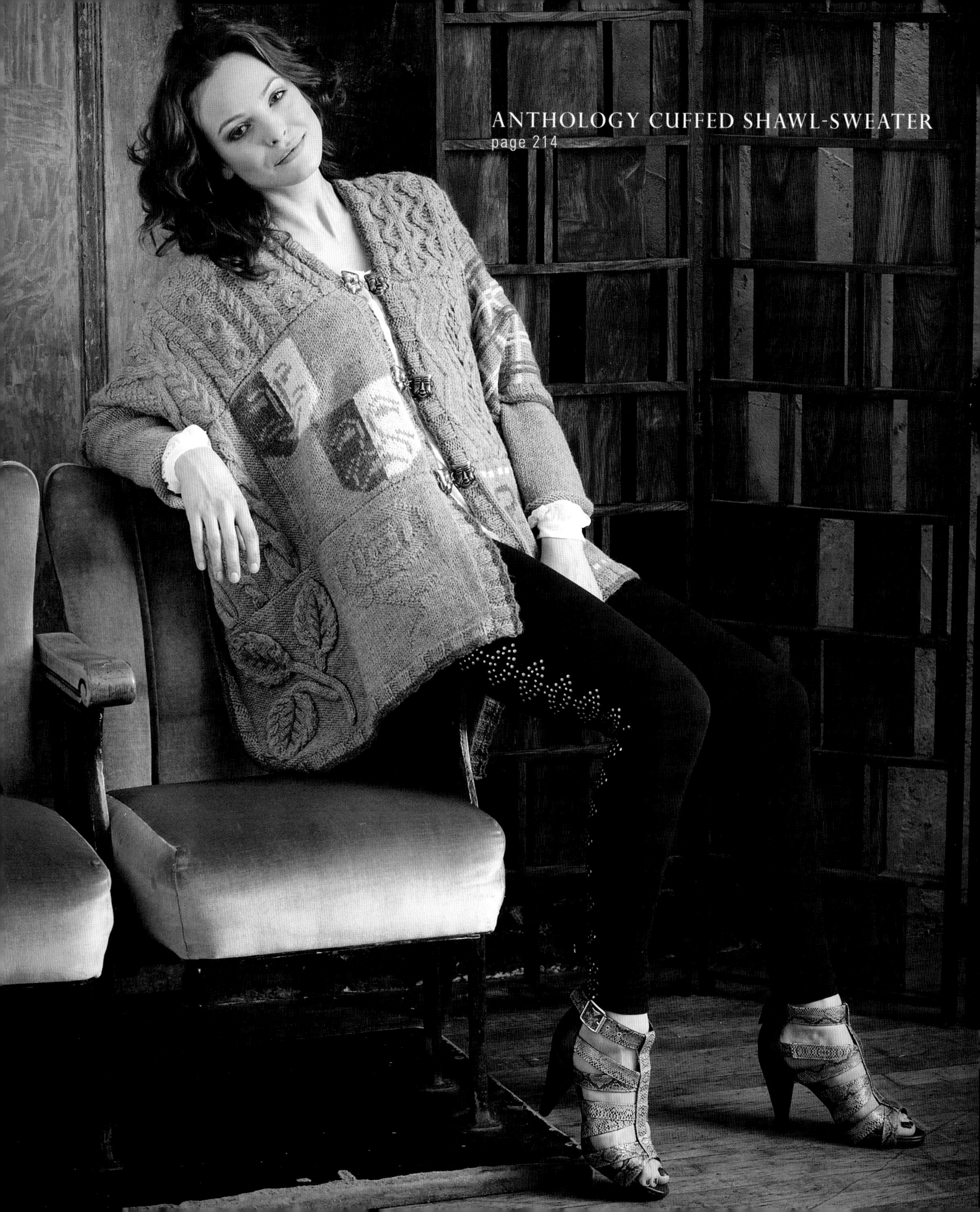

ANTHOLOGY CUFFED SHAWL-SWEATER
page 214

ACADEMIC AFGHAN
page 216

TRES CHIC PULLOVER
page 218

EMPIRE CROPPED VEST

page 219

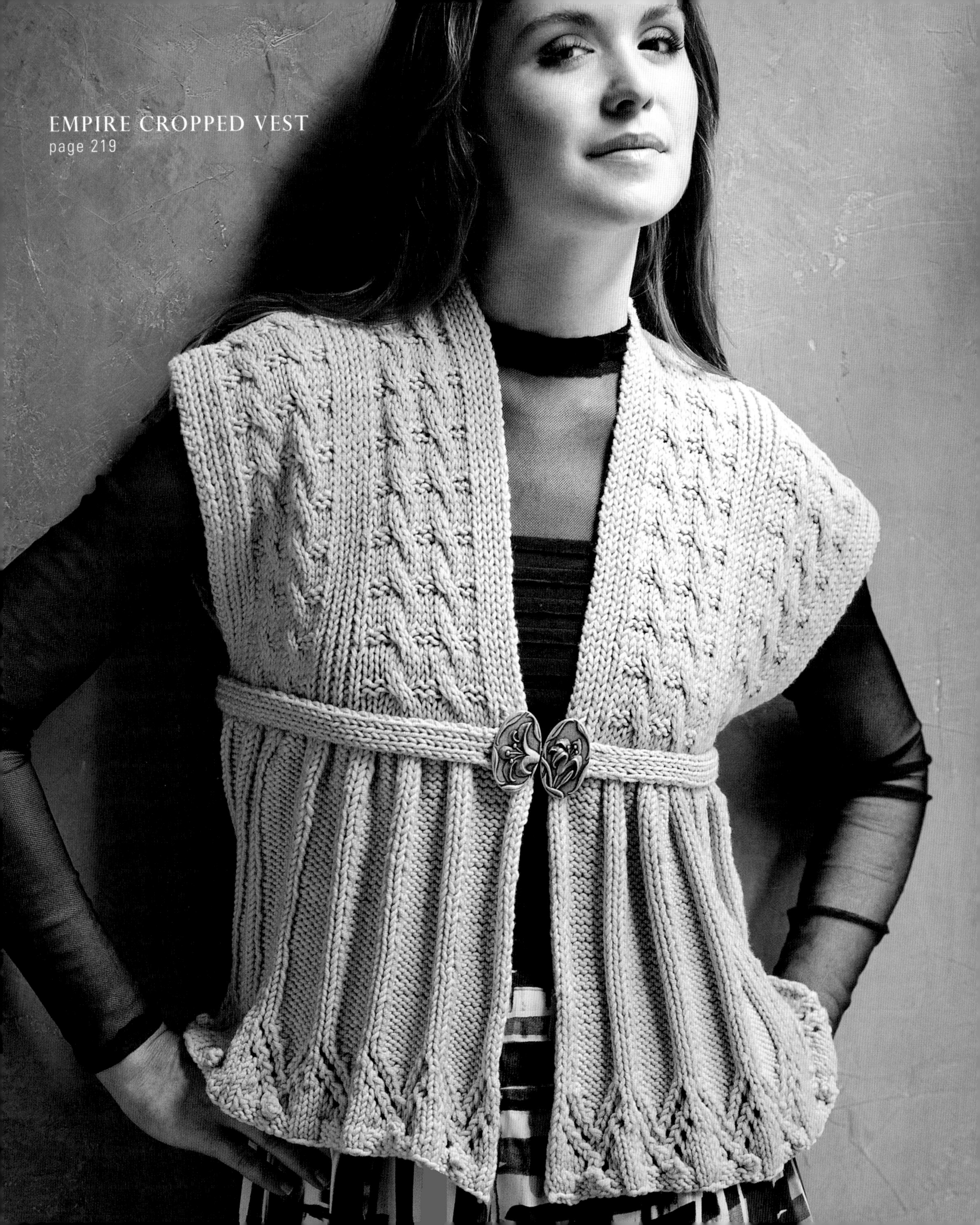

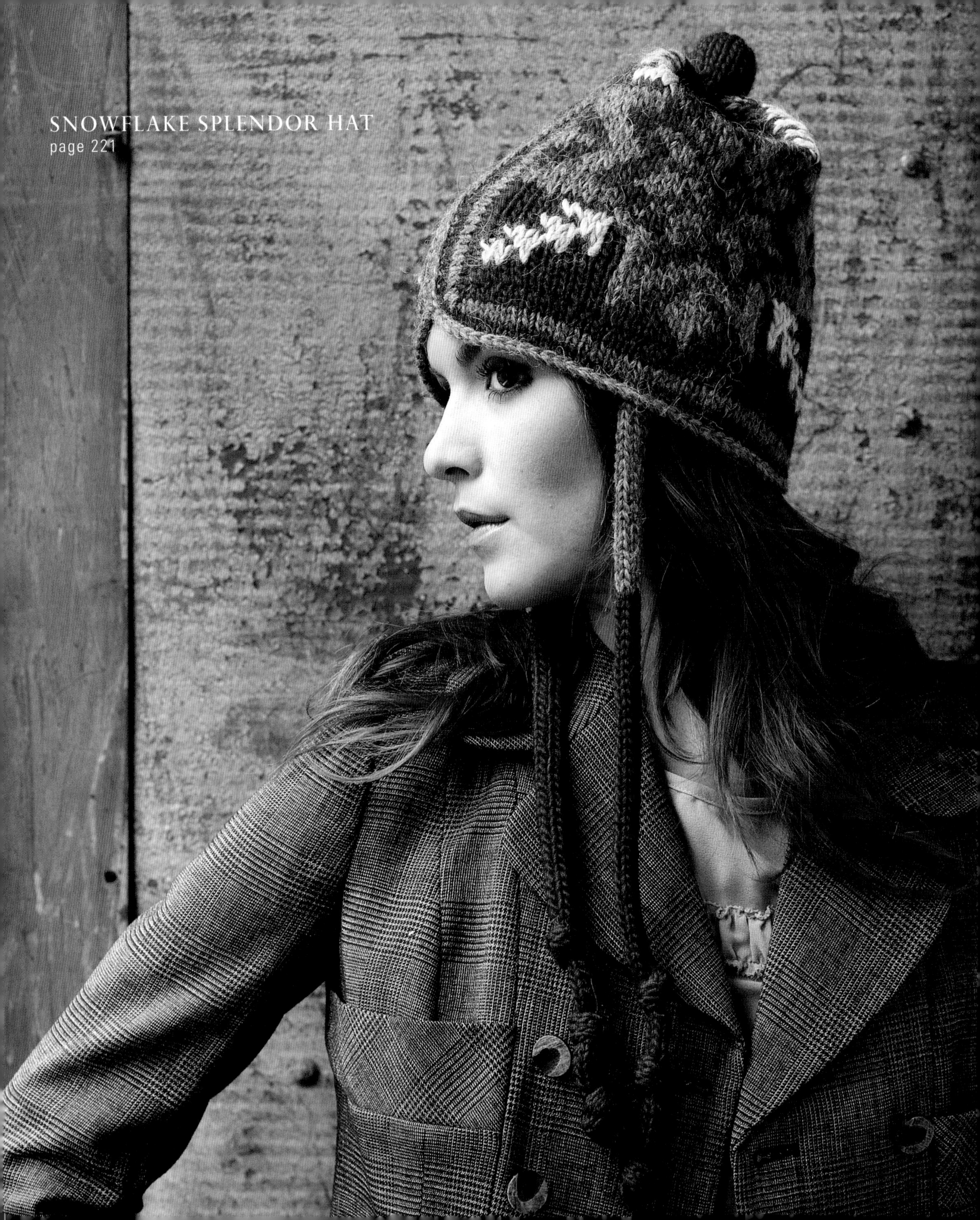

SNOWFLAKE SPLENDOR HAT
page 221

chapter 1

BASIC BUILDING BLOCKS

This chapter is the key to block knitting design. Included are the basic blocks and frames that are the essential ingredients of any design.

The basic blocks shown here can serve to accent the more intricate blocks in a design, as on a kitchen backsplash, in which plain tiles surround more decorative tiles and offset them nicely. The Academic Afghan (see page 216) showcases the use of plain blocks separating more intricate blocks.

With a beautiful painting, the frame can play an important part in the overall effect; and in knitting, the frame is an edging. As a preview of the full-fledged edgings that will appear later (see page 228), I've used a variety of simple edgings within some of the blocks, which makes them look like ornamental photo frames.

The groundwork and building blocks have been laid, and it's just the beginning of the knitting fun to come.

seed stitch

page 26

stockinette stitch

page 26

garter stitch

page 26

4x4 pulled rib

page 27

basketweave

page 27

horizontal stripes

page 27

2-color triangle

page 28

points frame

page 29

cameo frame

page 28

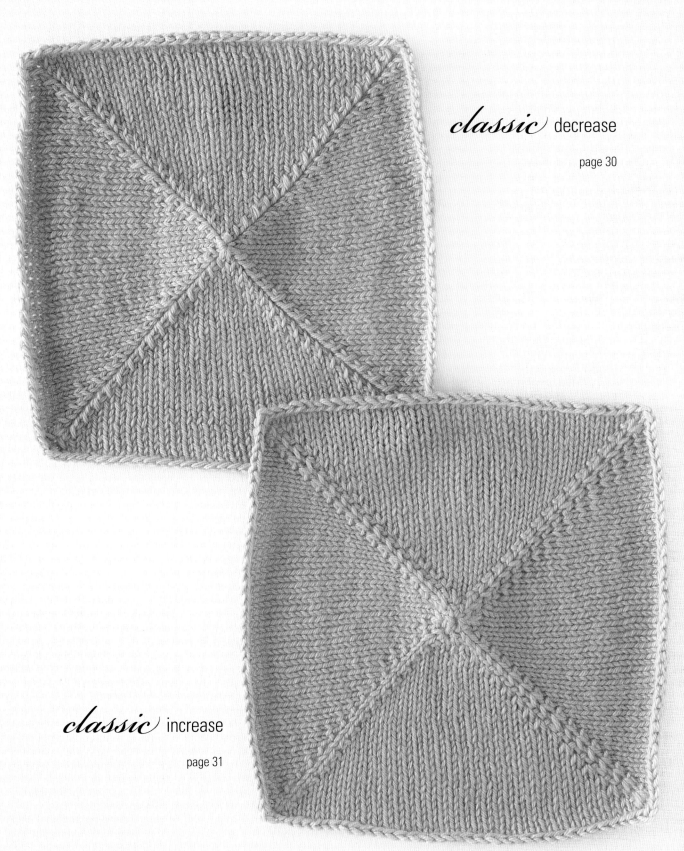

classic decrease

page 30

classic increase

page 31

classic swirl

page 31

classic diamond

page 32

bobble frame

page 33

celtic knot frame

page 34

scallop lace frame

page 34

SEED STITCH page 18

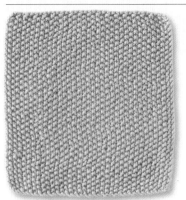

Cast on 41 stitches.
Row 1 K1, *p1, k1; repeat from * to end.
Rep row 1 always having a knit stitch over a purl stitch and a purl stitch over a knit stitch.
Work in Seed st until block length measures same as width.
Bind off.

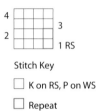

Stitch Key

☐ K on RS, P on WS

▣ P on RS, K on WS

☐ Repeat

STOCKINETTE STITCH page 18

Cast on 45 stitches.
Work in St st (knit on RS, purl on WS) until block length measures same as width.
Bind off.

Stitch Key

☐ K on RS, P on WS

☐ Repeat

GARTER STITCH page 18

Cast on 45 stitches.
Work in Garter st (knit every row) until block length measures same as width.
Bind off.

Stitch Key

☐ K on RS

▣ K on WS

☐ Repeat

4X4 PULLED RIB page 19

Cast on 44 stitches.
Row 1 (RS) K4, *p4, k4; repeat from * to end.
Row 2 (WS) P4, *k4, p4; repeat from * to end.
Repeat rows 1 and 2 until block length measures same as width when ribbing is blocked out.
Bind off.

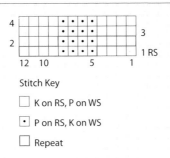

Stitch Key

☐ K on RS, P on WS

⊡ P on RS, K on WS

☐ Repeat

BASKETWEAVE page 19

BASKETWEAVE PATTERN

Rows 1, 3 and 5 (RS) K5, *p5, k5; repeat from * to end.
Rows 2 and 4 P5, *k5, p5; repeat from * to end.
Rows 6, 8 and 10 K5, *p5, k5; repeat from * to end.
Rows 7 and 9 P5, *k5, p5; repeat from * to end.
Repeat rows 1–10 for pattern.

Cast on 45 stitches. Work in Basketweave pattern for 55 rows.
Bind off.

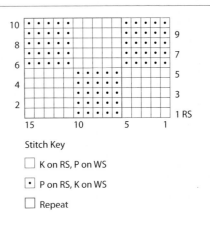

Stitch Key

☐ K on RS, P on WS

⊡ P on RS, K on WS

☐ Repeat

HORIZONTAL STRIPES page 20

Colors MC and CC

With MC, cast on 45 stitches.
Work in St st (knit on RS, purl on WS) alternating 4 rows MC and 4 rows CC for 60 rows, ending with 4 rows MC.
Bind off.

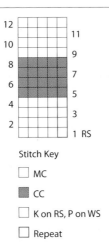

Stitch Key

☐ MC

▨ CC

☐ K on RS, P on WS

☐ Repeat

2-COLOR TRIANGLE page 20

Colors MC and CC

With MC, cast on 3 stitches.

INCREASE ROWS

Row 1 K1, m1, k1, m1, k1 (5 stitches).
Row 2 and all even-numbered rows Knit.
Row 3 K1, m1, k to last stitch, m1, k1.
Repeat last 2 rows until there are 57 stitches.

DECREASE ROWS

Change to CC.
Row 1 K1, k2tog, k to last 3 stitches, ssk, k1.
Row 2 and all even-numbered rows Knit.
Repeat last 2 rows until 3 stitches remain.
SK2P.
Fasten off remaining stitch.

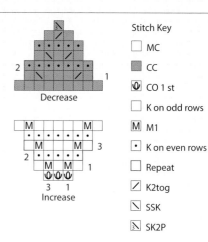

Decrease

Increase

Stitch Key

☐ MC
▨ CC
Ⓥ CO 1 st
☐ K on odd rows
Ⓜ M1
• K on even rows
☐ Repeat
╱ K2tog
╲ SSK
⋌ SK2P

CAMEO FRAME page 21

Colors A, B and C

With A, cast on 45 stitches.
Work in St st (knit on RS, purl on WS) until block
length measures same as width.
Bind off.

FRAME

With B, cast on 167 stitches (a multiple of 11
stitches plus 2 more).
Row 1 (WS) Purl.
Row 2 K2, *k1 and slip the stitch back to the left-
hand needle, with the right-hand needle, lift the
next 8 stitches, one at a time, over this stitch and
off the needle, yo twice, k the first stitch again, k2;
repeat from * to end.
Row 3 K1, *p2tog, drop the first yo of the previous
row, (k1, p1, k1, p1) in the second yo (4 stitches),
p1; repeat from *, end k1.
Change to C.
Rows 4 and 5 Work in Garter stitch.
Bind off.

Sew frame to block following photo.

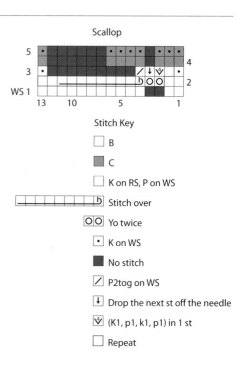

Scallop

Stitch Key

☐ B
▨ C
☐ K on RS, P on WS
ᑌ Stitch over
OO Yo twice
• K on WS
■ No stitch
╱ P2tog on WS
↓ Drop the next st off the needle
Ⅴ (K1, p1, k1, p1) in 1 st
☐ Repeat

POINTS FRAME page 21

Colors A, B and C

With A, cast on 45 stitches.
Work in St st (knit on RS, purl on WS) until block
length measures same as width.
Bind off.

FRAME

Points (make 7)
With B, cast on 2 stitches.
Row 1 (RS) Knit.
Row 2 Yo, k to end—1 stitch increased.
Repeat row 2 until there are 11 stitches.
Cut yarn and leave stitches on the needle.
On the same needle, cast on 2 stitches and make
another point.

Continue in this manner until 7 points have been
made. Do not cut yarn after last point.

To join points, using B, knit across stitches of all 7
points on needle (77 stitches).
Knit 1 row.
Change to C. Work 4 rows in Garter st.
Bind off.

Sew frame to block.

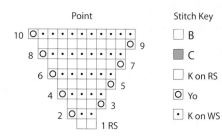

Point

Stitch Key

☐ B
▨ C
☐ K on RS
☒ Yo
· K on WS

Joining

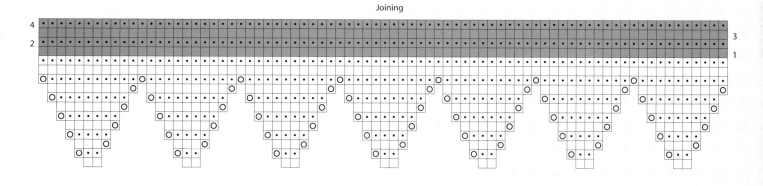

Cast on 160 stitches (40 sts each on 4 double-pointed needles).

Join, being careful not to twist stitches.

Place a marker on the first needle to indicate beginning of rnd.

Rnd 1 *K2tog, k to last 2 sts on needle, ssk; repeat from * to end 8 stitches decreased.

Rnd 2 Knit.

Repeat these 2 rnds until 2 sts remain on each needle.

Break the yarn and thread it through a tapestry needle and through the remaining 8 stitches.

Sew through first stitch to complete the center and pull tightly.

Fasten off.

Stitch Key

⟨0⟩ CO 1 st

◻ K2tog

◻ Knit

◻ SSK

◻ Repeat

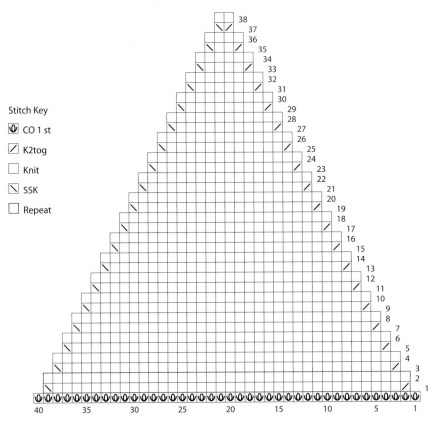

CLASSIC INCREASE page 22

Cast on 8 stitches (2 sts each on 4 double-pointed needles).

Join, being careful not to twist stitches.

Place a marker on the first needle to indicate beginning of rnd.

Rnd 1 Knit into the back of all stitches.

Rnd 2 Kf&b in every stitch.

Rnd 3 Knit.

Rnd 4 *Kf&b in first stitch, k to last stitch on needle, kf&b in last st; repeat from * to end—8 stitches increased.

Repeat rnds 3 and 4 until block is desired size.

Bind off.

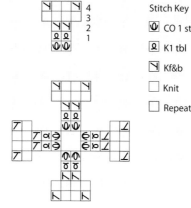

Stitch Key

Ⓤ CO 1 st

Ⓠ K1 tbl

Ⓝ Kf&b

☐ Knit

☐ Repeat

CLASSIC SWIRL page 23

Cast on 8 stitches (2 sts each on 4 double-pointed needles).

Join, being careful not to twist stitches.

Place a marker on the first needle to indicate beginning of rnd.

Rnd 1 Kf&b in every stitch (8 stitches).

Rnd 2 *Yo, k to the end of the needle; repeat from * to end—4 stitches increased.

Repeat rnd 2 until block is desired size.

Bind off.

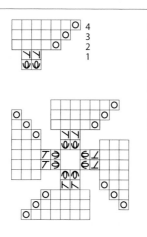

Stitch Key

Ⓤ CO 1 st

Ⓝ Kf&b

Ⓞ Yo

☐ Knit

☐ Repeat

CLASSIC DIAMOND PATTERN

(worked over 37 stitches)

Row 1 and all odd-numbered rows (WS) Purl.

Row 2 (RS) K12, k2tog, yo, k2, k2tog, yo, k1, yo, ssk, k2, yo, ssk, k12.

Row 4 K11, k2tog, yo, k2, k2tog, yo, k3, yo, ssk, k2, yo, ssk, k11.

Row 6 K10, k2tog, yo, k2, k2tog, yo, k5, yo, ssk, k2, yo, ssk, k10.

Row 8 K9, k2tog, yo, k2, k2tog, yo, k7, yo, ssk, k2, yo, ssk, k9.

Row 10 K8, k2tog, yo, k2, k2tog, yo, k9, yo, ssk, k2, yo, ssk, k8.

Row 12 K7, k2tog, yo, k2, k2tog, yo, k11, yo, ssk, k2, yo, ssk, k7.

Row 14 K6, k2tog, yo, k2, k2tog, yo, k13, yo, ssk, k2, yo, ssk, k6.

Row 16 K5, k2tog, yo, k2, k2tog, yo, k15, yo, ssk, k2, yo, ssk, k5.

Row 18 K4, k2tog, yo, k2, k2tog, yo, k17, yo, ssk, k2, yo, ssk, k4.

Row 20 K3, k2tog, yo, k2, k2tog, yo, k19, yo, ssk, k2, yo, ssk, k3.

Row 22 K2, k2tog, yo, k2, k2tog, yo, k21, yo, ssk, k2, yo, ssk, k2.

Row 24 K1, k2tog, yo, k2, k2tog, yo, k23, yo, ssk, k2, yo, ssk, k1.

Row 26 K2tog, yo, k2, k2tog, yo, k25, yo, ssk, k2, yo, ssk.

Row 28 K1, yo, ssk, k2, yo, ssk, k23, k2tog, yo, k2, k2tog, yo, k1.

Row 30 K2, yo, ssk, k2, yo, ssk, k21, k2tog, yo, k2, k2tog, yo, k2.

Row 32 K3, yo, ssk, k2, yo, ssk, k19, k2tog, yo, k2, k2tog, yo, k3.

Row 34 K4, yo, ssk, k2, yo, ssk, k17, k2tog, yo, k2, k2tog, yo, k4.

Row 36 K5, yo, ssk, k2, yo, ssk, k15, k2tog, yo, k2, k2tog, yo, k5.

Row 38 K6, yo, ssk, k2, yo, ssk, k13, k2tog, yo, k2, k2tog, yo, k6.

Row 40 K7, yo, ssk, k2, yo, ssk, k11, k2tog, yo, k2, k2tog, yo, k7.

Row 42 K8, yo, ssk, k2, yo, ssk, k9, k2tog, yo, k2, k2tog, yo, k8.

Row 44 K9, yo, ssk, k2, yo, ssk, k7, k2tog, yo, k2 k2tog, yo, k9.

Row 46 K10, yo, ssk, k2, yo, ssk, k5, k2tog, yo, k2, k2tog, yo, k10.

Row 48 K11, yo, ssk, k2, yo, ssk, k3, k2tog, yo, k2, k2tog, yo, k11.

Row 50 K12, yo, ssk, k2, yo, ssk, k1, k2tog, yo, k2, k2tog, yo, k12.

Row 51 Purl.

Row 52 Knit.

Cast on 39 stitches.

Knit 1 row. Work 52 rows of Classic Diamond pattern on center 37 stitches keeping first and last stitch in Garter st for selvedge.

Bind off.

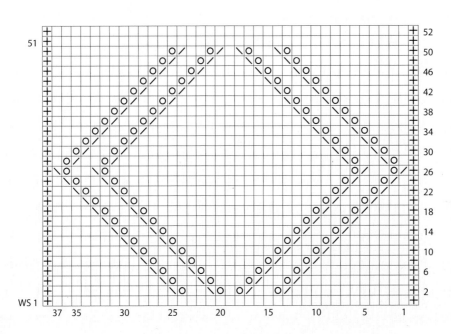

Stitch Key

+ Selvedge st

☐ K on RS, P on WS

╱ K2tog

╲ SSK

○ Yo

NOTE: Purl all WS rows

BOBBLE FRAME page 24

Colors MC and CC

SPECIAL STITCH

Bobble Cast on 1 stitch. K in front, back, front and back of stitch (4 stitches), turn, p4, turn, k4, turn, p4. With the left-hand needle lift the 2nd, 3rd and 4th stitches over the first stitch (1 stitch). Fasten off.

With MC, cast on 45 stitches.
Work in St st (knit on RS, purl on WS) until block length measures same as width.
Bind off.

FRAME

With CC, embroider inner and outer rectangular frames in duplicate stitch following chart.

With CC, make 14 bobbles and attach between lines of duplicate stitch frames following placement diagram.

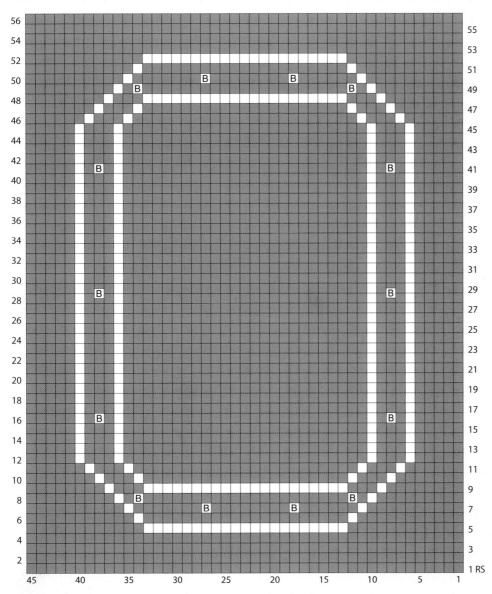

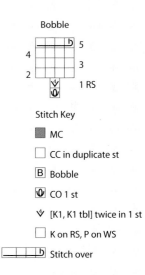

Bobble

Stitch Key

▨	MC
☐	CC in duplicate st
B	Bobble
Ⓤ	CO 1 st
⅄	[K1, K1 tbl] twice in 1 st
☐	K on RS, P on WS
⊟b	Stitch over

CELTIC KNOT FRAME page 25

Colors MC and CC

With MC, cast on 45 stitches.
Work in St st (knit on RS, purl on WS) until block length measures same as width.
Bind off.

I-CORD

With double-pointed needles and CC, cast on 3 stitches.
Row 1 K3, do not turn, slide sts to other end of needle.
Repeat row 1 for approx 64" (162.5cm).
Bind off.

Sew I-cord to block following photo.

I-cord

Stitch Key

⊙ CO 1 st

☐ Knit

→ Do not turn

☐ Repeat

SCALLOP LACE FRAME page 25

Colors MC and CC

With MC, cast on 45 stitches.
Work in St st (knit on RS, purl on WS) until block length measures same as width.
Bind off.

FRAME

With CC, cast on 130 sts (a multiple of 9 stitches plus 5 more).
Row 1 (RS) K3, *yo, k2, ssk, k2tog, k2, yo, k1; repeat from * to last 2 stitches, k2.
Row 2 Purl.
Row 3 K2, *yo, k2, ssk, k2tog, k2, yo, k1; repeat from * to last 3 sts, k3.
Row 4 Purl.
Rows 5–8 Repeat rows 1–4.
Work 2 rows in Garter st.
Bind off.

Sew cast-on edge to bound-off edge. Sew frame to block using photo as a guide.

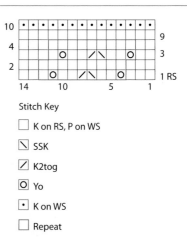

Stitch Key

☐ K on RS, P on WS

╲ SSK

╱ K2tog

⊙ Yo

• K on WS

☐ Repeat

chapter 2

ORNATE APPLIQUÉ, EMBROIDERY, AND CORDS

There was a time when the complexities of dimensional knitting frightened knitters. Happily, those days are gone. Today, dimensional knitting such as appliqué, embroidery, and cords is hot, hot, *hot*, both on the fashion runways and in the knitting world. This chapter deals with applied textures using easy techniques, such as knitted flowers, cords, leaves, and embroidery, that make the blocks look more complicated than they really are. This is a good thing and I encourage you to try a few of these blocks. You'll discover endless creative possibilities that you never thought you had in you.

Sewing the appliqués on is easy, but you also can use (now, don't cringe) washable fabric tack glue. If you do so, I suggest you swatch your yarn first, experimenting with the glue, it may not work on all yarns.

Creativity is the driving force that inspires us to knit, so let your creative juices flow with these fun, easy techniques.

Projects that come from the techniques in this chapter are the Mélange Counterpane Afghan (see page 208) and the Anthology Cuffed Shawl-Sweater (see page 214).

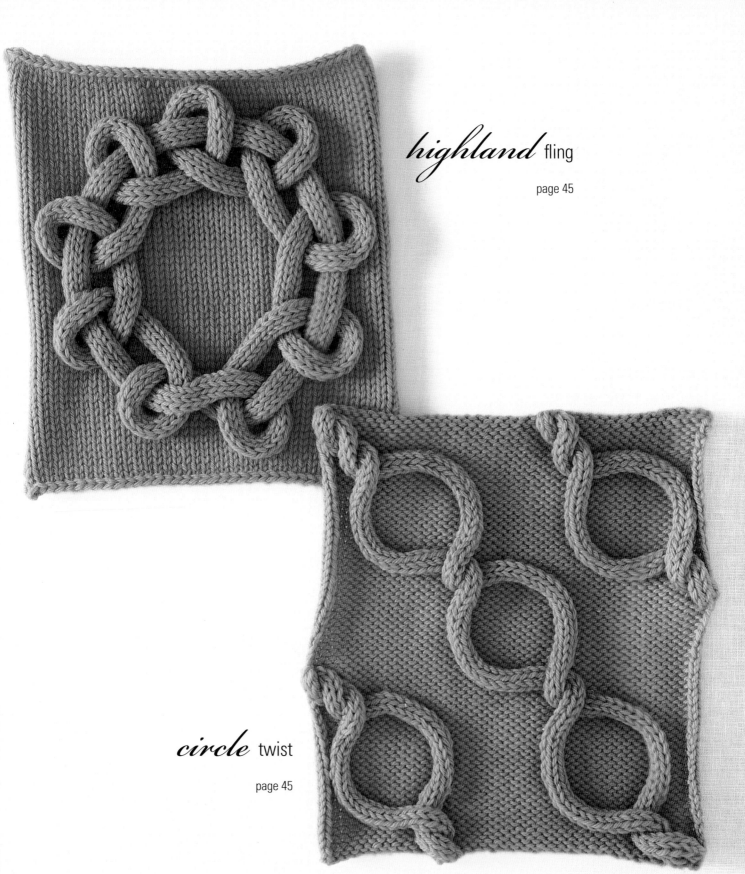

highland fling

page 45

circle twist

page 45

chucka chain

page 46

cable-leaf trio

page 47

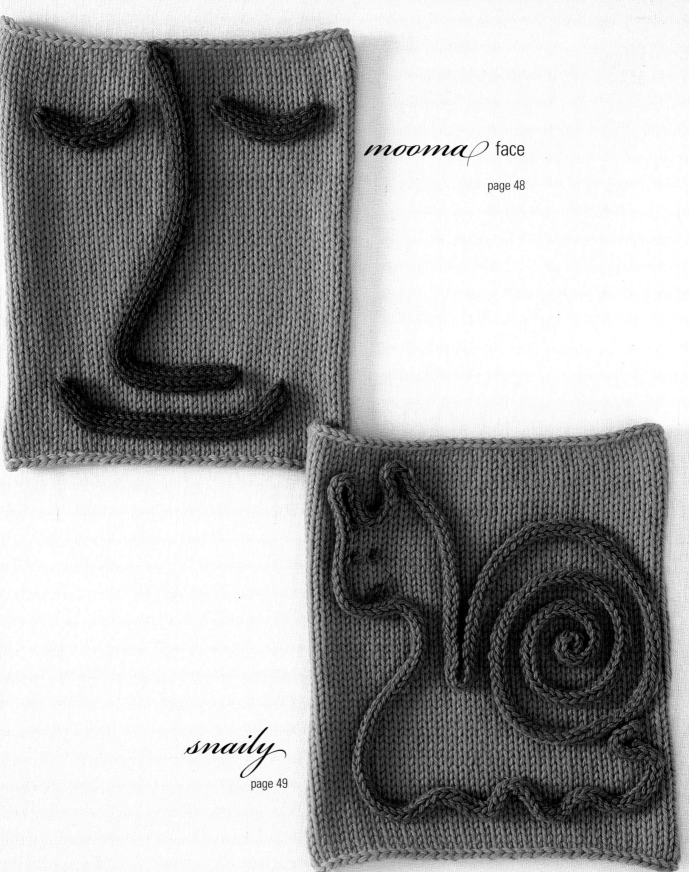

mooma face

page 48

snaily

page 49

fiddle fern

page 48

jacobean flower

page 49

cross-cable cords

page 50

irish jig

page 50

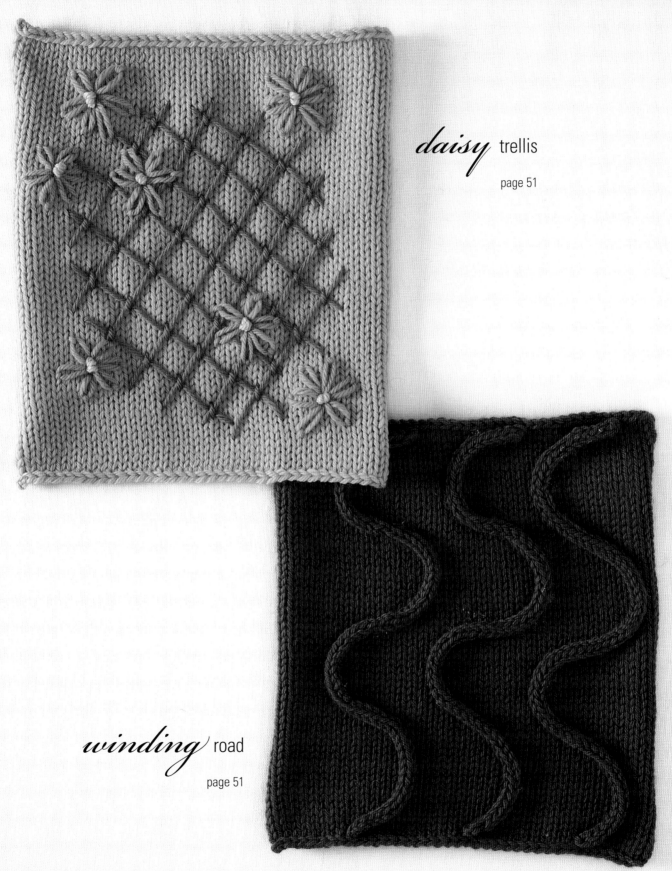

daisy trellis

page 51

winding road

page 51

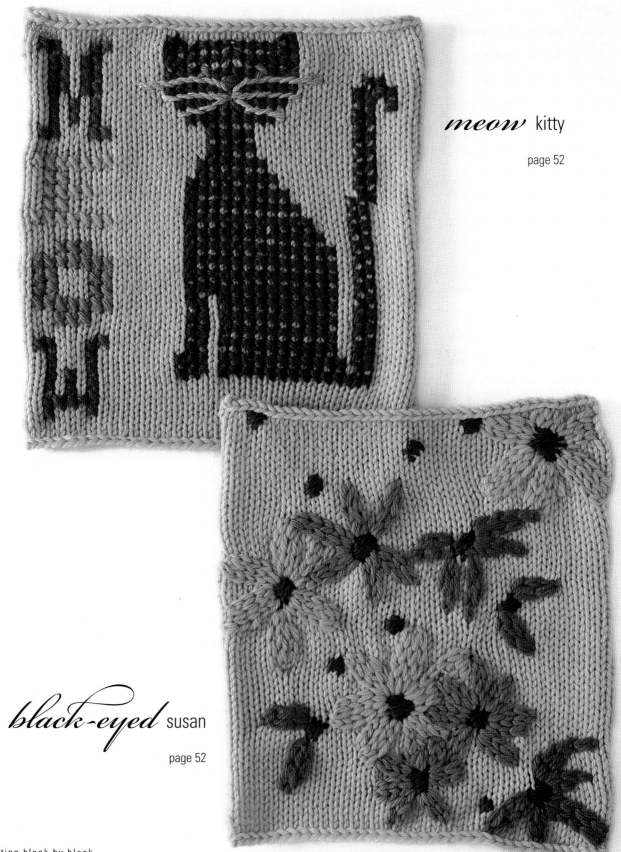

meow kitty

page 52

black-eyed susan

page 52

star bright

page 53

wild flower vine

page 54

happy heart cord
page 55

crazy floral burst

page 55

HIGHLAND FLING page 36

BLOCK
Cast on 45 stitches.
Work in Reverse St st until block length measures same as width.
Bind off.

I-CORD
With double-pointed needles, cast on 5 stitches.
Work I-cord (see page 238) for approximately 72" (183cm). Keep stitches and yarn on hold until motif is complete.

FINISHING
Sew cord to block following diagram, adding or removing rows as needed. Bind off and hide ends of cord under the motif.

After loops are made, weave I-cord in and out of loops.

I-Cord

Stitch Key

· P on RS, K on WS

CO 1 st

Knit

→ Do not turn

Repeat

CIRCLE TWIST page 36

BLOCK
Cast on 45 stitches.
Work in St st until block length measures same as width.
Bind off.

I-CORDS (make 3)
With double-pointed needles, cast on 5 stitches.
Work in I-cord (see page 238) for 30" (76cm) and 2 cords for 15" (38cm).

FINISHING
Sew cords to block following photo.
Wrap cord around small round object to shape circles, pinning as you twist and shape cord.

I-Cord Stem

Stitch Key

K on RS, P on WS

CO 1 st

Repeat

→ Do not turn

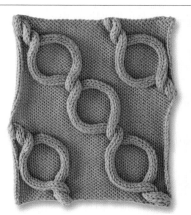

BLOCK

Cast on 45 stitches.

Work in St st until block length measures same as width.

Bind off.

CHUCKA CHAIN (make one of each with stitch amount given)

First Chain

With two strands yarn held together, cast on 60 stitches loosely (over two needles).

K 2 rows.

Pass all the stitches, one at a time, over the first stitch.

Shape the 60-stitch chain into a large ring. Fasten off the first stitch and sew the ends of the ring together.

Second Chain

*Cast on 50 stitches loosely in same manner as the first chain.

K 2 rows.

Pass all the stitches, one at a time, over the first stitch.

Shape the 50-stitch chain into a large ring. Place one end through first chain and sew the ends of the ring together.

Third Chain

Work the same as the Second Chain on 40 stitches.

Fourth Chain

Work the same as the Third Chain on 30 stitches to complete the Chucka Chain.

FINISHING

Sew to block as pictured.

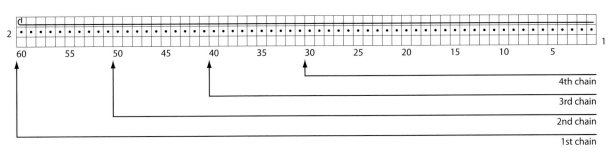

4th chain

3rd chain

2nd chain

1st chain

Stitch Key

☐ K on RS, P on WS

• Knit

Stitch over

BLOCK

Cast on 45 stitches.
Work in St st until block length
measures same as width.
Bind off.

CABLE LEAF (make 3—1 with a 1" [2.5cm] stem, 1 with a 2" [5cm] stem, and 1 with a 4" [10cm] stem)

2/2 RC dec Sl 2 stitches to cn and hold in back, [k1
from left-hand needle together with 1 st from cn]
twice.
2/2 LC dec Sl 2 sts to cn and hold in front, [k1 from
cn together with 1 st from left-hand needle] twice.
SP2P Sl 1, p2tog, pass the slipped st over.

Cast on 5 stitches. Work I-cord (see page 238) for
1" (2.5cm), 2" (5cm) or 4" (10cm).
Row 1 (RS) [K1, m1] twice, p1, [m1, k1] twice (9
stitches).
Row 2 and all WS rows except 26 and 28 K the
knit stitches and p the purl stitches.
Row 3 2/2 RC, m1P, p1, m1P, 2/2 LC (11 stitches).
Row 5 K4, m1P, p3, m1P, k4 (13 stitches).
Row 7 2/2 RC, m1P, p5, m1P, 2/2 LC (15 stitches).
Row 9 K4, m1P, p7, m1P, k4 (17 stitches).
Row 11 2/2 RC, m1P, p9, m1P, 2/2 LC (19 stitches).
Rows 13, 17 and 21 K the knit stitches and p the
purl stitches.
Row 15 2/2 RC, p2tog, p7, ssp, 2/2 LC (17 stitches).
Row 19 2/2 RC, p2tog, p5, ssp, 2/2 LC (15 stitches).
Row 23 2/2 RC, p2tog, p3, ssp, 2/2 LC (13 stitches).

Row 25 K4, p2tog, p1, p2tog, k4 (11 stitches).
Row 26 P4, SP2P, p4 (9 stitches).
Row 27 2/2 RC dec, p1, 2/2 LC dec (5 stitches).
Row 28 P1, SP2P, p1 (3 stitches).
Row 29 SK2P (1 st).
Fasten off.

FINISHING

Sew leaves to block following photo for placement.
With a contrasting color yarn, embroider straight
stitch veins onto one leaf if desired.

I-Cord

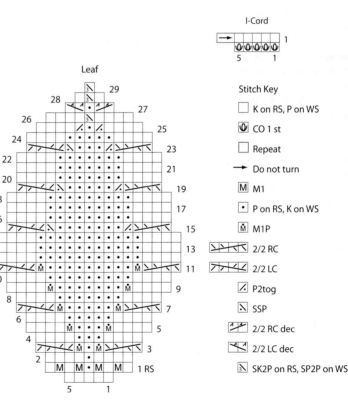

Leaf

Stitch Key

- ☐ K on RS, P on WS
- ⊍ CO 1 st
- ☐ Repeat
- → Do not turn
- Ⓜ M1
- • P on RS, K on WS
- Ⓜ M1P
- 2/2 RC
- 2/2 LC
- ☐ P2tog
- ☐ SSP
- 2/2 RC dec
- 2/2 LC dec
- SK2P on RS, SP2P on WS

MOOMA FACE page 38

Colors MC and CC

BLOCK

With MC, cast on 45 stitches.
Work in St st until block length measures same as width.
Bind off.

I-CORDS (make 4)

With CC and double-pointed needles, cast on 5 sts.
Work in I-cord (see page 238) for 10" (25.5cm), 6" (15cm) and two cords for 3" (7.5cm).
Bind off.
Sew cords to block following photo for placement.

I-Cord

1

5   1

Stitch Key

☐ MC

▨ CC

☐ K on RS, P on WS

Ⓤ CO 1 st

☐ Repeat

→ Do not turn

FIDDLE FERN page 39

BASKETWEAVE PATTERN

(a multiple of 6 stitches plus 4 more)
Row 1 (RS) P4, *k2, p6; repeat from * to the last 6 stitches, k2, p4.
Row 2 K4, *p2, k6; repeat from * to the last 6 stitches, p2, k4.

Rows 3 and 4 Knit.
Row 5 P8, *k2, p6; repeat from * to the last 10 stitches, k2, p8.
Row 6 K8, *p2, k6; repeat from * to the last 10 stitches, p2, k8.
Rows 7 and 8 Knit.
Repeat rows 1–8 for pattern.

BLOCK

Cast on 42 stitches.
K 4 rows.
Work 8 rows of Basketweave pattern 8 times, then repeat rows 1 and 2 once more.
K 4 rows.
Bind off.

LOOPS (make 4)

Cast on 25 stitches loosely.
K 2 rows.
Pass all the stitches, one at a time, over the first stitch. Fasten off.

I-CORD STEMS (make 4)

With double-pointed needles, cast on 3 stitches.
Work I-cord (see page 238) for 12" (30.5 cm).
Bind off.

FINISHING

Sew loops and stems to block following photo for placement.

I-Cord Stem

1

3   1

Stitch Key

• P on RS, K on WS

☐ K on RS, P on WS

☐ Repeat

Ⓤ CO 1 st

ȸ Stitch over

→ Do not turn

Basketweave Pattern

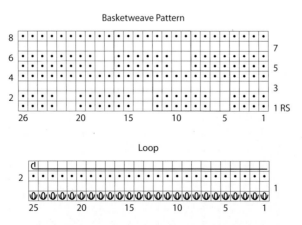

Loop

JACOBEAN FLOWER page 39

Colors A, B, C and D

BLOCK

With A, cast on 45 stitches.
Work in St st until block length measures
same as width.
Bind off.

FLOWER PETALS

Bobble Cord Petal (make 8—two each in 4 colors)

Make Bobble (MB) K in front, back, front, back
of next st (4 stitches), turn, p4, turn, k4, turn, p4,
turn, k4, pass the 2nd, 3rd and 4th stitches, one at a
time, over the first st.

With double-pointed needles, cast on 5 stitches.
Slide stitches to the other end of the needle.
Rows 1–5 Knit, do not turn, slide stitches to the
other end of the needle.
Row 6 K2, MB, k2, do not turn, slide stitches to the
other end of the needle.
Repeat rows 1–6 one more time, then repeat rows
1–5 once more.
Bind off.

I-Cord Stem

With B and double-pointed needles, cast on
5 stitches. Slide stitches to the other end of the
needle. Work row 1 of Bobble Cord Petal for
12" (30.5cm).

FINISHING

Sew petals and stem to block following photo for
placement. With B, cast on 1 stitch, MB. Fasten off
and sew bobble to center of flower.

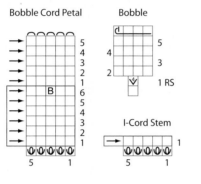

Bobble Cord Petal   Bobble   I-Cord Stem

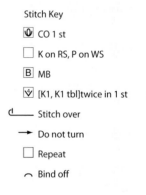

Stitch Key

☒ CO 1 st
☐ K on RS, P on WS
B MB
☒ [K1, K1 tbl]twice in 1 st
⌐— Stitch over
→ Do not turn
☐ Repeat
⌒ Bind off

SNAILY page 38

Colors MC and CC

BLOCK

With MC, cast on 45 stitches.
Work in St st until block length
measures same as width.
Bind off.

I-CORD

With CC and double-pointed needles, cast on 3
stitches. Work in I-cord (see page 238) for 48"
(122cm). Bind off.
Sew cord to block following photo for placement.
Embroider eyes using French knots and mouth
using backstitch (see page 237).

I-Cord

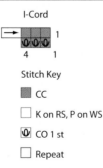

Stitch Key

■ CC
☐ K on RS, P on WS
☒ CO 1 st
☐ Repeat
→ Do not turn

CROSS-CABLE CORDS page 40

5-st Cable Cord

6
5
4
3
2
1

5   1

Stitch Key

⊙ CO 1 st

☐ Knit

⟩⟨ 1/2 LC

→ Do not turn

☐ Repeat

5-ST CABLE CORD
1/2 LC Sl 1 st to cn and hold in front, k2, k1 from cn.

Cast on 5 stitches. Slide stitches to the other end of the needle.
Rows 1–5 Knit, do not turn, slide stitches to the other end of the needle.
Row 6 K1, 1/2 LC, k1, do not turn, slide stitches to the other end of the needle.
Repeat rows 1–5 for pattern.

BLOCK
Cast on 45 stitches.
Work 8 rows in St st, starting with a k row.
Row 1 (RS) K6, *k5 and with a tapestry needle, run a length of waste yarn purlwise through the front of these 5 stitches (leaving them on needle), k2*; repeat from * once, k9; repeat from * to * twice, k6. Continue in St st for approximately 41 rows more, ending with a WS row. Leave stitches on needle.

CORD
Next row (RS) *Slip 5 marked stitches onto a double-pointed needle and work rows 1–6 of 5-st Cable Cord 10 times, ending with row 6. Cut yarn and place stitches on a holder. Repeat from * on remaining 3 sets of marked stitches.

Cross the cords following the photo and place the 20 stitches in crossed order on a spare needle ready to work a RS row. Block and crossed cords should be the same length.
Next row (RS) K6, *[k one stitch from the cord together with one stitch from the block] 5 times, k2*; repeat from * to * once more, k9; repeat from * to * twice, k6.
Continue in St st for 7 rows more.
Bind off. Sew cords in place.

Note Cable cords can be worked separately and sewn in place.

IRISH JIG page 40

BLOCK
Cast on 45 stitches.
Work in St st until block length measures same as width.
Bind off.

I-CORD
With double-pointed needles, cast on 5 stitches.
Work I-cord (see page 238) for approximately 72" (183cm). Keep stitches and yarn on hold until motif is complete.

FINISHING
Sew cord to block following diagram, adding or removing rows as needed. Bind off and hide ends of cord under the motif.

I-Cord

→ ⊙⊙⊙⊙⊙ 1

5   1

Stitch Key

☐ K on RS, P on WS

⊙ CO 1 st

☐ Repeat

→ Do not turn

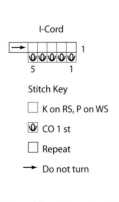

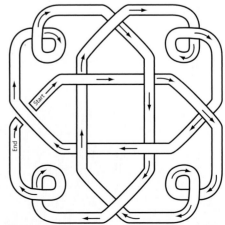

DAISY TRELLIS page 41

Colors

Goldenrod (A)

Mustard (B)

Light Orange (C)

Light Gray (D)

BLOCK

With A, cast on 45 stitches.

Work in St st until block length measures same as width.

Bind off.

Embroider pattern onto block following chart using Lazy daisy stitch in C for the petals, French knots in D for the centers, and long and straight stitches in B for the trellis (see page 237 for stitches).

Stitch Key

■ Mustard (B)

▨ Light Orange (C)

▨ Light Grey (D)

☐ K on RS, P on WS

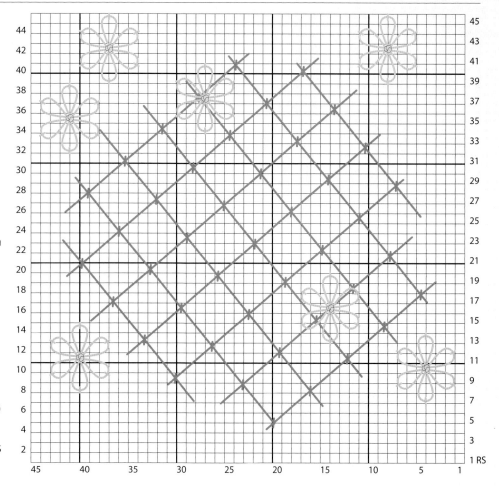

WINDING ROAD page 41

BLOCK

Cast on 45 stitches.

Work in St st until block length measures same as width.

Bind off.

I-CORDS (make 3)

With double-pointed needles, cast on 3 stitches.

Work in I-cord (see page 238) for 15" (38cm).

Sew cord to block following photo for placement.

I-Cord

1

3   1

Stitch Key

☐ K on RS, P on WS

Ⓥ CO 1 st

☐ Repeat

→ Do not turn

WIDE LATTICE PATTERN

(a multiple of 18 stitches)

Row 1 (RS) *K2, p7, k1, p7, k1; repeat from * to end.

Row 2 *K7, p3, k7, p1; repeat from * to end.

Row 3 *P7, k5, p5, k1; repeat from * to end.

Row 4 *K1, p1, k3, p7, k6; repeat from * to end.

Row 5 *P5, k9, p1, k1, p2; repeat from * to end.

Row 6 *K3, p11, k4; repeat from * to end.

Row 7 *P3, k1, p1, k9, p4; repeat from * to end.

Row 8 *K5, p7, k3, p1, k2; repeat from * to end.

Row 9 *P1, k1, p5, k5, p6; repeat from * to end.

Row 10 *K7, p3, k7, p1; repeat from * to end.

Row 11 *K2, p7, k1, p7, k1; repeat from * to end.

Row 12 *P2, k5, p1, k7, p3; repeat from * to end.

Row 13 *K4, p7, k1, p3, k3; repeat from * to end.

Row 14 *P4, k1, p1, k7, p5; repeat from * to end.

Row 15 *K6, p7, k5; repeat from * to end.

Row 16 *P4, k7, p1, k1, p5; repeat from * to end.

Row 17 *K4, p3, k1, p7, k3; repeat from * to end.

Row 18 *P2, k7, p1, k5, p3; repeat from * to end.

Repeat rows 1–18 for pattern.

BLOCK

Cast on 42 stitches.

K 4 rows. Work rows 1–18 of Wide Lattice pattern 3 times (54 rows) on center 36 stitches, keeping first and last 3 stitches in Garter st.

K 4 rows.

Bind off.

I-Cord Stem

With double-pointed needles, cast on 3 stitches.

Work I-cord (see page 238) for 36" (91.5cm).

Bind off.

FLOWER

Petal

Cast on 2 stitches.

Row 1 Kf&b of first st, k to end of row.

Rows 2–9 Repeat row 1 (11 stitches after row 9).

Break yarn.

Wide Lattice Pattern

I-Cord Stem

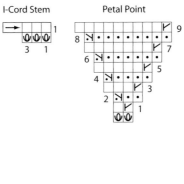

Petal Point

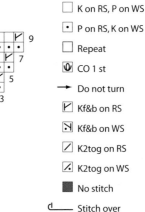

Stitch Key

☐ K on RS, P on WS

• P on RS, K on WS

☐ Repeat

Ⓤ CO 1 st

→ Do not turn

↗ Kf&b on RS

↘ Kf&b on WS

╱ K2tog on RS

╱ K2tog on WS

■ No stitch

⌐ Stitch over

Flower

Make 4 more points, casting on stitches for each point onto an empty needle and breaking yarn on all but the last point.
Row 10 (joining) K across all 5 points (55 stitches).
Rows 11 and 12 Knit.
Row 13 *K2tog; repeat from * to the last st, k1 (28 stitches).

Rows 14 and 15 *K2tog; repeat from * to end (7 stitches after row 15).
Pass the 2nd, 3rd, 4th, 5th, 6th and 7th stitches over the first st (1 st).
Fasten off. Sew seam. Sew bead to flower center if desired.

FINISHING
Sew flower and stem to block following photo for placement. Sew bead to center of flower.

HAPPY HEART CORD page 44

Colors MC and CC

BLOCK
With MC, cast on 45 stitches.
Work in St st until block length measures same as width.
Bind off.

I-CORD
With CC and double-pointed needles, cast on 4 stitches. Work in I-cord (see page 238) for 30" (76cm).

Sew cord to block following photo for placement.

I-Cord

Stitch Key

■ CC

□ K on RS, P on WS

Ⓞ CO 1 st

□ Repeat

→ Do not turn

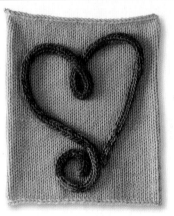

CRAZY FLORAL BURST page 44

Colors MC and CC

BLOCK
With MC, cast on 45 stitches.
Work in St st until block length measures same as width.
Bind off.

I-CORD
With CC and double-pointed needles, cast on 4 stitches. Work in I-cord (see page 238) for 65" (165cm).

Sew cord to block following photo for placement.

I-Cord

Stitch Key

■ CC

□ K on RS, P on WS

Ⓞ CO 1 st

□ Repeat

→ Do not turn

chapter 3

CREATIVE COLORWORK

Intarsia colors knit in, duplicate stitch colors embroidered on a knitted background, and Fair Isle using only two to three colors on a row are all techniques using two or more colors to create pattern repeats, motifs, and even edgings. I hope you'll like the patterns and motifs I've chosen to use, and you'll have fun mixing and matching the blocks within this chapter, or in combination with the blocks in other chapters.

Colorwork choices can say much about a knitter's personal style. The pieces can be happy and fun, or elegant and sophisticated. Blank graph paper can be used for you to create your own colorwork piece. It's easier than you might think, so make a drawing you like or transfer a photo to the graph. Then outline the blocks around the illustration, keeping in mind that each small block is a stitch, and fill the blocks with your color choices.

This is certainly one of my favorite knitting techniques, and I hope you'll enjoy it too.

Good examples of projects that use colorwork are the Scarfosaurus (see page 211), Winter Solstice Hooded Scarf (see page 210), and Snowflake Splendor Hat (see page 221).

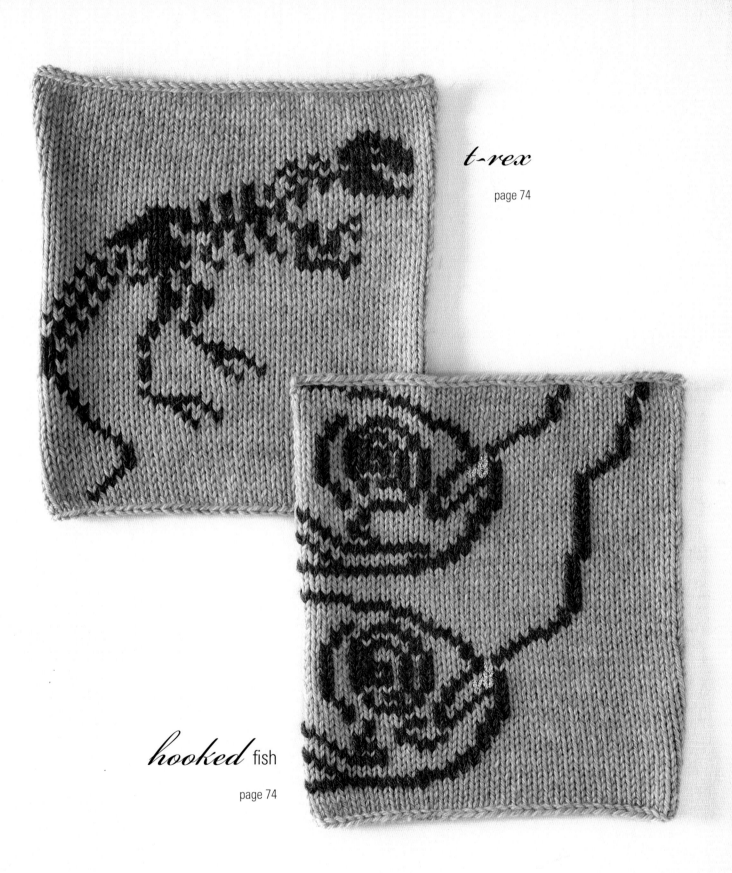

t-rex

page 74

hooked fish

page 74

rose bouquet

page 75

macaw

page 75

dry martini

page 76

vintage keys

page 76

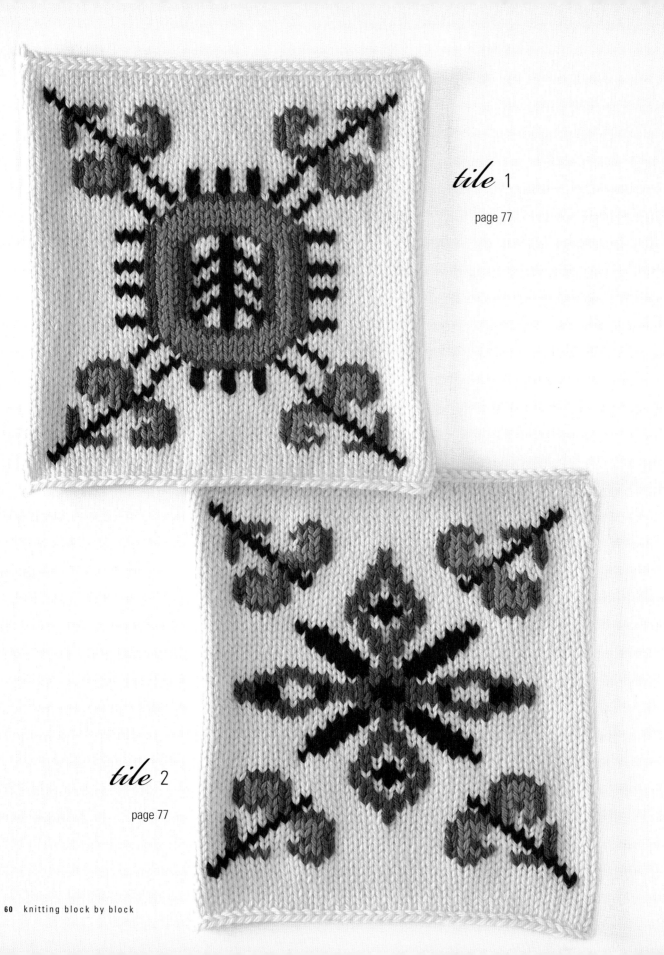

tile 1

page 77

tile 2

page 77

op art
page 78

paisleys
page 78

creative colorwork **61**

peeping tom check

page 79

skullduggery

page 79

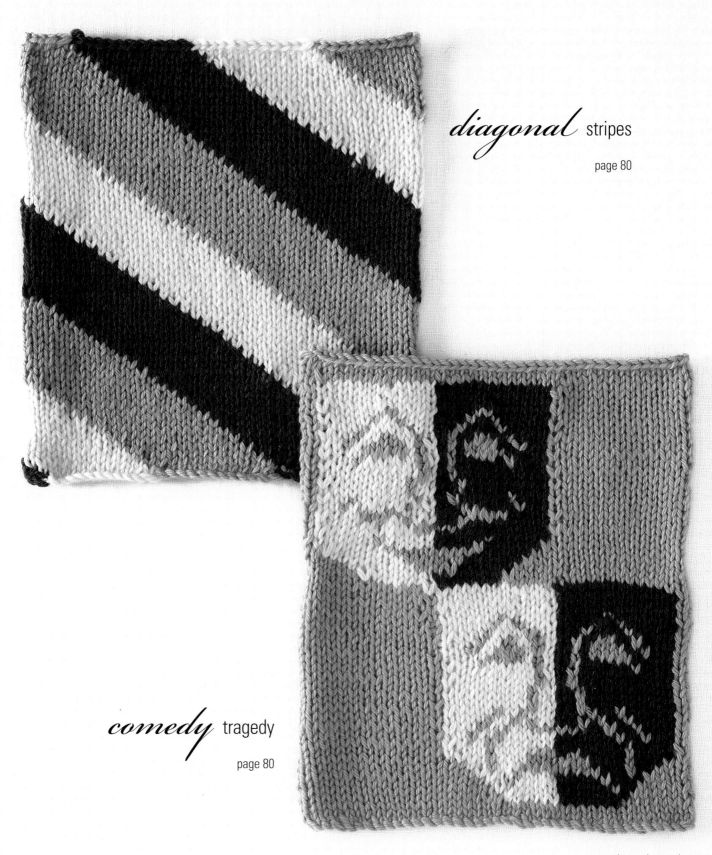

diagonal stripes

page 80

comedy tragedy

page 80

sanquhar

page 81

snowflake

page 81

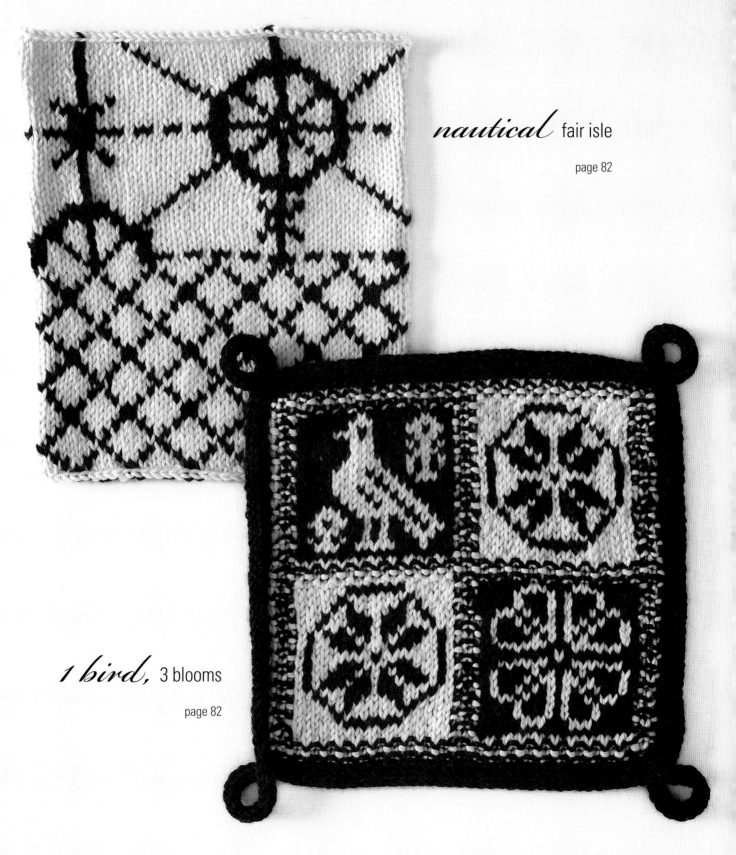

nautical fair isle

page 82

1 bird, 3 blooms

page 82

birds and flowers

page 83

mock tartan plaid floral

page 83

diamond jim argyle

page 84

buck

page 84

seed stitch fair isle combo

page 85

petite box plaid

page 85

negative/positive

page 86

panda

page 86

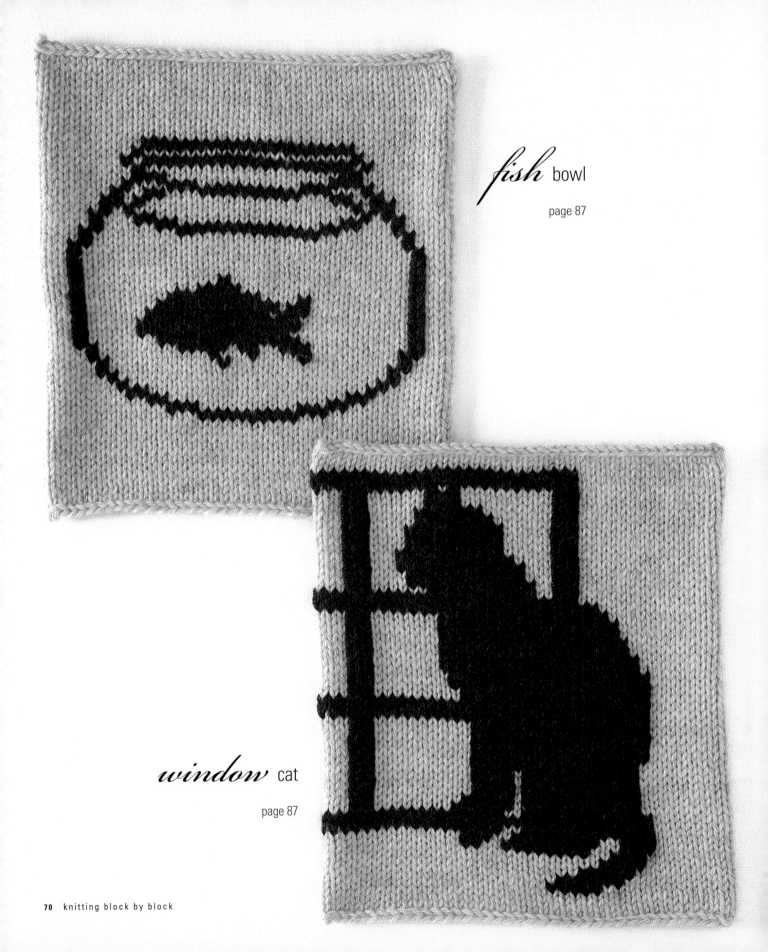

fish bowl

page 87

window cat

page 87

royal crown

page 88

armor knight

page 88

T-REX page 57

BLOCK

With MC, cast on 39 stitches.
Work 60 rows in St st.
Bind off.

Stitch Key

▫ Wheat (MC)

◼ Medium Gray (CC)

FINISHING

Work T-Rex chart using Duplicate st
or St st in intarsia.

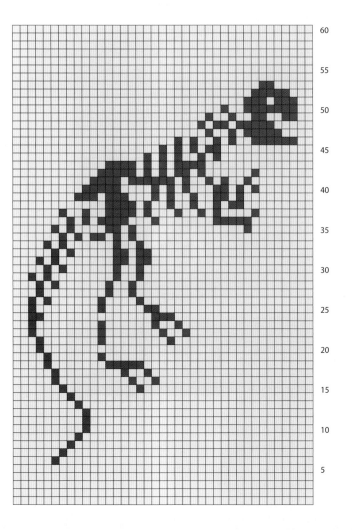

HOOKED FISH page 57

BLOCK

With A, cast on 39 stitches.
Work 60 rows in St st.
Bind off.

Stitch Key

◼ Medium Gray (A)

▫ Wheat (B)

Silver (C)

FINISHING

Work Hooked Fish chart using Duplicate st or St st in intarsia.

.

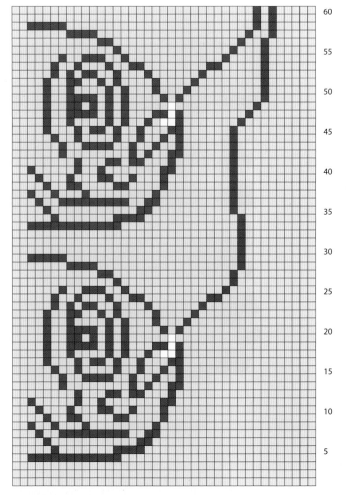

ROSE BOUQUET page 58

BLOCK
With A, cast on 40 stitches.
Work 58 rows in St st.
Bind off.

FINISHING
Work Rose Bouquet chart in
Duplicate st.

Stitch Key
- ░ Light Gray (A)
- ▓ Medium Gray (B)
- ░ Light Purple (C)
- ▒ Medium Purple D)
- █ Dark Purple (E)
- ░ Yellow (F)
- ░ Green (G)
- ░ Olive (H)

MACAW page 58

BLOCK
With MC, cast on 40 stitches.
Work Macaw chart in Duplicate st or
St st intarsia.
Bind off.

Stitch Key
- ░ Wheat (MC)
- ▓ Dark Gray (CC)

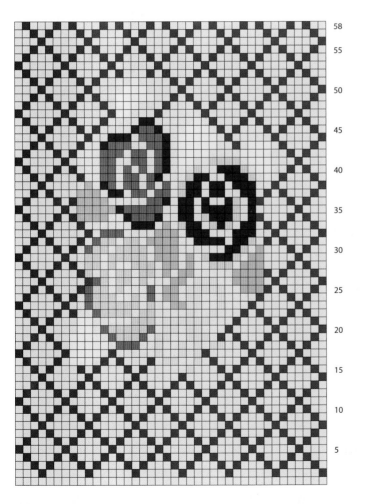

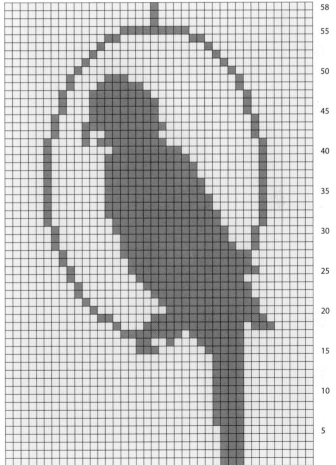

DRY MARTINI page 59

BLOCK

With A, cast on 40 stitches.
Work 58 rows in St st.
Bind off.

FINISHING

Work Dry Martini chart in Duplicate
st or St st intarsia. Embroider tooth-
pick using Stem st.

Stitch Key

- ■ Dark Gray (A)
- ▨ Light Gray (B)
- □ White (C)
- ▨ Olive Green (D)
- ▨ Dark Orange (E)
- ■ Brown (F)

VINTAGE KEYS page 59

BLOCK

With A, cast on 40 stitches.
Work Vintage Keys chart in Duplicate
st or St st intarsia.
Bind off.

Stitch Key

- ■ Dark Gray (A)
- ▨ Gray Green (B)
- ▨ Orange (C)
- ■ Bright Blue (D)

TILE 1 page 60

BLOCK

With A, cast on 43 stitches.
Work 58 rows in St st.
Bind off.

FINISHING

Work Tile 1 chart in Duplicate st.

Stitch Key

☐ White (A)

▨ Light Purple (B)

▨ Medium Purple (C)

■ Dark Purple (D)

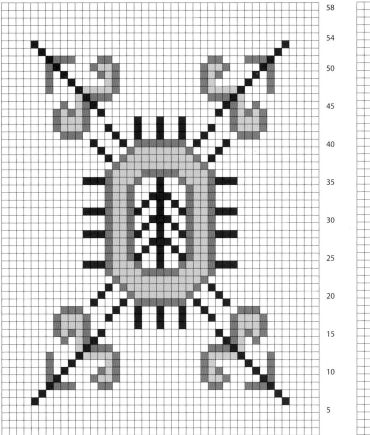

TILE 2 page 60

BLOCK

With A, cast on 43 stitches.
Work 58 rows in St st.
Bind off.

FINISHING

Work Tile 2 chart in Duplicate st.

Stitch Key

☐ White (A)

▨ Light Purple (B)

▨ Medium Purple (C)

■ Dark Purple (D)

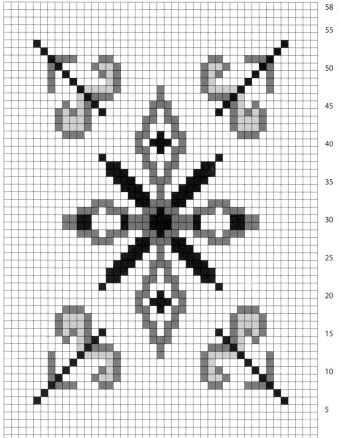

OP ART page 61

BLOCK
With A, cast on 41 stitches.
Work 59 rows in St st.
Bind off.

FINISHING
Work Duplicate st following
Op Art chart.

Stitch Key
- ■ Dark Purple (A)
- ☐ Light Gray (B)
- ■ Black (C)

PAISLEYS page 61

BLOCK
With A, cast on 39 stitches.
Work 58 rows in St st.
Bind off.

FINISHING
Work Paisleys chart using
Duplicate st.
With B, embroider French knots
(see page 237) in the center of each
Paisley.

Stitch Key
- ☐ Light Gray (A)
- ■ Black (B)
- ■ Orange (C)
- ☐ Green (D)
- ■ Dark Purple (E)

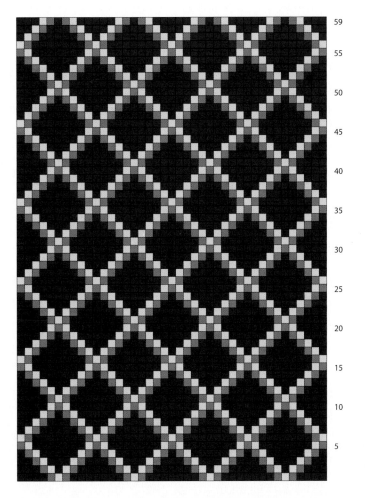

PEEPING TOM CHECK page 62

BLOCK
With MC, cast on 40 stitches.
Work Peeping Tom Check chart in
St st intarsia, then repeat Rows
1–14 of chart.
Bind off.

Stitch Key
■ Dark Gray (MC)
□ Light Gray (CC)

SKULLDUGGERY page 62

BLOCK
Cast on 40 stitches in colors
corresponding with chart.
Work Skullduggery chart in St st
intarsia.
Bind off.

Stitch Key
▨ Dark Gray (A)
▨ Light Gray (B)
■ Blue (C)
▨ Green (D)
■ Purple (E)
▨ Dark Orange (F)

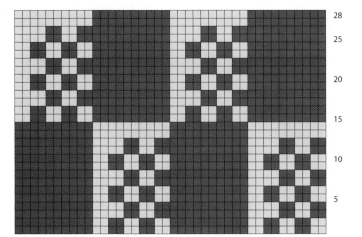

DIAGONAL STRIPES page 63

BLOCK

Cast on 40 stitches in colors
corresponding with chart.
Work Diagonal Stripes chart in St st
intarsia.
Bind off.

Stitch Key

■ Dark Gray (A)

▨ Light Gray (B)

☐ White (C)

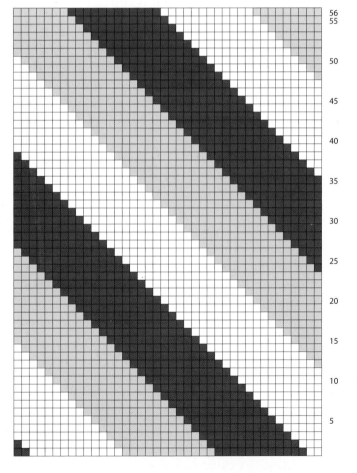

COMEDY/TRAGEDY page 63

BLOCK

With A, cast on 40 stitches.
Work Comedy/Tragedy chart in St st
intarsia.
Bind off.

Stitch Key

☐ Light Blue (A)

■ Dark Gray (B)

▨ Light Gray (C)

☐ White (D)

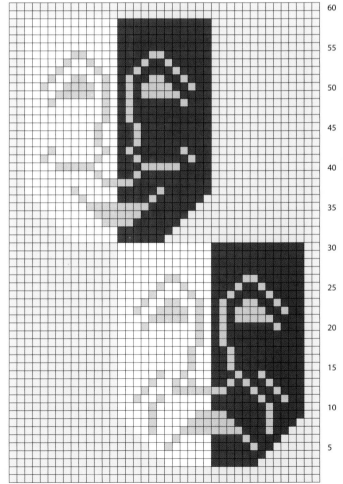

SANQUHAR page 64

BLOCK

With A, cast on 49 stitches. Work Sanquhar chart in St st intarsia. Bind off with A.

Stitch Key

- ■ Dark Gray (A)
- □ White (B)
- ▨ Light Gray (C)
- ▨ Black (D)

SNOWFLAKE page 64

BLOCK

With MC, cast on 33 stitches. Work Snowflake chart in St st intarsia. Bind off with MC.

FRAME

With the right side facing, using double-pointed needles and MC, beginning at the top right, *pick up and k1 st in the corner, pm, pick up and k35 stitches along one side of the block; repeat from * 3 times (144 stitches). Pm and join to work in the round.

Rnd 1 With MC, *k1 (corner st), inc 1 in the next st, k to 1 st before the next marker, inc 1 in this st; repeat from * around (8 stitches increased).

Rnd 2 With CC, knit.

Rnds 3 and 4 With CC, repeat rnd 1 (168 stitches after rnd 4).

Rnd 4 With MC, repeat rnd 2.

Rnd 5 With MC, repeat rnd 1 (176 stitches).

Rnd 6 With CC, knit.

Rnd 7 With CC, repeat rnd 1 (184 stitches). Bind off with CC.

Stitch Key

- □ White (MC)
- ▨ Light Gray (CC)

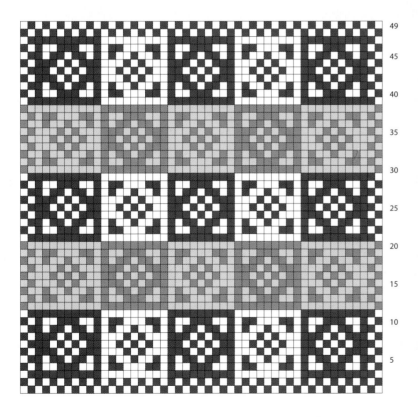

NAUTICAL FAIR ISLE page 65

BLOCK
With MC, cast on 45 stitches.
Work Nautical Fair Isle chart in St st
Fair Isle.
Bind off.

Stitch Key
☐ White (MC)
▨ Black (CC)

1 BIRD, 3 BLOOMS page 65

BLOCK
With MC, cast on 47 stitches.
Work 1 Bird, 3 Blooms chart.
Bind off with MC.

Stitch Key
▨ Black
☐ White

EDGING
With MC, cast on 5 stitches. Work
in I-cord (see page 238) to required
length. Sew cord in place along edge
of block forming 1" (2.5cm) loops at
each corner.

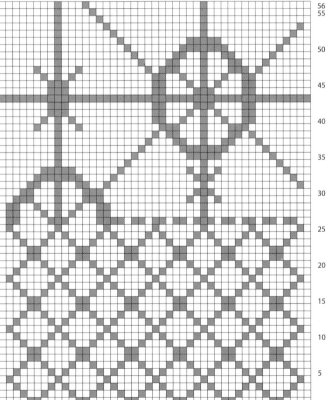

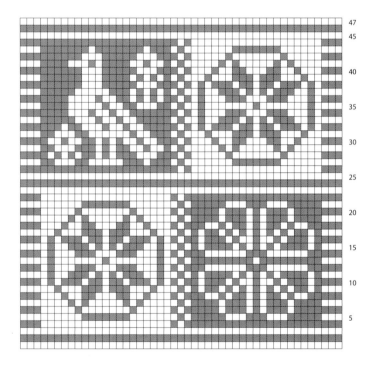

BIRDS AND FLOWERS page 66

BLOCK

With MC, cast on 45 stitches.
Work Birds and Flowers chart in St
st intarsia.
Bind off with MC.

Stitch Key

■ Medium Gray (MC)
□ White (CC)

MOCK TARTAN PLAID FLORAL page 66

BLOCK

With A, cast on 41 stitches.
Work horizontal stripes of Mock
Tartan Plaid Floral chart in St st.
Bind off with A.

VERTICAL STRIPES

Work vertical stripes of chart in
Duplicate st.

FLOWER

Embroider flower, stem and leaves
using Satin stitch, Lazy daisy stitch,
Stem stitch and French knots.

Stitch Key

Light Gray (A)
■ Dark Gray (B)
□ White (C)
Light Purple (D)
■ Dark Purple (E)
■ Dark Green (F)

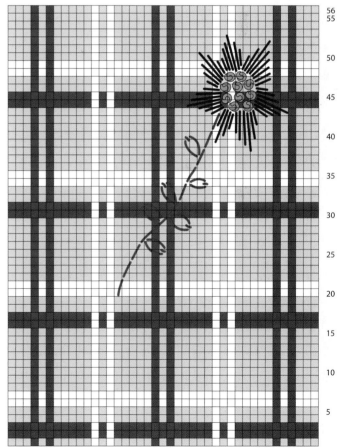

BLOCK

With MC, cast on 40 stitches.

Rows 1–6 With MC, knit.

Rows 7, 9 and 11 With CC, k20; with MC, k20.

Rows 8, 10 and 12 With MC, k20; with CC, k20.

Rows 13, 15 and 17 With MC, k20; with CC, k20.

Rows 14, 16 and 18 With CC, k20; with MC, k20.

Repeat rows 7–18 four times more, then rows 7–12 once more.

With CC, k 6 rows.

Bind off with CC.

Stitch Key

▨ Black

☐ White

BLOCK

With A, cast on 40 stitches.

Work Panda chart in St st intarsia.

Bind off.

FINISHING

With D, embroider stems onto leaves using Stem stitch.

Stitch Key

☐ White (A)

▨ Black (B)

▨ Olive Green (C)

▨ Dark Green (D)

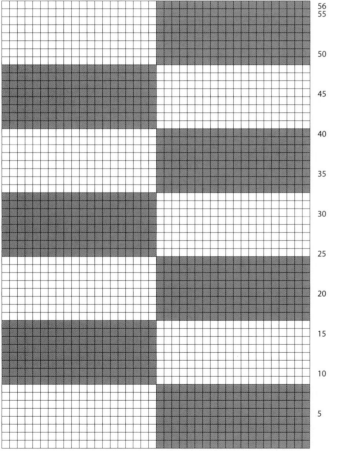

FISH BOWL page 70

BLOCK
With MC, cast on 42 stitches.
Work Fish Bowl chart in St st
intarsia.
Bind off.

Stitch Key

☐ Wheat (MC)

▩ Black (CC)

WINDOW CAT page 70

BLOCK
With MC, cast on 40 stitches.
Work Window Cat chart in St st
intarsia.
Bind off.

Stitch Key

☐ Wheat (MC)

▩ Black (CC)

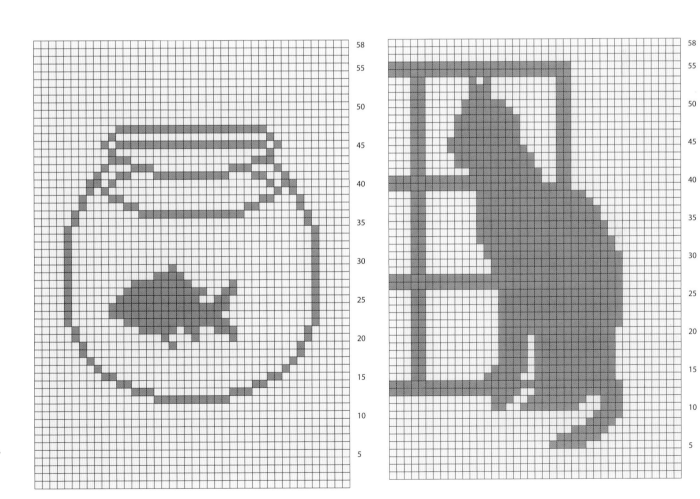

ROYAL CROWN page 71

BLOCK

With A, cast on 40 stitches.
Work Royal Crown chart in St st
intarsia.
Bind off.

FINISHING

Sew 6 purple rhinestones to crown
using photo (see page 71) for
placement.

Stitch Key

- Black (A)
- Light Purple (B)
- Dark Purple (C)
- Light Gray (D)
- Light Blue (E)

ARMOR KNIGHT page 71

BLOCK

With A, cast on 39 stitches.
Work Armor Knight chart in St st
intarsia.
Bind off.

FINISHING

Sew a small rhinestone to the hinge
of the helmet.

Stitch Key

- Light Purple (A)
- Light Gray (B)
- Medium Gray (C)

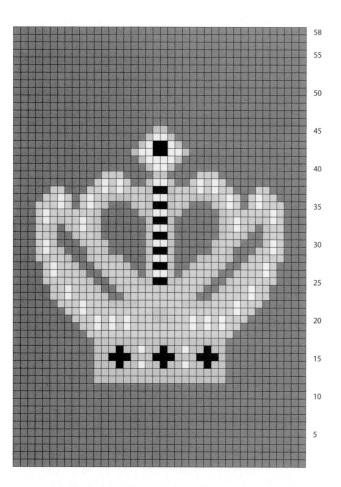

LEOPARD EYES page 72

BLOCK
With A, cast on 39 stitches.
Work Leopard Eyes chart in St st
intarsia.
Bind off.

FINISHING
With E, embroider eyes using Long
stitch.

Stitch Key
- Wheat (A)
- Medium Gray (B)
- Light Brown (C)
- Orange (D)
- Black (E)

ZEBRA EYE page 72

BLOCK
With A, cast on 40 stitches.
Work Zebra Eye chart in St st intarsia.
Bind off.

FINISHING
With B, embroider eye slit using
Straight stitch.

Stitch Key
- Wheat (A)
- Black (B)
- Dark Orange (C)

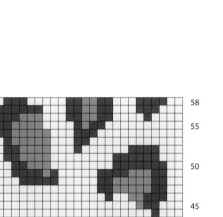

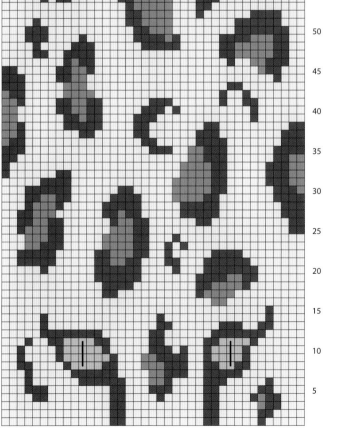

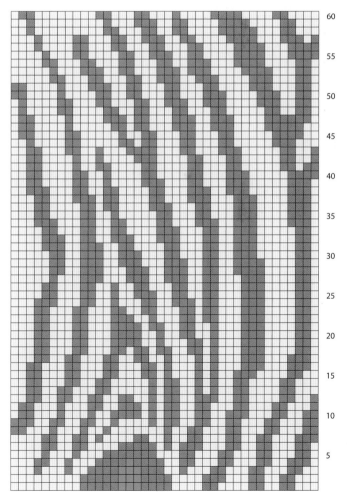

BLOCK

With A, cast on 49 stitches.
Work Fair Isle and Flower chart in
St st Fair Isle.
Bind off with C.

FLOWER

With A, cast on 45 stitches. Work
first 6 rows of chart in St st Fair Isle.
Row 7 (RS) With A, k1, *k2tog;
repeat from * to end (22 stitches).
Row 8 With A, *p2tog; repeat from *
to end (11 stitches).

Row 9 With A, repeat row 7
(6 stitches).
Pass 2nd, 3rd, 4th, 5th and 6th
stitches, one at a time, over the
first st.
Fasten off and sew side seam. Sew
flowers to block as desired.

Stitch Key

■ Dark Gray (A)

□ Light Gray (B)

▨ Light Purple (C)

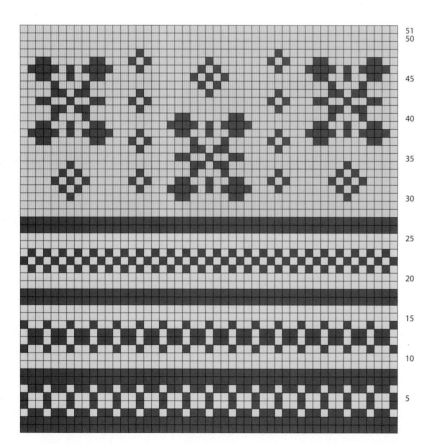

chapter 4

SPECIAL TECHNIQUES

For experienced knitters, traditional knitting techniques are like coming home. They make us comfortable because we recognize them like old friends. For newer knitters, they bring a special kind of excitement—the gateway to a lifetime of learning.

If you want to learn some traditional techniques or experiment with those you already know, this is the chapter for you. Included are many well-loved knitting techniques, such as domino, entrelac, mosaic, smocking, lace, embossed, Fair Isle, and reversible knitting. What could be easier than learning them from making a small block? All of these techniques are tried and true and lend themselves, beautifully, to designing with blocks. You can choose your favorite and repeat it, right side up and sideways, or do a fabulous combination piece, using a variety of the blocks.

A nice example of a garment using patterns from this chapter is the Fairy Leaves Shrug Duo (see page 212).

checkmate

page 108

drop stitch

page 108

maple leaf

page 109

double-knit diamond

page 110

daisy entrelac

page 110

single domino

with flower

page112

classic domino

with beads

page 114

quattro domino

page 115

boxed illusion

page 116

skeleton mosaic

page 116

steeked fair isle

page 118

mock fair isle

with beads

page 118

honeycomb smocking

page 119

bold smocking

page 119

multilayered lace

page 120

floral

fantasy

page 120

diagonal block

page 121

layered lace scallop

page 122

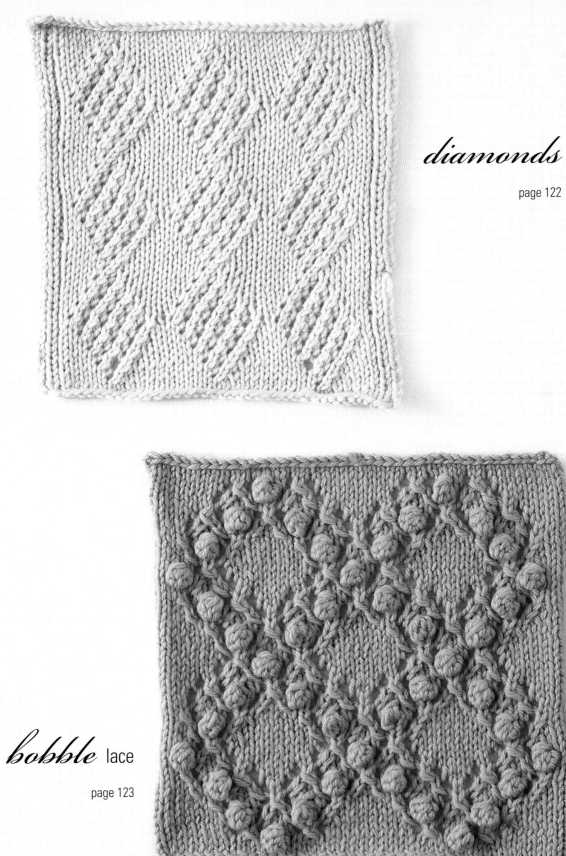

diamonds

page 122

bobble lace

page 123

angel blossom

page 124

fairy leaves

page 124

embossed castle

page 125

classic candelabra

page 126

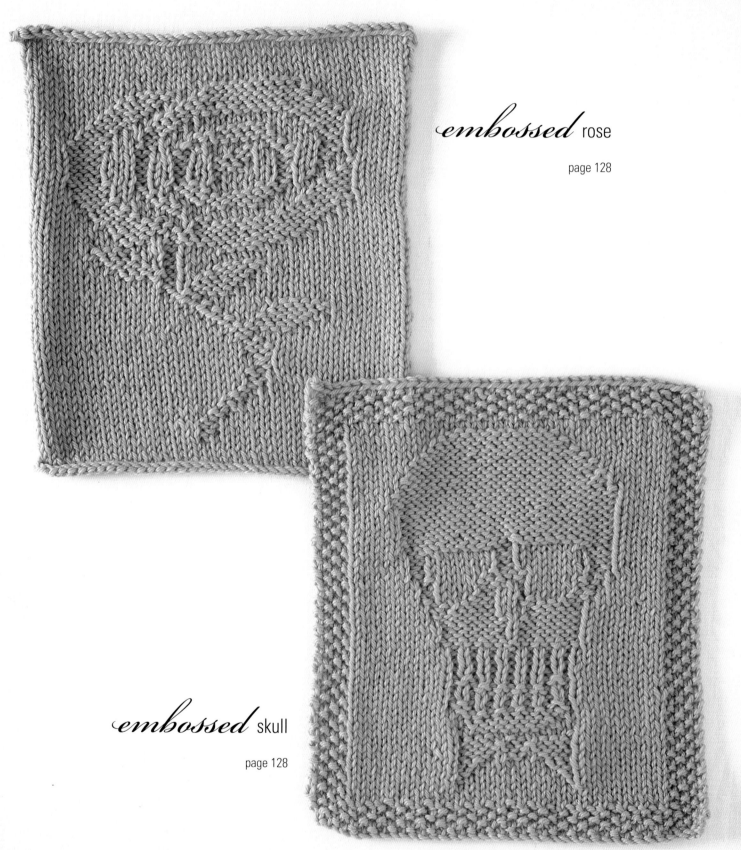

embossed rose

page 128

embossed skull

page 128

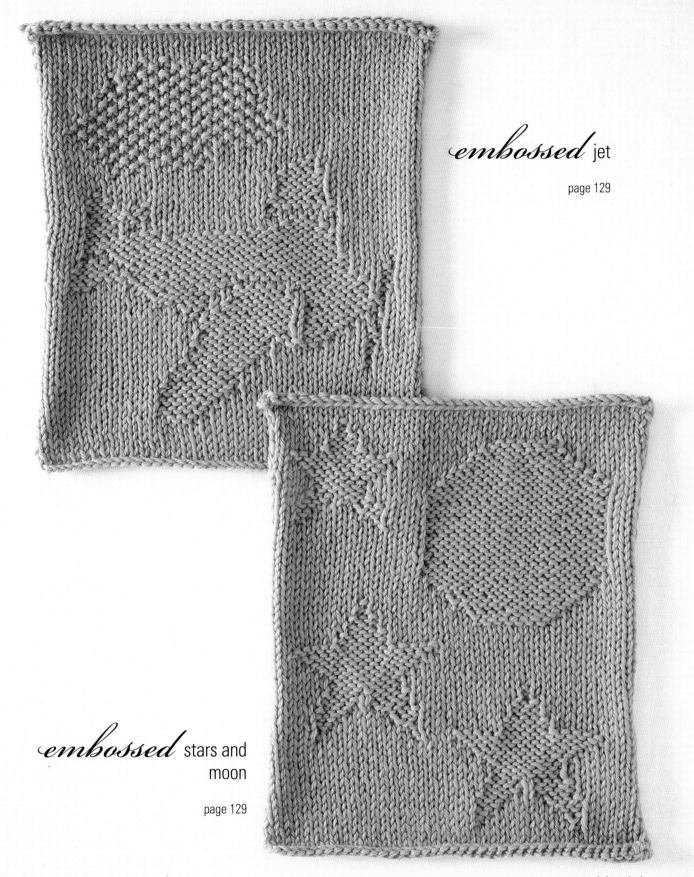

embossed jet

page 129

embossed stars and
moon

page 129

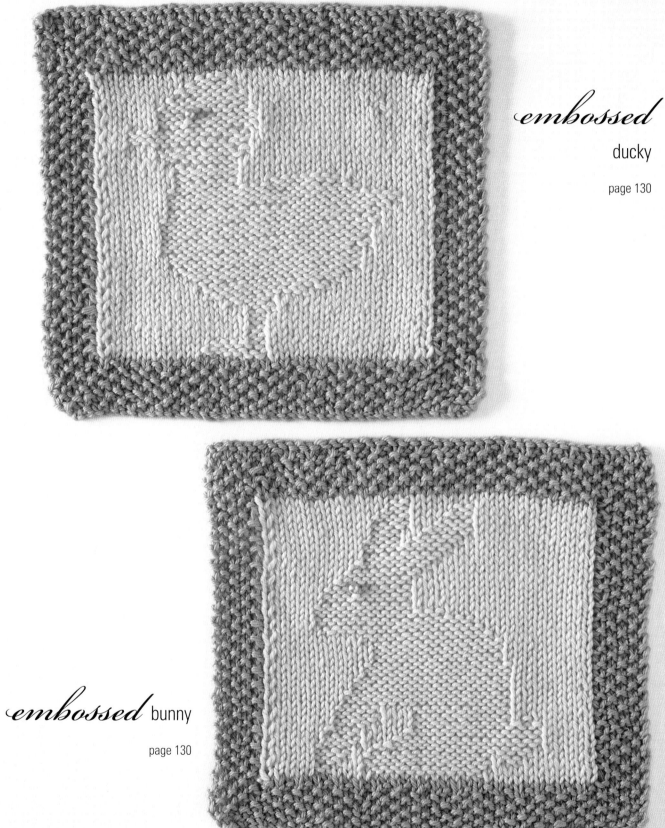

embossed
duckly
page 130

embossed bunny
page 130

embossed

teddy

page 131

embossed lamb

page 131

CHECKMATE page 92

Colors MC and CC

Notes Use MC (dark color) double-stranded. Be sure to twist colors when they are both at the same end of the row to prevent holes.

BLOCK

With CC and circular needle, cast on 42 stitches. Turn.

Row 1 With CC, p1, *k2, p2; repeat from * to the last st, k1. Slide the stitches to the other end of the needle.

Row 2 With MC, sl 1 wyif, *sl 2 wyib, sl 2 wyif; repeat from * to the last st, sl 1 wyib. Turn.

Row 3 With CC, repeat row 1.

Row 4 With MC, repeat row 2.

Row 5 With CC, k1, *p2, k2; repeat from * to the last st, p1. Slide the stitches to the other end of the needle.

Row 6 With MC, sl 1 wyib, *sl 2 wyif, sl 2 wyib; repeat from * to the last st, sl 1 wyif. Turn.

Row 7 With CC, repeat row 5.

Row 8 With MC, repeat row 6.

Repeat rows 1–8 for pattern until block length is the same as the width, ending on pattern row 8. Bind off.

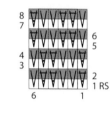

Stitch Key

☐ CC

■ MC

· Purl

☐ Knit

☑ Sl 1 wyif on RS, Sl 1 wyib on WS

Ⅴ Sl 1 wyib on RS, Sl 1 wyif on WS

☐ Repeat

DROP STITCH page 92

BLOCK

Cast on 37 stitches.

K 4 rows.

Row 1 (RS) K6, *bind off 1 stitch, k5; repeat from * to the last st, k1.

Row 2 K6, *yo, k5; repeat from * to the last st, k1. Continue in St st until block length is the same as the width less 6 rows.

Next row (RS) K6, *drop the next stitch off the needle, k5; repeat from * to the last st, k1.

Next row K6, *yo, k5; repeat from * to the last st, k1.

K 4 rows.

Bind off

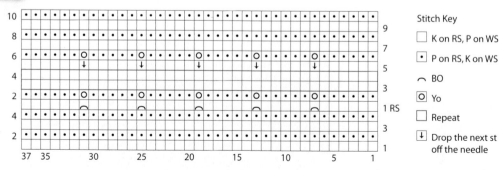

Stitch Key

☐ K on RS, P on WS

· P on RS, K on WS

⌢ BO

Ⓞ Yo

☐ Repeat

↓ Drop the next st off the needle

Colors MC and CC

SOLID DOUBLE-KNIT

Row 1 Sl 1, *with both colors in back k1 MC, with both colors in front p1 CC; repeat from * to the last st, with both colors in front p the last stitch with both colors.

Row 2 Sl 1, *with both colors in back k1 CC, with both colors in front p1 MC; repeat from * to the last st, with both colors in front p1.

MAPLE LEAF MOTIF

(over 34 stitches)

Row 1 With CC, [k1, sl 1 wyif] 8 times, (sl 1 wyib, p1), [k1, sl 1 wyif] 8 times. Turn.

Row 2 and all even-numbered rows Repeat previous row with MC.

Row 3 With CC, [sl 1 wyib, p1] 8 times, (sl 1 wyif, k1), [sl 1 wyib, p1] 8 times. Turn.

Row 5 With CC, repeat row 1.

Row 7 With CC, [sl 1 wyib, p1] 4 times, [k1, sl 1 wyif] twice, [sl 1 wyib, p1] twice, (k1, sl 1 wyif), [sl 1 wyib, p1] twice, [k1, wyif slip 1] twice, [sl 1 wyib, p1] 4 times. Turn.

Row 9 With CC, [k1, sl 1 wyif] 4 times, [sl 1 wyib, p1] 3 times, (k1, sl 1 wyif) , (sl 1 wyib, p1), (k1, sl 1 wyif), [sl 1 wyib, p1] 3 times, [k1, sl 1 wyif] 4 times. Turn.

Row 11 With CC, [sl 1 wyif, p1] 5 times, [k1, sl 1 wyif] 7 times, [sl 1 wyib, p1] 5 times. Turn.

Row 13 With CC, [k1, sl 1 wyif] 4 times, [sl 1 wyib, p1] 9 times, [k1, sl 1 wyif] 4 times. Turn.

Row 15 With CC, [sl 1 wyib, p1] 3 times, [k1, sl 1 wyif] 11 times, [sl 1 wyib, p1] 3 times. Turn.

Row 17 With CC, (k1, sl 1 wyif), [sl 1 wyib, p1] 15 times, (k1, sl 1 wyif). Turn.

Row 19 With CC, [k1, sl 1 wyif] 17 times. Turn.

Row 21 With CC, [sl 1 wyib, p1] 17 times. Turn.

Row 23 With CC, (sl 1 wyib, p1), [k1, sl 1 wyif] 15 times, (sl 1 wyib, p1). Turn.

Row 25 With CC, (k1, sl 1 wyif), (sl 1 wyib, p1 4 times, (k1, sl 1 wyif), [sl 1 wyib, p1] 5 times, (k1, sl 1 wyif), [sl 1 wyib, p1] 4 times, [k1, sl 1 wyif]. Turn.

Row 27 With CC, (sl 1 wyib, p1), [k1, sl 1 wyif] 3 times, [sl 1 wyif, p1] twice, [k1, sl 1 wyif] 5 times, [sl 1 wyib, p1] twice, [k1, sl 1 wyif] 3 times, (sl 1 wyib, p1). Turn.

Row 29 With CC, [k1, sl 1 wyif] 3 times, (sl 1 wyib, p1), (k1, sl 1 wyif), [sl 1 wyib, p1] 7 times, (k1, sl 1 wyif), (sl 1 wyib, p1), [k1, sl 1 wyif] 3 times. Turn.

Row 31 With CC, repeat row 11.

Row 33 With CC, [k1, sl 1 wyif] 5 times, [sl 1 wyib, p1] 7 times, [k1, sl 1 wyif] 5 times. Turn.

Row 35 With CC, [sl 1 wyib, p1] 5 times, (k1, sl 1 wyif), (sl 1 wyib, p1), (k1, sl 1 wyif] 3 times, (sl 1 wyib, p1), (k1, sl 1 wyif), [sl 1 wyib, p1] 5 times. Turn.

Row 37 With CC, [k1, sl 1 wyif] 7 times, [sl 1 wyib, p1] 3 times, [k1, sl 1 wyif] 7 times. Turn.

Row 39 With CC, [sl 1 wyib, p1] 8 times, (k1, sl 1 wyif), [sl 1 wyib, p1] 8 times. Turn.

Row 40 Repeat row 2.

BLOCK

With MC and circular needle, cast on 70 stitches. Work 24 rows of Solid double-knit.

Place a marker on either side of the center 34 stitches. Continuing in pattern as established, work 40 rows of Maple Leaf Motif between markers. Work 24 rows of Solid double-knit. Bind off.

Stitch Key

☐	MC
▩	CC
☐	Knit
Ⅴ	Slip 1 wyib
⩔	Slip 1 wyif
•	Purl

DOUBLE-KNIT DIAMOND page 93

Colors MC and CC

BLOCK

With MC and circular needle, cast on 68 stitches. Slide the stitches to the other end of the needle.

Row 1 With CC, p1, *(sl 1 wyib, p1), [k1, sl 1 wyif] 9 times, (sl 1 wyib, p1); repeat from * to the last st, slip 1. Turn.

Row 2 and all even-numbered rows Repeat the previous row with MC. Slide the stitches to the other end of the needle.

Row 3 With CC, p1, *(sl 1 wyib, p1), (k1, sl 1 wyif), [sl 1 wyib, p1] 7 times, (k1, sl 1 wyif), (sl 1 wyib, p1); repeat from * to the last st, k1. Turn.

Row 5 With CC, sl 1 wyif, *(k1, sl 1 wyif), (sl 1 wyib, p1), [k1, sl 1 wyif] 7 times, (sl 1 wyib, p1), (k1, sl 1 wyif); repeat from * to the last st, k1. Turn.

Row 7 With CC, p1, *[sl 1 wyib, p1] twice, [k1, sl 1 wyif] twice, [sl 1 wyib, p1] 3 times, [k1, sl 1 wyif] twice, [sl 1 wyib, p1] twice; repeat from * to the last st, sl 1. Turn.

Row 9 With CC, sl 1 wyif, *[k1, sl 1 wyif] 3 times, (sl 1 wyib, p1), [k1, sl 1 wyif] 3 times, (sl 1 wyib, p1), [k1, sl 1 wyif] 3 times; repeat from * to the last st, k1. Turn.

Row 11 With CC, p1, [sl 1 wyib, p1] 4 times, (k1, sl 1 wyif), (sl 1 wyib, p1), (k1, sl 1 wyif), [sl 1 wyib, p1] 4 times; repeat from * to the last st, sl 1. Turn.

Row 13 With CC, sl 1 wyif, *[k1, sl 1 wyif] 4 times, (sl 1 wyib, p1), (k1, sl 1 wyif), (sl 1 wyib, p1), [k1, sl 1 wyif] 4 times; repeat from * to the last st, k1. Turn.

Row 15 With CC, p1, *[sl 1 wyib, p1] 5 times, (k1, sl 1 wyif), [sl 1 wyib, p1] 5 times; repeat from * to the last st, sl 1. Turn.

Row 17 With CC, repeat row 13.

Row 19 With CC, repeat row 11.

Row 21 With CC, repeat row 9.

Row 23 With CC, repeat row 7.

Row 25 With CC, repeat row 5.

Row 27 With CC, repeat row 3.

Row 28 Repeat row 2.

Repeat rows 1–28 twice more.

With MC, bind off in p1, k1 rib.

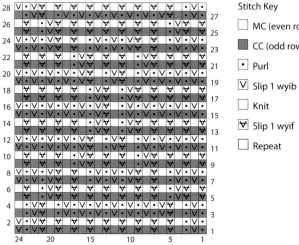

Stitch Key

☐	MC (even rows)
■	CC (odd rows)
•	Purl
Ⅴ	Slip 1 wyib
⩖	Knit
Ⅴ	Slip 1 wyif
☐	Repeat

DAISY ENTRELAC page 94

Colors A, B and C

ENTRELAC

Base Triangles (over a multple of 6 stitches)
Beginning with a right side row, *k2, turn, p2, turn. K3, turn, p3, turn. K4, turn, p4, turn, k5, turn, p5, turn, k6. Do not turn.
Rep from * to end. Change to the next color.

FIRST ROW OF RECTANGLES
Beginning Triangle

Beginning with a wrong side row, p2, turn, k1, m1, k1, turn. P2, p2tog, turn, k2, m1, k1, turn. P3, p2tog, turn, k3, m1, k1, turn. P4, p2tog, turn, k4, m1, k1, turn. P5, p2tog. Do not turn.

Rectangles

*With the wrong side facing, pick up and p6 stitches along the side of the base triangle. Beginning with a right side row [k6, turn, p5, p2tog, turn] 5 times. K6, turn, p4, p2tog. Do not turn. Repeat from * to the last triangle.

End Triangle

With the wrong side facing, pick up and p6 stitches along the side of the last base triangle.

Beginning with a right side row, k1, k2tog, k3, turn, p5, turn. K1, k2tog, k2, turn, p4, turn. K1, k2tog, k1, turn, p3, turn. K1, k2tog, turn, p2, turn. K2tog. Do not turn. Change to the next color.

SECOND ROW OF RECTANGLES

Beginning Rectangle

With the right side facing, pick up and k6 stitches along the side of the end triangle.

Beginning with a wrong side row, [p6, turn, k5, ssk, turn] 5 times. P6, turn, k5, ssk. Do not turn.

Rectangles

*With the right side facing, pick up and k6 stitches along the side of the rectangle.

Beginning with a wrong side row, [p6, turn, k5, ssk, turn] 5 times. P6, turn, k5, ssk. Do not turn. Repeat from * to end.

Repeat first and second rows of rectangles, ending with a second row.

ENDING ROW OF TRIANGLES

Beginning Triangle

Beginning with a wrong side row, p2, turn, k1, m1, k1, turn. P2, p2tog, turn, sl 1 st from the right-hand needle to the left-hand needle, k2tog, k1, m1, k1, turn. P3, p2tog, turn, sl 1 st from the right-hand needle to the left-hand needle, k2tog, k2, m1, k1, turn, bind off 4 stitches purlwise (1 stitch).

TRIANGLES

*With the wrong side facing, pick up and p6 stitches along the side of the rectangle (7 stitches). K5, k2tog, turn, p5, p2tog, turn. K4, k2tog, turn, p4, p2tog, turn. K3, k2tog, turn, p3, p2tog, turn.

K2, k2tog, turn, p2, p2tog, turn. K1, k2tog, turn, p1, p2tog, turn. K2tog, turn, p2tog, turn (1 stitch). Repeat from * to the last rectangle.

End Triangle

With the wrong side facing, pick up and p5 stitches (6 stitches). K1, k2tog, k3, turn, p2tog, p3, turn. K1, k2tog, k1, turn, p2tog, p1, turn. K2tog (1 stitch). Fasten off.

BLOCK

With A, cast on 30 stitches. Work base triangles row.

Alternate first and second rectangle rows in stripe pattern as follows:

*1 row B, 1 row C, 1 row B, 1 row A; repeat from * once more, then work end triangle row with B.

BASE TRIANGLES

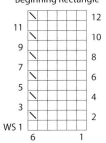

FIRST ROW RECTANGLES
Beginning Triangle

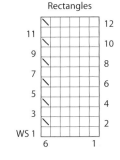

FIRST ROW RECTANGLES
Rectangles

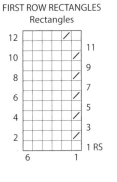

FIRST ROW RECTANGLES
End Triangle

Color Key

☐ A
☐ B
☐ C

Stitch Key

CO 1 st

☐ K on RS, P on WS

☐ Repeat

M Make 1

K2tog on RS, P2tog on WS

No stitch

SSK

Slip 1 st from RN to LN

BO Purlwise

SECOND ROW RECTANGLES
Beginning Rectangle

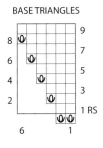

SECOND ROW RECTANGLES
Rectangles

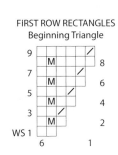

ENDING ROW TRIANGLES
Beginning Triangle

ENDING ROW TRIANGLES
End Triangle

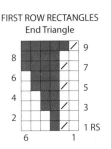

ENDING ROW TRIANGLES
Triangles

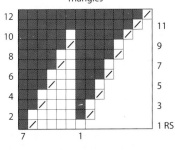

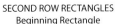
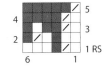

Colors MC and CC

Bobble Cast on 1 stitch K in front, back, front, back and front of st (5 stitches), turn, p5, turn, k5, turn, p5, turn. With the left-hand needle, lift the 2nd, 3rd, 4th and 5th stitches over the first st (1 stitch). Fasten off.

BLOCK
With MC, cast on 77 stitches using knitted cast-on. Mark the center stitch.
Row 1 (WS) With MC, knit.
Row 2 With CC, knit to 1 st before the center st, S2KP, k to end (2 stitches decreased).
Row 3 With CC, k to the center st, p1, k to end. Change to MC.

Repeat rows 2 and 3, alternating 2 rows MC with 2 rows CC until 3 stitches remain.
Next row (WS) S2PP (1 stitch). Fasten off.

FLOWER
PETAL SQUARES (make 5)
With A, cast on 19 stitches using knitted cast-on. Beginning with row 1, work same as block.

FINISHING
Arrange the 5 squares in a circle to form a flower, overlapping each square at the center. Sew the flower to the center of the block. Make a bobble and sew to the center of the flower.

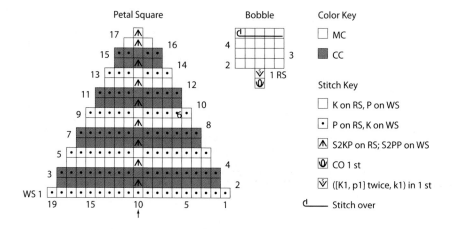

Petal Square

Bobble

Color Key
☐ MC
■ CC

Stitch Key
☐ K on RS, P on WS
• P on RS, K on WS
⋀ S2KP on RS; S2PP on WS
⓪ CO 1 st
⥋ ([K1, p1] twice, k1) in 1 st
⌐ Stitch over

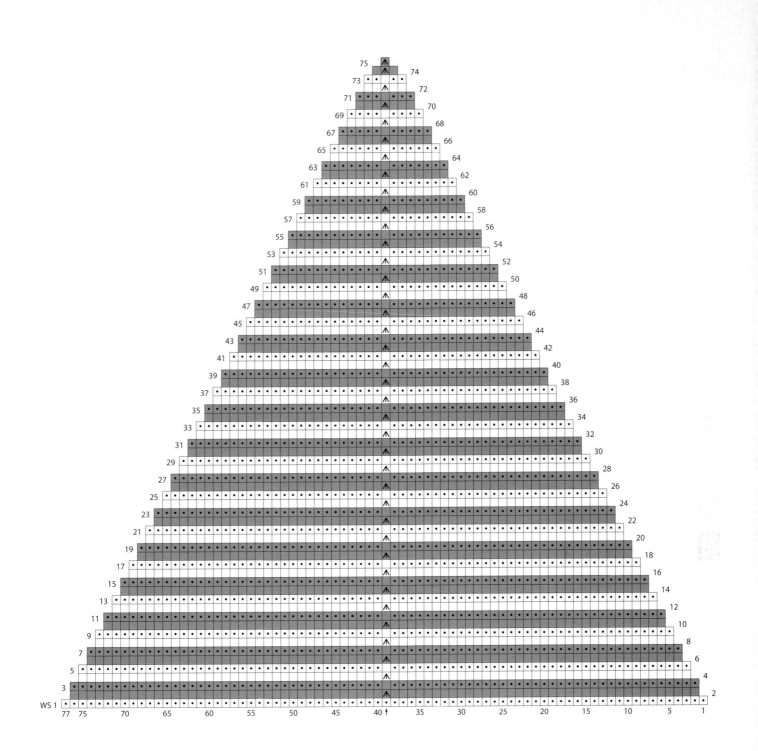

Colors MC and CC

SPECIAL STITCH
S2PP Slip 2 stitches as if to p2tog tbl, p1, pass the 2 slipped stitches over.

BLOCK
Square A (row 1, bottom)
With MC, cast on 19 stitches using knitted cast-on. Mark the center stitch.
Row 1 (WS) With MC, knit.
Row 2 With CC, knit to 1 st before the center st, S2KP, k to end (2 stitches decreased).
Row 3 With CC, k to the center st, p1, k to end. Change to MC.
Repeat rows 2 and 3, alternating 2 rows MC with 2 rows CC until 3 stitches remain.
Next row (WS) S2PP (1 stitch, counts as the first stitch for the next square).

Square B
With the right side facing and MC, place the remaining stitch from the previous square onto the needle, pick up and k8 stitches along the left side of square A, pick up and k1 stitch in the corner, cast on 9 stitches (19 stitches). Beginning with row 1, work the same as square A.

Square C
Working along side of square B, work the same as square B.

Square D
Working along side of square C, work the same as square B.

Square E (row 2)
With the right side facing and MC, cast on 9 stitches, pick up and k10 stitches along top edge of square A (19 stitches).
Beginning with row 1, work the same as square A.

Square F
With the right side facing and MC, place the remaining stitch from the previous square onto the needle, pick up and k8 stitches along left side of square E, pick up and k10 stitches along top of square B (19 stitches).
Beginning with row 1, work the same as square A.

Continue to add squares as established until the block is 4 squares wide and 4 squares high. Fasten off the last stitch.

FINISHING
Sew a bead in the corner of each square.

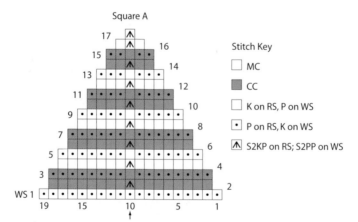

Square A

Stitch Key

☐ MC

▨ CC

☐ K on RS, P on WS

• P on RS, K on WS

⋀ S2KP on RS; S2PP on WS

QUATTRO DOMINO page 95

Colors MC and CC

SPECIAL STITCH
S2PP Slip 2 stitches as if to p2tog tbl, p1, pass the 2 slipped stitches over.

BLOCK

Square A (lower right)
With MC, cast on 37 stitches using knitted cast-on. Mark the center stitch.
Row 1 (WS) With MC, knit.
Row 2 With CC, knit to 1 st before the center st, S2KP, k to end (2 stitches decreased).
Row 3 With CC, k to the center st, p1, k to end. Change to MC.
Repeat rows 2 and 3, alternating 2 rows MC with 2 rows CC until 3 stitches remain.

Next row (WS) S2PP (1 stitch, counts as the first stitch for the next square).

Square B (lower left)
With the right side facing and MC, place the remaining stitch from the previous square onto the needle, pick up and k17 stitches along the left side of square A, pick up and k1 st in the corner, cast on 18 stitches (37 stitches). Beginning with row 1, work the same as square A. Fasten off the last st.

Square C (upper right)
With the right side facing and MC, cast on 18 stitches, pick up and k19 stitches along the top edge of square A (37 stitches).
Beginning with row 1, work the same as square A.

Square D (upper left)
With the right side facing and MC, place the remaining stitch from the previous square onto the needle, pick up and k17 stitches along the left side of square C, pick up and k19 stitches across the top of square B (37 stitches). Beginning with row 1, work the same as square A. Fasten off the last st.

Square A

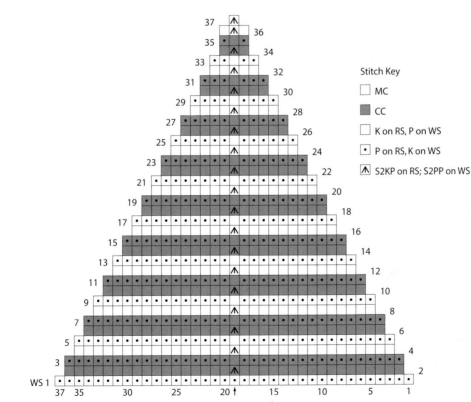

Stitch Key
- ☐ MC
- ▨ CC
- ☐ K on RS, P on WS
- ⊡ P on RS, K on WS
- ⊼ S2KP on RS; S2PP on WS

BOXED ILLUSION page 96

Boxed Illusion Pattern

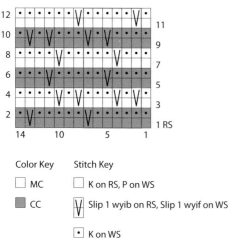

Color Key
- ☐ MC
- ▦ CC

Stitch Key
- ☐ K on RS, P on WS
- Ⅴ Slip 1 wyib on RS, Slip 1 wyif on WS
- • K on WS
- ☐ Repeat

BOXED ILLUSION PATTERN

(a multiple of 6 stitches plus 2 more)

Row 1 (RS) With CC, k1, *k5, sl 1 wyib; repeat from * to the last st, k1.

Row 2 With CC, k1, *sl 1 wyif, k5; repeat from * to the last st, k1.

Row 3 With MC, k1, *sl 1 wyib, k1, sl 1 wyib, k3; repeat from * to the last st, k1.

Row 4 With MC, k4, *sl 1 wyif, k1, sl 1 wyif, k3; repeat from * to the last 4 stitches, [sl 1 wyif, k1] twice.

Row 5 With CC, k4, *sl 1 wyib, k5; repeat from * to the last 4 stitches, sl 1 wyib, k3.

Row 6 With CC, k3, *sl 1 wyif, k5; repeat from * to the last 5 stitches, sl 1 wyif, k4.

Row 7 With MC, k3, *sl 1 wyib, k5; repeat from * to the last 5 stitches, sl 1 wyib, k4.

Row 8 With MC, k4, *sl 1 wyif, k5; repeat from * to the last 4 stitches, sl 1 wyif, k3.

Row 9 With CC, k4, *sl 1 wyib, k1, sl 1 wyib, k3; repeat from * to the last 4 stitches, [sl 1 wyib, k1] twice.

Row 10 With CC, k1, *sl 1 wyif, k1, sl 1 wyif, k3; repeat from * to the last st, k1.

Row 11 With MC, k1, *sl 1 wyib, k5; repeat from * to the last st, k1.

Row 12 With MC, k6, *sl 1 wyif, k5; repeat from * to the last 2 stitches, sl 1 wyif, k1.

Repeat rows 1–12 for pattern.

BLOCK

With MC, cast on 45 stitches. K 1 row.

Row 1 (RS) Work 20 stitches in Boxed Illusion pattern or chart, pm, with MC, work 5 stitches in Garter st, pm, work 20 stitches in Boxed Illusion pattern or chart.

Continue in patterns as established until 3 repeats of Boxed Illusion pattern or chart have been completed.

With MC, work in Garter st for 1" (2.5cm), ending with a WS row.

Repeat row 1 and continue in patterns as established until another 3 repeats of Boxed Illusion pattern or chart have been completed.

With MC, k 1 row.

Bind off purlwise.

FINISHING

With 2 strands of CC, embroider flower (see diagram) in center of block.

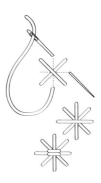

SKELETON MOSAIC page 96

Colors MC and CC

SKELETON PATTERN

(over 29 stitches)

Row 1 (RS) With CC, [k5, sl 2 wyib] twice, k5.

Row 2 With CC, p5, [sl 2 wyif, p5] twice.

Row 3 With MC, k1, sl 2 wyib, k1, sl 1 wyib, k9, sl 1 wyib, k1, sl 2 wyib, k1.

Row 4 With MC, p1, sl 2 wyif, p1, sl 1 wyif, p9, sl 1 wyif, p1, sl 2 yif, p1.

Row 5 With CC, k5, sl 1 wyib, k1, sl 1 wyib, k3, sl 1 wyib, k1, sl 1 wyib, k5.

Row 6 With CC, p5, sl 1 wyif, p1, sl 1 wyif, p3, sl 1 wyif, p1, sl 1 wyif, p5.

Row 7 With MC, k8, sl 3 wyib, k8.

Row 8 With MC, p8, sl 3 wyif, p8.

Row 9 With CC, k2, sl 1 wyib, k1, sl 1 wyib, k2, sl 1 wyib, k3, sl 1 wyib, k2, sl 1 wyib, k1, sl 1 wyib, k2.

Row 10 With CC, p2, sl 1 wyif, p1, sl 1 wyif, p2, sl 1 wyif, p3, sl 1 wyif, p2, sl 1 wyif, p1, sl 1 wyif, p2.

Row 11 With MC, k5, sl 1 wyib, k7, sl 1 wyib, k5.

Row 12 With MC, p5, sl 1 wyif, p7, sl 1 wyif, p5.

Row 13 With CC, [k1, sl 1 wyib] twice, k2, sl 1 wyib, k5, sl 1 wyib, k2, [sl 1 wyib, k1] twice.

Row 14 With CC, [p1, sl 1 wyif] twice, p2, sl 1 wyif, p5, sl 1 wyif, p2, [sl 1 wyif, p1] twice.

Row 15 With MC, k4, sl 1 wyib, k2, sl 1 wyib, k3, sl 1 wyib, k2, sl 1 wyib, k4.

Row 16 With MC, p4, sl 1 wyif, p2, sl 1 wyif, p3, sl 1 wyif, p2, sl 1 wyif, p4.

Row 17 With CC, k2, sl 1 wyib, k2, sl 2 wyib, k5, sl 2 wyib, k2, sl 1 wyib, k2.

Row 18 With CC, p2, sl 1 wyif, p2, sl 2 wyif, p5, sl 2 wyif, p2, sl 1 wyif, p2.

Row 19 With MC, k3, sl 1 wyib, k3, sl 2 wyib, k1, sl 2 wyib, k3, sl 1 wyib, k3.

Row 20 With MC, p3, sl 1 wyif, p3, sl 2 wyif, p1, sl 2 wyif, p3, sl 1 wyif, p3.

Row 21 With CC, k4, sl 2 wyib, k7, sl 2 wyib, k4.

Row 22 With CC, p4, sl 2 wyif, p7, sl 2 wyif, p4.

Row 23 With MC, k6, sl 1 wyib, k1, sl 3 wyib, k1, sl 1 wyib, k6.

Row 24 With MC, p6, sl 1 wyif, p1, sl 3 wyif, p1, sl 1 wyif, p6.

Row 25 With CC, k3, sl 1 wyib, k1, sl 1 wyib, k7, sl 1 wyib, k1, sl 1 wyib, k3.

Row 26 With CC, p3, sl 1 wyif, p1, sl 1 wyif, p7, sl 1 wyif, p1, sl 1 wyif, p3.

Row 27 With MC, k1, sl 2 wyib, k13, sl 2 wyib, k1.

Row 28 With MC, p1, sl 2 wyif, p13, sl 2 wyif, p1.

Row 29 With CC, k3, sl 1 wyib, k2, [sl 1 wyib, k1] 3 times, sl 1 wyib, k2, sl 1 wyib, k3.

Row 30 With CC, p3, sl 1 wyif, p2, sl 1 wyif, [p1, sl 1 wyif] 3 times, p2, sl 1 wyif, p3.

Row 31 With MC, k5, sl 1 wyib, k7, sl 1 wyib, k5.

Row 32 With MC, p5, sl 1 wyif, p7, sl 1 wyif, p5.

Row 33 With CC, k4, sl 1 wyib, k2, [sl 1 wyib, k1] twice, sl 1 wyib, k2, sl 1 wyib, k4.

Row 34 With CC, p4, sl 1 wyif, p2, sl 1 wyif, [p1, sl 1 wyif] twice, p2, sl 1 wyif, p4.

Row 35 With MC, k3, sl 1 wyib, k2, sl 1 wyib, k5, sl 1 wyib, k2, sl 1 wyib, k3.

Row 36 With MC, p3, sl 1 wyif, p2, sl 1 wyif, p5, sl 1 wyif, p2, sl 1 wyif, p3.

Row 37 With CC, k4, sl 2 wyib, k2, sl 1 wyib, k1, sl 1 wyib, k2, sl 2 wyib, k4.

Row 38 With CC, p4, sl 2 wyif, p2, sl 1 wyif, p1, sl 1 wyif, p2, sl 2 wyif, p4.

Row 39 With MC, k2, sl 2 wyib, k3, sl 1 wyib, k3, sl 1 wyib, k3, sl 2 wyib, k2.

Row 40 With MC, p2, sl 2 wyif, p3, sl 1 wyif, p3, sl 1 wyif, p3, sl 2 wyif, p2.

Row 41 With CC, [k5, sl 2 wyib] twice, k5.

Row 42 With CC, p5, [sl 2 wyif, p5] twice.

BLOCK

With MC, cast on 50 stitches.

Work 6 rows in Garter st.

Set-up row (RS) With MC, work 4 stitches in Garter st; work 19 stitches in Skeleton pattern or chart; with MC, work 4 stitches in Garter st; work 19 stitches in Skeleton pattern or chart; with MC, work 4 stitches in Garter st.

Continue in patterns as established until 42 rows of Skeleton chart or pattern have been completed. With MC, work 16 rows in Garter stitch.

Bind off.

Skeleton Pattern

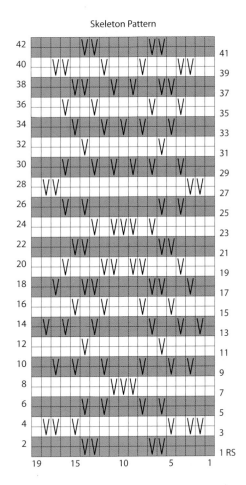

Color Key

☐ MC

▨ CC

Stitch Key

☐ K on RS, P on WS

Ⅴ Slip 1 wyib on RS, Slip 1 wyif on WS

STEEKED FAIR ISLE page 97

Colors A, B C, D, E and F

With double-pointed needles and A, cast on 52 stitches. Pm and join. K2 steek stitches alternating the 2 colors of the rnd, work Steeked Fair Isle chart to the last 2 stitches, k2 steek stitches alternating the 2 colors of the rnd.
Continue in Patterns as established until the 45-row Steeked Fair Isle chart is complete.
Bind off.

FINISHING

Sew a machine seam vertically along each side of the steek. Cut along the center of the machine seams.

Color Key

☐ Cream

☐ Cream Gray

▨ Light Charcoal Gray

■ Dark Charcoal Gray

▨ Lavender

☐ Light Blue

Stitch Key

☐ K on RS

MOCK FAIR ISLE WITH BEADS page 97

Colors MC and CC

BLOCK

With MC, cast on 51 stitches.
Work 50 rows of Mock Fair Isle chart.
Bind off with MC.

Finishing

Sew beads to block as marked on chart.

Stitch Key

■ Black

☐ Variegated

☒ Bead

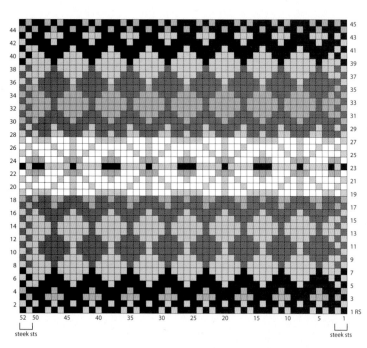

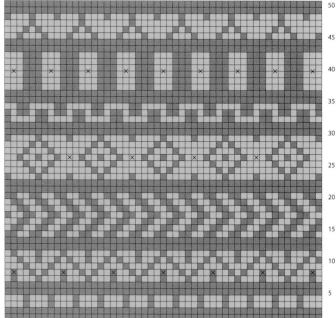

HONEYCOMB SMOCKING page 98

BLOCK

Cast on 43 stitches (a multiple of 8 stitches plus 3 more).

Rows 1, 3 and 5 (RS) P3, *k1, p3; repeat from to end.

Rows 2, 4 and 6 K3, *p1, k3; repeat from * to end.

Row 7 (smocking) *Work 8 stitches in rib, slip the last 5 stitches on the right-hand needle to a cable needle and hold in front, wrap yarn clockwise twice around these stitches, ending with the yarn in back, slip these 5 stitches back to the right-hand needle; repeat from * to the last 3 stitches, p3.

Rows 8–10 Work in rib as established.

Row 11 (smocking) P3, k1, *work 8 stitches in rib, slip the last 5 stitches on the right-hand needle to a cable needle and hold in front, wrap yarn clockwise twice around these stitches, ending with the yarn in back, slip these 5 stitches back to the right-hand needle; repeat from * to the last 7 stitches, p3, k1, p3.

Rows 12–14 Work in rib as established.

Repeat rows 1–14 for pattern until block length is the same as the width.

Bind off.

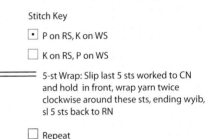

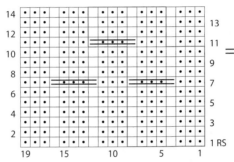

Stitch Key

- • P on RS, K on WS
- ☐ K on RS, P on WS
- ═ 5-st Wrap: Slip last 5 sts worked to CN and hold in front, wrap yarn twice clockwise around these sts, ending wyib, sl 5 sts back to RN
- ☐ Repeat

BOLD SMOCKING page 98

BLOCK

Cast on 66 stitches (a multiple of 8 stitches plus 2 more).

Preparation row (RS) P2, *k2, p2; repeat from * to end.

Rows 1 and 3 K2, *p2, k2; repeat from * to end.

Row 2 P2, *k2, p2; repeat from * to end.

Row 4 P2, *insert the right-hand needle between the 6th and 7th stitches and draw up a loop, slip the loop to the left-hand needle and k it together with the first stitch on the left-hand needle, k1, p2, k2, p2; repeat from * to end.

Rows 5 and 7 Repeat row 1.

Row 6 Repeat row 2.

Row 8 P2, k2, p2, *insert the right-hand needle between the 6th and 7th stitches and draw up a loop, slip the loop to the left-hand needle and k it together with the first stitch on the left-hand needle, k1, p2, k2, p2; repeat from * to the last 4 stitches, k2, p2.

Repeat rows 1–8 until block length is same as the width, ending with pattern row 4 or 8.

Bind off.

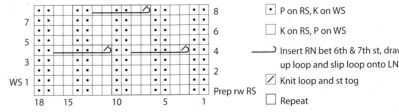

Stitch Key

- • P on RS, K on WS
- ☐ K on RS, P on WS
- ⌐ Insert RN bet 6th & 7th st, draw up loop and slip loop onto LN
- ⟋ Knit loop and st tog
- ☐ Repeat

MULTILAYERED LACE page 99

BLOCK

Layer 1

Cast on 49 stitches (a multiple of 9 stitches plus 4 more). P 1 row.

Row 1 (RS) K3, *yo, k2, ssk, k2tog, k2, yo, k1; repeat from * to the last st, k1.

Row 2 Purl.

Row 3 K2, *yo, k2, ssk, k2tog, k2, yo, k1; repeat from * to the last 2 stitches, k2.

Row 4 Purl.

Rows 5–15 Repeat rows 1–4 twice, then rows 1–3 once more.

Leave these stitches on a spare needle.

Layers 2–5

Cast on 49 stitches. P 1 row.

Rows 1–7 Work rows 1–4, then rows 1–3 once more.

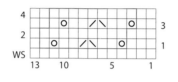

Row 8 (joining row) With the wrong sides facing and the shorter layer behind the longer layer, *purl 1 st from the shorter layer together with 1 st from the longer layer; repeat from * to end.

Rows 9–15 Repeat rows 1–4 once, then rows 1–3. Leave these stitches on a spare needle.

Layer 6

Cast on 49 stitches. P 1 row.

Rows 1–8 Work the same as Layer 2.

Bind off knitwise.

Stitch Key

- ☐ K on RS, P on WS
- ☐O☐ Yo
- ☐╲☐ SSK
- ☐╱☐ K2tog
- ☐ Repeat

FLORAL FANTASY page 99

SPECIAL STITCH

Make Bobble (MB) Cast on 1 st. (K1, p1, k1, p1, k1) all in the same st, turn, p5, turn, pass the 2nd, 3rd, 4th and 5th stitches, one at a time, over the first st, then k this st tbl.

BLOCK

Note Stitch count is given for each needle.

Cast on 8 stitches (2 stitches each on 4 double-pointed needles). K 1 rnd.

Rnd 1 *K1, yo, k1; repeat from * to end (3 stitches).

Rnd 2 and all even-numbered rnds Knit.

Rnd 3 *[K1, yo] twice, k1; repeat from * to end (5 stitches).

Rnd 5 *K1, yo, k3, yo, k1; repeat from * to end (7 stitches).

Rnd 7 *K1, yo, k5, yo, k1; repeat from * to end (9 stitches).

Rnd 9 *K1, yo, k7, yo, k1; repeat from * to end (11 stitches).

Rnd 11 *K1, yo, k9, yo, k1; repeat from * to end (13 stitches).

Rnd 13 *K1, yo, k11, yo, k1; repeat from * to end (15 stitches).

Rnd 15 *K1, yo, k13, yo, k1; repeat from * to end (17 stitches).

Rnd 17 *K1, yo, k15, yo, k1; repeat from * to end (19 stitches).

Rnd 19 *[K1, yo] twice, k5, ssk, k1, k2tog, k5, [yo, k1] twice; repeat from * to end (84 stitches).

Rnd 21 *[K1, yo] twice, ssk, yo, k4, ssk, k1, k2tog, k4, yo, k2tog, [yo, k1] twice; repeat from * to end (23 stitches).

Rnd 23 *[K1, yo] twice, [ssk, yo] twice, k3, ssk, k1, k2tog, k3, [yo, k2tog] twice, [yo, k1] twice; repeat from * to end (25 stitches).

Rnd 25 *[K1, yo] twice, [ssk, yo] 3 times, k2, ssk, k1, k2tog, k2, [yo, k2tog] 3 times, [yo, k1] twice; repeat from * to end (27 stitches).

Rnd 27 *[K1, yo] twice, [ssk, yo] 4 times, k1, ssk, k1, k2tog, k1, [yo, k2tog] 4 times, [yo, k1] twice; repeat from * to end (29 stitches).

Rnd 29 *[K1, yo] twice, [ssk, yo] 5 times, ssk, k1, k2tog, [yo, k2tog] 5 times, [yo, k1] twice; repeat from * to end (31 stitches).

Row 31 *[K1, yo] twice, [ssk, yo] 6 times, SK2P, [yo, k2tog] 6 times, [yo, k1] twice; repeat from * to end (33 stitches).

Rnd 33 *[K1, yo] twice, [ssk, yo] 6 times, ssk, k1, k2tog, [yo, k2tog] 6 times, [yo, k1] twice; repeat from * to end (35 stitches).

Rnd 35 *[K1, yo] twice, [ssk, yo] 7 times, SK2P, [yo, k2tog] 7 times, [yo, k1] twice; repeat from * to end (37 stitches).

Rnd 37 *[K1, yo] twice, [ssk, yo] 7 times, ssk, k1, k2tog, [yo, k2tog] 7 times, [yo, k1] twice; repeat from * to end (39 stitches).

Rnd 39 *[K1, yo] twice, [ssk, yo] 8 times, SK2P, [yo, k2tog] 8 times, [yo, k1] twice; repeat from * to end (41 stitches).

Rnd 40 Knit.

Bind off.

FINISHING

Make 5 bobbles and sew them to the center of the block.

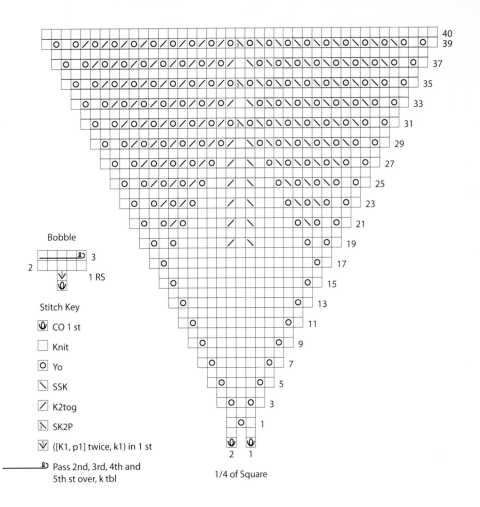

1/4 of Square

Bobble

Stitch Key

CO 1 st	
Knit	
Yo	
SSK	
K2tog	
SK2P	
([K1, p1] twice, k1) in 1 st	
Pass 2nd, 3rd, 4th and 5th st over, k tbl	

DIAGONAL BLOCK page 100

BLOCK

Cast on 44 stitches (a multiple of 8 stitches plus 4 more).

Row 1 (WS) K2, *yo, p2tog, k1, p2tog, yo, k3; repeat from * to the last 2 stitches, k2.

Row 2 K2, *k5, p2tog, yo, k1; repeat from * to the last 2 stitches, k2.

Row 3 K2, *k2, yo, p2tog, k1, p2tog, yo, k1; repeat from * to the last 2 stitches, k2.

Row 4 K2, *k3, p2tog, yo, k3; repeat from * to the last 2 stitches, k2.

Row 5 K1, *p2tog, yo, k3, yo, p2tog, k1; repeat from * to the last 3 stitches, k3.

Row 6 K2, *k1, p2tog, yo, k5; repeat from * to the last 2 stitches, k2.

Row 7 K2, *k1, p2tog, yo, k3, yo, p2tog; repeat from * to the last 2 stitches, k2.

Row 8 K1, *p2tog, yo, k6; repeat from * to the last 3 stitches, k3.

Repeat rows 1–8 eight times more.

Bind off knitwise.

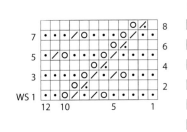

Stitch Key

•	K on WS
O	Yo
/	P2tog on WS
	K on RS
/	P2tog on RS
	Repeat

LAYERED LACE SCALLOP page 100

FISHTAIL STITCH
(a multiple of 10 stitches plus 3 more)
Row 1 (RS) K2tog, yo, *k3, SK2P, k3, yo, k1, yo, repeat from * to the last st, k1.
Rows 2 and 4 Purl.
Row 3 K2, *yo, k2, SK2P, k2, yo, k3, repeat from * to the last st, k1.
Row 5 K2tog, yo, *k1, yo, k1, sk2p, [k1, yo] twice, SK2P, yo, repeat from * to the last st, k1.
Row 6 Purl.
Repeat rows 1–6.

BLOCK
First Layer
Cast on 43 stitches.
P 1 row.
Work rows 1–6 of Fishtail st 3 times, then rows 1–5 once more.
Leave these stitches on a spare needle.

Second Layer
Cast on 43 stitches.
P 1 row.
Work rows 1–6 of Fishtail st, then rows 1–5 once more.

JOIN LAYERS
With wrong sides facing, place the needle with the second layer behind the needle with the first layer. *Purl a stitch from the back needle together with a stitch from the front needle; repeat from * to end. Work rows 1–6 of Fishtail st 5 times more.
Bind off knitwise.

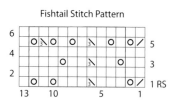

Fishtail Stitch Pattern

Stitch Key
- ∕ K2tog
- O Yo
- ☐ K on RS, P on WS
- ⋉ SK2P
- ☐ Repeat

DIAMONDS page 101

Row 8 K2, *[k2tog, yo] 4 times, k3; repeat from * to the last 10 stitches, [k2tog, yo] 4 times, k2.
Row 10 K1, *[k2tog, yo] 5 times, k1; repeat from * to end.
Row 12 Repeat row 8.
Row 14 Repeat row 6.
Row 16 Repeat row 4.
Repeat rows 1–16 for pattern.

BLOCK
Cast on 42 stitches.
Row 1 (WS) [P1, k1] twice, work Diamond Lace pattern over the next 34 stitches, (k1, p1) twice. Continue in patterns as established, keeping the first and last 4 stitches in rib until 48 rows of Diamond Lace pattern have been completed. Rep rows 1–3.
Bind off.

DIAMOND LACE PATTERN
(a multiple of 11 stitches plus 1 more)
Row 1 and all odd-numbered rows (WS) Purl.
Row 2 K5, *k2tog, yo, k9; repeat from * to the last 7 stitches, k2tog, yo, k5.
Row 4 K4, *[k2tog, yo] twice, k7; repeat from * to the last 8 stitches, [k2tog, yo] twice, k4.
Row 6 K3, *[k2tog, yo] 3 times, k5; repeat from * to the last 9 stitches, [k2tog, yo] 3 times, k3.

Diamond Lace Pattern

Stitch Key
- ☐ K on RS, P on WS
- ∕ K2tog
- O Yo
- ☐ Repeat

BOBBLE LACE page 101

SPECIAL STITCH

Make Bobble (MB) (K1, p1, k1, p1, k1) in the same st, turn, p5, turn, pass the 2nd, 3rd, 4th and 5th stitches, one at a time, over the first st, then k this st tbl.

BLOCK

With MC, cast on 43 stitches. P 1 row.

Row 1 (RS) Knit.

Row 2 and all WS rows Purl.

Row 3 K3, [k5, yo, SK2P, yo, k1, MB, k1, yo, SK2P, yo, k4] twice, k4.

Row 5 K3, [k3, (k1, k2tog, yo, k1, yo, ssk) twice, k3] twice, k4.

Row 7 K6, [k2tog, yo, k1, MB, k1, yo, SK2P, yo, k1, MB, k1, yo, ssk, k5] twice, k1.

Row 9 K3, [k1, k2tog, yo, k1, yo, ssk] 6 times, k4.

Row 11 K3, k2tog, [yo, k1, MB, k1, yo, SK2P, yo, k3, yo, SK2P, yo, k1, MB, k1, yo], SK2P, repeat between [ ], ssk, k3.

Row 13 K3, [k1, yo, ssk, k1, k2tog, yo, k7, yo, ssk, k1, k2tog, yo] twice, k4.

Row 15 K3, [MB, k1, yo, SK2P, yo, k9, yo, SK2P, yo, k1] twice, MB, k3.

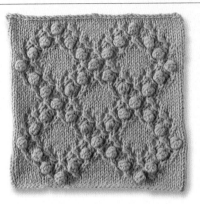

Row 17 K3, [k1, k2tog, yo, k1, yo, ssk, k7, k2tog, yo, k1, yo, ssk] twice, k4.

Row 19 K3, k2tog, [yo, k1, MB, k1, yo, ssk, k5, k2tog, yo, k1, MB, k1, yo], SK2P, repeat between [ ], ssk, k3.

Row 21 K3, [k1, yo, ssk, k1, k2tog, yo] 6 times, k4. **CH**

Row 23 K3, [k1, (k1, yo, sk2p, yo, k1, MB) twice, k1, yo, SK2P, yo, k1] twice, k4.

Row 25 K3, [k3, (k1, yo, ssk, k1, k2tog, yo) twice, k3] twice, k4.

Row 26 Purl.

Rows 27–50 Repeat rows 3–26.

Row 51 Repeat row 3.

Row 52 Purl.

Row 53 Knit.

Row 54 Purl.

Bind off.

Block

(chart)

Bobble

(chart)

Stitch Key

- ☐ K on RS, P on WS
- O Yo
- ⊼ SK2P
- B MB (make bobble)
- ⩔ ([K1, p1] twice, k1) in 1 st
- ── Pass 2nd, 3rd, 4th and 5th st over, k tbl
- ╱ K2tog
- ╲ SSK

special techniques **123**

ANGEL BLOSSOM page 102

SPECIAL STITCH

Make Bobble (MB) (K1, p1, k1, p1, k1) all in the next st, turn, p5, turn, pass the 2nd, 3rd, 4th and 5th stitches, one at a time, over the first st, then k this st tbl.

BLOCK

With double-pointed needles, cast on 41 stitches (a multiple of 18 stitches plus 5 more).

Row 1 (RS) K5, *yo, k1, yo, [ssk, yo] twice, k2, ssk, k5, k2tog, k2; repeat from * to end.

Row 2 and all WS rows Purl.

Row 3 K5, *yo, k3, yo, [ssk, yo] twice, k2, ssk, k3, k2tog, k2; repeat from * to end.

Row 5 K5, *yo, k2, MB, k2, yo, [ssk, yo] twice, k2, ssk, k1, k2tog, k2; repeat from * to end.

Row 7 K5, *yo, k2, MB, k1, MB, k2, yo, [ssk, yo] twice, k2, SK2P, k2; repeat from * to end.

Row 9 K2, *ssk, k5, k2tog, k2, yo, [k2tog, yo] twice, k1, yo, k2; repeat from * to the last 3 stitches, k3.

Row 11 K2, *ssk, k3, k2tog, k2, yo, [k2tog, yo] twice, k3, yo, k2; repeat from * to the last 3 stitches, k3.

Row 13 K2, *ssk, k1, k2tog, k2, yo, [k2tog, yo] twice, k2, MB, k2, yo, k2; repeat from * to the last 3 stitches, k3.

Row 15 K2, *SK2P, k2, yo, [k2tog, yo] twice, k2, MB, k1, MB, k2, yo, k2; repeat from * to the last 3 stitches, k3.

Row 16 Purl.

Repeat rows 1–16 three times.

Bind off knitwise.

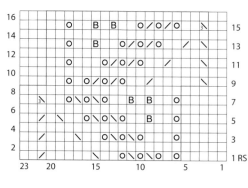

Bobble

Stitch Key

☐	K on RS, P on WS
Ⓞ	Yo
◣	SSK
◲	K2tog
Ⓑ	MB (make bobble)
Ⓥ	([K1, p1] twice, k1) in 1 st
⌐	Pass 2nd, 3rd, 4th and 5th st over, k tbl
◩	SK2P
☐	Repeat

FAIRY LEAVES page 102

Stitch Key

•	P on RS, K on WS	Ⓞ	Yo
☐	K on RS, P on WS	◩	SK2P
◲	K2tog	◮	S2KP
Ⓥ	(K1, Yo, K1) in 1 st	☐	Repeat
◣	SSK		

Fairy Leaves Panel

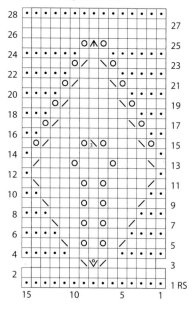

BLOCK

FAIRY LEAVES PANEL (make 2)

Cast on 43 stitches (a multiple of 14 stitches plus 1 more).

Rows 1 and 2 Purl.

Row 3 (RS) *K5, k2tog, (k1, yo, k1) in the next st, ssk, k4; repeat from * to the last st, k1.

Row 4 *K5, p5, k4; repeat from * to the last st, k1.

Row 5 *K4, k2tog, [k1, yo] twice, k1, ssk, k3; repeat from * to the last st, k1.

Row 6 *K4, p7, k3; repeat from * to the last st, k1.

Row 7 *K3, k2tog, k2, yo, k1, yo, k2, ssk, k2; repeat from * to the last st, k1.

Row 8 *K3, p9, k2; repeat from * to the last st, k1.

Row 9 *K2, k2tog, k3, yo, k1, yo, k3, ssk, k1; repeat from * to the last st, k1.

Row 10 *K2, p11, k1; repeat from * to the last st, k1.

Row 11 *K1, k2tog, k4, yo, k1, yo, k4, ssk; repeat from * to the last st, k1.

Rows 12 and 14 *K1, p13; repeat from * to the last st, k1.

Row 13 *K1, ssk, [k3, yo] twice, k3, k2tog; repeat from * to the last st, k1.

Row 15 *K1, yo, ssk, k3, yo, SK2P, yo, k3, k2tog, yo; repeat from * to the last st, k1.

Row 16 Repeat row 10.

Row 17 *K2, yo, ssk, k7, k2tog, yo, k1; repeat from * to the last st, k1.

Row 18 Repeat row 8.

Row 19 *K3, yo, ssk, k5, k2tog, yo, k2; repeat from * to the last st, k1.

Row 20 Repeat row 6.

Row 21 *K4, yo, ssk, k3, k2tog, yo, k3; repeat from * to the last st, k1.

Row 22 Repeat row 4.

Row 23 *K5, yo, ssk, k1, k2tog, yo, k4; repeat from * to the last st, k1.

Row 24 *K6, p3, k5; repeat from * to the last st, k1.

Row 25 *K6, yo, SK2P, yo, k5; repeat from * to the last st, k1.

Row 26 Purl.

Rows 27 and 28 Knit.

Bind off.

FINISHING

Sew the cast-on edges together.
Bind-off edges make up the sides of the square.
Row ends make up the top and bottom of the square.

Optional Sew decorative buttons along the center seam.

EMBOSSED CASTLE page 103

BLOCK

Cast on 40 stitches.
Work 60 rows of the Castle chart.
Bind off.

Stitch Key

☐ K on RS, P on WS

▣ P on RS, K on WS

Colors A, B and C

CLASSIC CANDELABRA PATTERN
(over 39 stitches)

Row 1 (RS) With B, knit.

Row 2 With B, purl.

Row 3 With A, k2, [sl 1 wyib, k1] 17 times, sl 1 wyib, k2.

Row 4 With A, p2, sl 1 wyif, [p1, sl 1 wyif] 17 times, p2.

Rows 5 and 6 Repeat rows 1 and 2.

Row 7 With A, k2, [sl 1 wyib, k1] 4 times, sl 1 wyib, k5, [sl 1 wyib, k1] 3 times, sl 1 wyib, k5, [sl 1 wyib, k1] 4 times, sl 1 wyib, k2.

Row 8 With A, p2, sl 1 wyif, [p1, sl 1 wyif] 4 times, p5, sl 1 wyif, [p1, sl 1 wyif] 3 times, p5, sl 1 wyif, [p1, sl 1 wyif] 4 times, p2.

Row 9 With B, k11, sl 1 wyib, k3, sl 1 wyib, k7, sl 1 wyib, k3, sl 1 wyib, k11.

Row 10 With B, p11, sl 1 wyif, p3, sl 1 wyif, p7, sl 1 wyif, p3, sl 1 wyif, p11.

Row 11 With A, k2, [sl 1 wyib, k1] 3 times, sl 1 wyib, [k3, sl 1 wyib, k1, sl 1 wyib] 3 times, k3, [sl 1 wyib, k1] 3 times, sl 1 wyib, k2.

Row 12 With A, p2, sl 1 wyif, [p1, sl 1 wyif] 3 times, p3, [sl 1 wyif, p1, sl 1 wyif, p3] 3 times, sl 1 wyif, [p1, sl 1 wyif] 3 times, p2.

Row 13 With B, k9, sl 1 wyib, k7, sl 1 wyib, k3, sl 1 wyib, k7, sl 1 wyib, k9.

Row 14 With B, p9, sl 1 wyif, p7, sl 1 wyif, p3, sl 1 wyif, p7, sl 1 wyif, p9.

Row 15 With A, k1, sl 1 wyib, k2, sl 1 wyib, k1, sl 1 wyib, k3, [sl 1 wyib, k1] 3 times, sl 1 wyib, k5, [sl 1 wyib, k1] 3 times, sl 1 wyib, k3, sl 1 wyib, k1, sl 1 wyib, k2, sl 1 wyib, k1.

Row 16 With A, p1, sl 1 wyif, p2, sl 1 wyif, p1, sl 1 wyif, p3, sl 1 wyif, [p1, sl 1 wyif] 3 times, p5, sl 1 wyif, [p1, sl 1 wyif] 3 times, p3, sl 1 wyif, p1, sl 1 wyif, p2, sl 1 wyif, p1.

Row 17 With B, [k3, sl 1 wyib] twice, k11, sl 1 wyib, k11, [sl 1 wyib, k3] twice.

Row 18 With B, [p3, sl 1 wyif] twice, p11, sl 1 wyif, p11, [sl 1 wyif, p3] twice.

Row 19 With A, k2, sl 1 wyib, k5, [sl 1 wyib, k1] 4 times, sl 2 wyib, k3, sl 2 wyib, [k1, sl 1 wyib] 4 times, k5, sl 1 wyib, k2.

Row 20 With A, p2, sl 1 wyif, p5, [sl 1 wyib, k1] 4 times, sl 2 wyif, p3, sl 2 wyif, [p1, sl 1 wyif] 4 times, p5, sl 1 wyif, p2.

Row 21 With B, k4, sl 1 wyib, k1, sl 1 wyib, k6, sl 1 wyib, k4, sl 1 wyib, k1, sl 1 wyib, k4, sl 1 wyib, k6, sl 1 wyib, k1, sl 1 wyib, k4.

Row 22 With B, p4, sl 1 wyif, p1, sl 1 wyif, p6, sl 1 wyif, p4, sl 1 wyif, p1, sl 1 wyif, p4, sl 1 wyif, p6, sl 1 wyif, p1, sl 1 wyif, p4.

Row 23 With A, [k1, sl 1 wyib] twice, k3, sl 2 wyib, k1, sl 1 wyib, k17, sl 1 wyib, k1, sl 2 wyib, k3, [sl 1 wyib, k1] twice.

Row 24 With A, [p1, sl 1 wyif] twice, p3, sl 2 wyif, p1, sl 1 wyif, p17, sl 1 wyif, p1, sl 2 wyif, p3, [sl 1 wyif, p1] twice.

Rows 25 and 26 Repeat rows 21 and 22.

Row 27 With A, [k1, sl 1 wyib] twice, k3, sl 2 wyib, [k1, sl 1 wyib] 4 times, k5, [sl 1 wyib, k1] 4 times, sl 2 wyib, k3, [sl 1 wyib, k1] twice.

Row 28 With A, [p1, sl 1 wyif] twice, p3, sl 2 wyif, [p1, sl 1 wyif] 4 times, p5, [sl 1 wyif, p1] 4 times, sl 2 wyif, p3, [sl 1 wyif, p1] twice.

Row 29 With B, k4, sl 1 wyib, k1, sl 1 wyib, k10, [sl 1 wyib, k1] twice, sl 1 wyib, k10, sl 1 wyib, k1, sl 1 wyib, k4.

Row 30 With B, p4, sl 1 wyif, p1, sl 1 wyif, p10, sl 1 wyif, [p1, sl 1 wyif] twice, p10, sl 1 wyif, p1, sl 1 wyif, p4.

Row 31 With A, [k1, sl 1 wyib] twice, k3, sl 2 wyib, [k1, sl 1 wyib] 3 times, k3, sl 1 wyib, k1, sl 1 wyib, k3, [sl 1 wyib, k1] 3 times, sl 2 wyib, k3, [sl 1 wyib, k1] twice.

Row 32 With A, [p1, sl 1 wyif] twice, p3, sl 2 wyif, [p1, sl 1 wyif] 3 times, p3, sl 1 wyif, p1, sl 1 wyif, p3, [sl 1 wyif, p1] 3 times, sl 2 wyif, p3, [sl 1 wyif, p1] twice.

Row 33 With B, k5, sl 1 wyib, k9, sl 1 wyib, k3, sl 1 wyib, k3, sl 1 wyib, k9, sl 1 wyib, k5.

Row 34 With B, p5, sl 1 wyif, p9, sl 1 wyif, p3, sl 1 wyif, p3, sl 1 wyif, p9, sl 1 wyif, p5.

Row 35 With A, k1, sl 1 wyib, k1, sl 2 wyib, k1, sl 2 wyib, k2, sl 1 wyib, k1, sl 1 wyib, [k3, sl 2 wyib] twice, k3, sl 1 wyib, k1, sl 1 wyib, k2, sl 2 wyib, k1, sl 2 wyib, k1, sl 1 wyib, k1.

Row 36 With A, p1, sl 1 wyif, p1, sl 2 wyif, p1, sl 2 wyif, p2, sl 1 wyif, p1, sl 1 wyif, p3, [sl 2 wyif, p3] twice, sl 1 wyif, p1, sl 1 wyif, p2, sl 2 wyif, p1, sl 2 wyif, p1, sl 1 wyif, p1.

Row 37 With B, k9, sl 1 wyib, k3, sl 1 wyib, k4, sl 1 wyib, k1, sl 1 wyib, k4, sl 1 wyib, k3, sl 1 wyib, k9.

Row 38 With B, p9, sl 1 wyif, p3, sl 1 wyif, p4, sl 1 wyif, p1, sl 1 wyif, p4, sl 1 wyif, p3, sl 1 wyif, p9.

Row 39 With A, [k1, sl 1 wyib] 3 times, k1, sl 2 wyib, k5, sl 2 wyib, k7, sl 2 wyib, k5, sl 2 wyib, [k1, sl 1 wyib] 3 times, k1.

Row 40 With A, p1, [sl 1 wyif, p1] 3 times, sl 2 wyif, p5, sl 2 wyif, p7, sl 2 wyif, p5, sl 2 wyif, p1, [sl 1 wyif, p1] 3 times.

Row 41 With B, k10, sl 1 wyib, k1, sl 1 wyib, k5, sl 1 wyib, k1, sl 1 wyib, k5, sl 1 wyib, k1, sl 1 wyib, k10.

Row 42 With B, p10, sl 1 wyif, p1, sl 1 wyif, p5, sl 1 wyif, p1, sl 1 wyif, p5, sl 1 wyif, p1, sl 1 wyif, p10.

Row 43 With A, [k1, sl 1 wyib] 5 times, (k3, [sl 1 wyib, k1] twice, sl 1 wyib) twice, k3, [sl 1 wyib, k1] 5 times.

Row 44 With A, [p1, sl 1 wyif] 5 times, p3, ([sl 1 wyif, p1] twice, sl 1 wyif, p3) twice, [sl 1 wyif, p1] 5 times.

Rows 45 and 46 Repeat rows 41 and 42.

Rows 47 and 48 Repeat rows 43 and 44.

Rows 49 and 50 Repeat rows 41 and 42.

Rows 51 and 52 Repeat rows 43 and 44.

Row 53 With B, k11, sl 1 wyib, k6, sl 1 wyib, k1, sl 1 wyib, k6, sl 1 wyib, k11.

Row 54 With B, p11, sl 1 wyif, p6, sl 1 wyif, p1, sl 1 wyif, p6, sl 1 wyif, p11.

Row 55 With A, [k1, sl 1 wyib] 4 times, k1, sl 2 wyib, k1, sl 2 wyib, [k1, sl 1 wyib] twice, k3, [sl 1 wyib, k1] twice, sl 2 wyib, k1, sl 2 wyib, k1, [sl 1 wyib, k1] 4 times.

Row 56 With A, [p1, sl 1 wyif] 4 times, p1, sl 2 wyif, p1, sl 2 wyif, [p1, sl 1 wyif] twice, p3, [sl 1 wyif, p1] twice, sl 2 wyif, p1, sl 2 wyif, p1, [sl 1 wyif, p1] 4 times.

Row 57 With B, k18, sl 1 wyib, k1, sl 1 wyib, k18.

Row 58 With B, p18, sl 1 wyif, p1, sl 1 wyif, p18.

Row 59 With A, [k1, sl 1 wyib] 9 times, k3, [sl 1 wyib, k1] 9 times.

Row 60 With A, [p1, sl 1 wyif] 9 times, p3, [sl 1 wyif, p1] 9 times.

Row 61 With B, k19, sl 1 wyib, k19.

Row 62 With B, p19, sl 1 wyif, p19.

Row 63 With A, [k1, sl 1 wyib] 8 times, [k1, sl 2 wyib] twice, [k1, sl 1 wyib] 8 times, k1.

Row 64 With A, p1, [sl 1 wyif, p1] 8 times, [sl 2 wyif, p1] twice, [sl 1 wyif, p1] 8 times.

Row 65 With B, knit.

Row 66 With B, purl.

BLOCK

Work 5 rows in Garter st.

Set-up row (RS) With A, work 4 stitches in Garter st; work 39 stitches in Classic Candelabra pattern or chart; with A, work 4 stitches in Garter st.

Continue in patterns as established until 66 rows of Classic Candelabra pattern or chart have been completed.

With A, work 6 rows in Garter st.

Bind off.

FINISHING

With C, embroider a straight stitch at the tip of each candle for flames.

Color Key Stitch Key

 A   K on RS, P on WS

B V Slip 1 st wyib on RS, Slip 1 st wyif on WS

Classic Candelabra Pattern

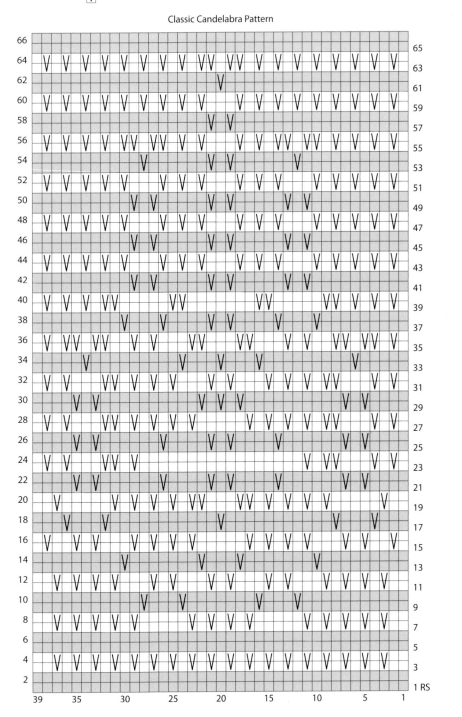

EMBOSSED DUCKY page 106

Colors MC and CC

BLOCK

With CC, cast on 43 stitches.
Work 7 rows in Seed st.

Set-up row (WS) With CC, work
5 stitches in Seed st, p33, work 5
stitches in Seed st.

Next row With CC, work 5 stitches
in Seed st; with MC, work 33 stitches
of Ducky chart; join a second ball of
CC and work the last 5 stitches in
Seed st.

Continue in patterns as established
until 36-row Ducky chart is complete.

Next row (RS) With CC, work 5
stitches in Seed st, k33, work 5
stitches in Seed st.
Work 7 rows in Seed st.
Bind off.

FINISHING

Sew a pearl on the ducky for the eye.

Color Key

☐ MC

▨ CC

Stitch Key

☐ K on RS, P on WS

· P on RS, K on WS

☒ Sew pearl

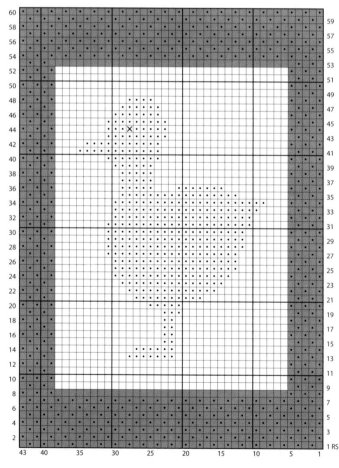

EMBOSSED BUNNY page 106

Colors MC and CC

BLOCK

With CC, cast on 43 stitches.
Work 7 rows in Seed st.

Set-up row (WS) With CC, work
5 stitches in Seed st, p33, work 5
stitches in Seed st.

Next row With CC, work 5 stitches
in Seed st; with MC, work 33 stitches
of Bunny chart; join a second ball of
CC and work the last 5 stitches in
Seed st.

Continue in patterns as established
until 36-row Bunny chart is complete.

Next row (RS) With CC, work 5
stitches in Seed st, k33, work 5
stitches in Seed st.
Work 7 rows in Seed st.
Bind off.

FINISHING

Sew a pearl on the bunny for the eye.

Color Key

☐ MC

▨ CC

Stitch Key

☐ K on RS, P on WS

· P on RS, K on WS

☒ Sew pearl

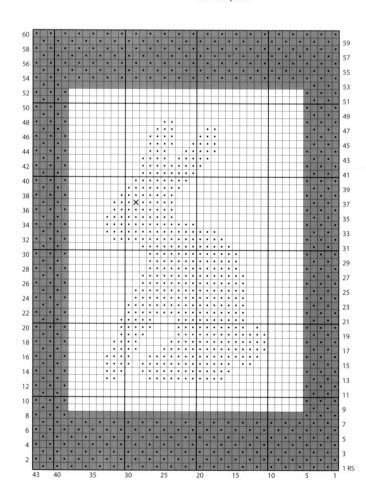

EMBOSSED TEDDY page 107

Colors MC and CC

BLOCK

With CC, cast on 43 stitches.
Work 7 rows in Seed st.
Set-up row (WS) With CC, work
5 stitches in Seed st, p33, work 5
stitches in Seed st.
Next row With CC, work 5 stitches
in Seed st; with MC, work 33 stitches
of Teddy chart; join a second ball of
CC and work the last 5 stitches in
Seed st.
Continue in patterns as established
until 37-row Teddy chart is complete.

Next row (WS) With CC, work
5 stitches in Seed st, p33, work 5
stitches in Seed st.
Work 7 rows in Seed st.
Bind off.

FINISHING

Sew pearls on the teddy for eyes and
nose.

Color Key

☐ MC

▨ CC

Stitch Key

☐ K on RS, P on WS

• P on RS, K on WS

☒ Sew pearl

EMBOSSED LAMB page 107

Colors MC and CC

BLOCK

With CC, cast on 40 stitches.
Work 6 rows in Seed st.
Set-up row (WS) With CC, work
5 stitches in Seed st, p33, work
5 stitches in Seed st.
Next row With CC, work 5 stitches
in Seed st; with MC, work 33 stitches
of Lamb chart; join a second ball of
CC and work the last 5 stitches in
Seed st.
Continue in patterns as established
until 33-row Lamb chart is complete.
Next row (WS) With CC, work
5 stitches in Seed st, p33, work 5
stitches in Seed st.

Work 6 rows in Seed st.
Bind off.

EAR

With CC, cast on 5 stitches.
Bind off.
Sew the ear on the lamb.

FINISHING

Sew a pearl on the lamb for the eye.

Color Key

☐ MC

▨ CC

Stitch Key

☐ K on RS, P on WS

• P on RS, K on WS

◎ CO 1 st

⌒ BO

☒ Sew pearl

Ear

⦿⦿⦿⦿⦿ 1
5　　1

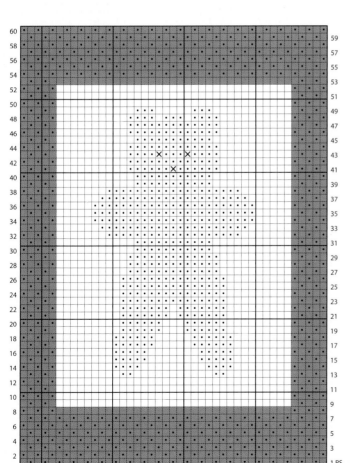

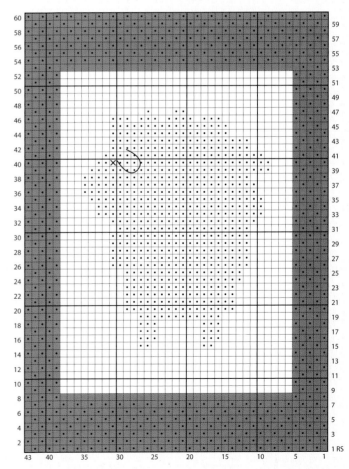

chapter 5

CABLES AND COUNTERPANES

As a knitter or designer, you just can't go wrong with cables or counterpanes. They always look good in any design. The textural twist and stitch repetition are consistent and pleasing to knit, see, and wear.

There are many, many original cable blocks in this chapter that make bold, unique textural statements and are spectacular for designing. The cables can be used by mixing and matching with all of the other chapters, or using the same block, different colors and/or yarns.

The counterpanes all speak, strikingly, for themselves. I love choosing two or three blocks and doing simple one-color combinations. Positioning the counterpanes at an angle is another lovely design trick.

Examples of these techniques used in projects are the Mélange Counterpane Afghan (see page 208), Très Chic Pullover (see page 218), the Empire Cropped Vest (see page 219), and the Anthology Cuffed Shawl-Sweater (see page 214).

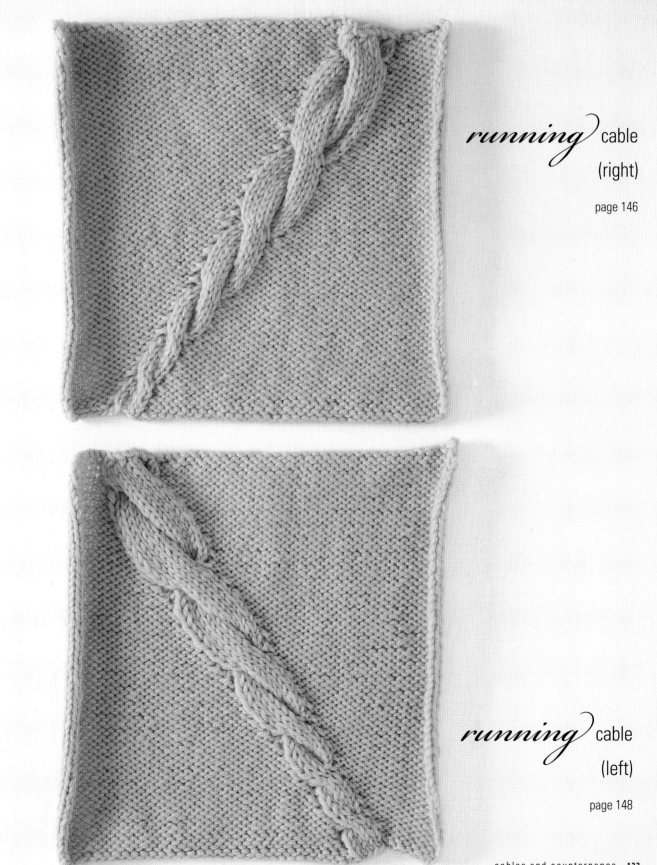

running cable (right)

page 146

running cable (left)

page 148

funnel cable

page 149

topsy-turvy cables

page 150

angled cables and ribs

page 151

boxed

cables and ribs

page 152

hourglass

page 153

tree breeze

page 154

reversible cables (front)

page 156

reversible cables (back)

page 156

crossed cables

page 156

whirlwind

cable twist

page 158

cable vision

page 159

rosemary sprigs

page 160

three kings

page 161

cassie's
cable ladder

page 162

portal cable

page 162

growing garden

page 164

curvy cable

page 165

diamond back

page 166

interlocked cables

page 167

X's

page 168

regal cable

page 168

4-triangles mix

page 170

classic leaf
bobble edge

page 171

forest

fantasy

page 172

BLOCK

Cast on 46 stitches.

Set-up row (WS) K7, p4, k35.

Row 1 (RS) P33, p2tog tbl, k4, m1P, p7.

Row 2 K8, p4, k34.

Row 3 P32, p2tog tbl, k4, m1P, p8.

Row 4 K9, p4, k33.

Row 5 P31, p2tog tbl, 2/2 LC, m1P, p9.

Row 6 K10, p4, k32.

Row 7 P30, p2tog tbl, k4, m1P, p10.

Row 8 K11, p4, k31.

Row 9 P29, p2tog tbl, k4, m1P, p11.

Row 10 K12, p4, k30.

Row 11 P28, p2tog tbl, 2/2 LC inc, m1P, p12 (48 stitches).

Row 12 K13, p6, k29.

Row 13 P27, p2tog tbl, k6, m1P, p13.

Row 14 K14, p6, k28.

Row 15 P26, p2tog tbl, k6, m1P, p14.

Row 16 K15, p6, k27.

Row 17 P25, p2tog tbl, k6, m1P, p15.

Row 18 K16, p6, k26.

Row 19 P24, p2tog tbl, 3/3 LC inc, m1P, p16 (50 stitches).

Row 20 K17, p8, k25.

Row 21 P23, p2tog tbl, k8, m1P, p17.

Row 22 K18, p8, k24.

Row 23 P22, p2tog tbl, k8, m1P, p18.

Row 24 K19, p8, k23.

Row 25 P21, p2tog tbl, k8, m1P, p19.

Row 26 K20, p8, k22.

Row 27 P20, p2tog tbl, k8, m1P, p20.

Row 28 K21, p8, k21.

Row 29 P19, p2tog tbl, 4/4 LC inc, m1P, p21 (52 stitches).

Row 30 K22, p10, k20.

Row 31 P18, p2tog tbl, k10, m1P, p22.

Row 32 K23, p10, k19.

Row 33 P17, p2tog tbl, k10, m1P, p23.

Row 34 K24, p10, k18.

Row 35 P16, p2tog tbl, k10, m1P, p24.

Row 36 K25, p10, k17.

Row 37 P15, p2tog tbl, k10, m1P, p25.

Row 38 K26, p10, k16.

Row 39 P14, p2tog tbl, k10, m1P, p26.

Row 40 K27, p10, k15.

Row 41 P13, p2tog tbl, 5/5 LC inc, m1P, p27 (54 stitches).

Row 42 K28, p12, k14.

Row 43 P12, p2tog tbl, k12, m1P, p28.

Row 44 K29, p12, k13.

Row 45 P11, p2tog tbl, k12, m1P, p29.

Row 46 K30, p12, k12.

Row 47 P10, p2tog tbl, k12, m1P, p30.

Row 48 K31, p12, k11.

Row 49 P9, p2tog tbl, k12, m1P, p31.

Row 50 K32, p12, k10.

Row 51 P8, p2tog tbl, k12, m1P, p32.

Row 52 K33, p12, k9.

Row 53 P7, p2tog tbl, k12, m1P, p33.

Row 54 K34, p12, k8.

Row 55 P6, p2tog tbl, 6/6 LC, m1P, p34.

Row 56 K35, p12, k7.

Row 57 P7, k12, p35.

Bind off, working p2tog across the 12 cable stitches.

Stitch Key

- P on RS, K on WS
- K on RS, P on WS
- P2tog tbl
- M1P
- 2/2 LC
- 2/2 LC Inc
- 3/3 LC Inc
- 4/4 LC Inc
- 5/5 LC Inc
- 6/6 LC

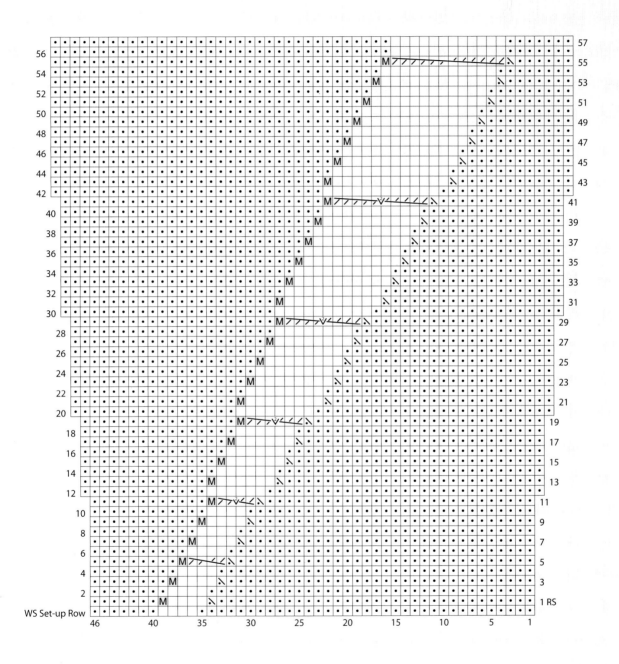

BLOCK

Cast on 46 stitches.

Set-up row (WS) K35, p4, k7.

Row 1 (RS) P7, m1P, k4, p2tog, p33.

Row 2 K34, p4, k8.

Row 3 P8, m1P, k4, p2tog, p32.

Row 4 K33, p4, k9.

Row 5 P9, m1P, 2/2 LC, p2tog, p31.

Row 6 K32, p4, k10.

Row 7 P10, m1P, k4, p2tog, p30.

Row 8 K31, p4, k11.

Row 9 P11, m1P, k4, p2tog, p29.

Row 10 K30, p4, k12.

Row 11 P12, m1P, 2/2 LC inc, p2tog, p28.

Row 12 K29, p6, k13.

Row 13 P13, m1P, k6, p2tog, p27.

Row 14 K28, p6, k14.

Row 15 P14, m1P, k6, p2tog, p26.

Row 16 K27, p6, k15.

Row 17 P15, m1P, k6, p2tog, p25.

Row 18 K26, p6, p16.

Row 19 P16, m1P, 3/3 LC inc, p2tog, p24.

Row 20 K25, p8, k17.

Row 21 P17, m1P, k8, p2tog, p23.

Row 22 K24, p8, k18.

Row 23 P18, m1P, k8, p2tog, p22.

Row 24 K23, p8, k19.

Row 25 P19, m1P, k8, p2tog, p21.

Row 26 K22, p8, k20.

Row 27 P20, m1P, k8, p2tog, p20.

Row 28 K21, p8, k21.

Row 29 P21, m1P, 4/4 LC inc, p2tog, p19.

Row 30 K20, p10, k22.

Row 31 P22, m1P, k10, p2tog, p18.

Row 32 K19, p10, k23.

Row 33 P23, m1P, k10, p2tog, p17.

Row 34 K18, p10, k24.

Row 35 P24, m1P, k10, p2tog, p16.

Row 36 K17, p10, k25.

Row 37 P25, m1P, k10, p2tog, p15.

Row 38 K16, p10, k26.

Row 39 P26, m1P, k10, p2tog, p14.

Row 40 K15, p10, k27.

Row 41 P27, m1P, 5/5 LC inc, p2tog, p13.

Row 42 K14, p12, k28.

Row 43 P28, m1P, k12, p2tog, p12.

Row 44 K13, p12, k29.

Row 45 P29, m1P, k12, p2tog, p11.

Row 46 K12, p12, k30.

Row 47 P30, m1P, k12, p2tog, p10.

Row 48 K11, p12, k31.

Stitch Key

•	P on RS, K on WS
□	K on RS, P on WS
⟋	P2tog
M	M1P
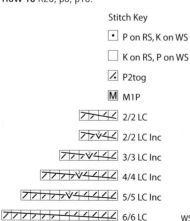	2/2 LC
	2/2 LC Inc
	3/3 LC Inc
	4/4 LC Inc
	5/5 LC Inc
	6/6 LC

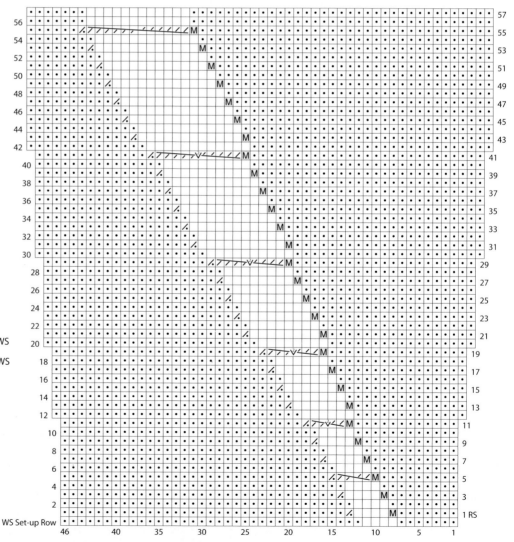

WS Set-up Row

Row 49 P31, m1P, k12, p2tog, p9.
Row 50 K10, p12, k32.
Row 51 P32, m1P, k12, p2tog, p8.
Row 52 K9, p12, k33.

Row 53 P33, m1P, k12, p2tog, p7.
Row 54 K8, p12, k34.
Row 55 P34, m1P, 6/6 LC, p2tog, p6.
Row 56 K7, p12, k35.

Row 57 P35, k12, p7.
Bind off, working p2tog across the 12 cable stitches.

FUNNEL CABLE page 134

Rows 30, 32, 34, 36, 38 and 40 K21, p10, k21.
Rows 31, 33, 35, 37 and 39 P21, k10, p21.
Row 41 P21, 5/5 LC inc, p21.
Rows 42, 44, 46, 48, 50, 52 and 54 K21, p12, k21.
Rows 43, 45, 47, 49, 51 and 53 P21, k12, p21.

Row 55 P21, 6/6 LC, p21.
Row 56 K21, p12, k21.
Row 57 P21, k12, p21.
Bind off, working p2tog across the 12 cable stitches.

BLOCK

Cast on 46 stitches.
Set-up row (WS) K21, p4, k21.
Rows 1 and 3 (RS) P21, k4, p21.
Rows 2, 4 and 6 K21, p4, k21.
Row 5 P21, 2/2 LC, p21.
Rows 7–10 Repeat rows 1–4.
Row 11 P21, 2/2 LC inc, p21.
Rows 12, 14, 16 and 18 K21, p6, k21.
Rows 13, 15 and 17 P21, k6, p21.
Row 19 P21, 3/3 LC inc, p21.
Rows 20, 22, 24, 26 and 28 K21, p8, k21.
Rows 21, 23, 25 and 27 P21, k8, p21.
Row 29 P21, 4/4 LC inc, p21.

Stitch Key

- ● P on RS, K on WS
- ☐ K on RS, P on WS
- 2/2 LC
- 2/2 LC Inc
- 3/3 LC Inc
- 4/4 LC Inc
- 5/5 LC Inc
- 6/6 LC

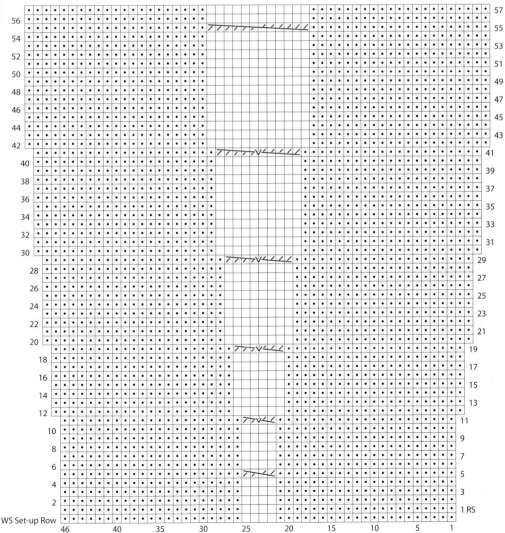

BLOCK

Cast on 50 stitches.

Set-up row (WS) K9, pf&b of the next 6 stitches, k8, p4, k8, pf&b of the next 6 stitches, k9 (62 stitches).

Rows 1, 7 and 9 P9, k12, p8, k4, p8, k12, p9.

Rows 2, 4, 6, 8 and 10 K9, p12, k8, p4, k8, p12, k9.

Row 3 P9, 6/6 LC, p8, k4, p8, 6/6 LC, p9.

Row 5 P9, k12, p8, 2/2 LC, p8, k12, p9.

Row 11 P9, k12, p8, 2/2 LC inc, p8, k12, p9 (64 stitches).

Rows 12, 14 and 16 K9, p12, k8, p6, k8, p12, k9.

Rows 13 and 15 P9, k12, p8, k6, p8, k12, p9.

Row 17 P9, 6/6 LC dec, p8, k6, p8, 6/6 LC dec, p9 (60 stitches).

Row 18 K9, p10, k8, p6, k8, p10, k9.

Row 19 P9, k10, p8, 3/3 LC inc, p8, k10, p9 (62 stitches).

Rows 20, 22, 24, 26 and 28 K9, p10, k8, p8, k8, p10, k9.

Rows 21, 23, 25 and 27 P9, k10, p8, k8, p8, k10, p9.

Row 29 P9, 5/5 LC dec, p8, 4/4 LC inc, p8, 5/5 LC dec, p9 (60 stitches).

Rows 30, 32, 34, 36 and 38 K9, p8, k8, p10, k8, p8, k9.

Rows 31, 33, 35 and 37 P9, k8, p8, k10, p8, k8, p9.

Row 39 P9, 4/4 LC dec, p8, k10, p8, 4/4 LC dec, p9 (56 stitches).

Row 40 K9, p6, k8, p10, k8, p6, k9.

Row 41 P9, k6, p8, 5/5 LC inc, p8, k6, p9 (58 stitches).

Stitch Key

- ⊡ P on RS, K on WS
- ☒ Pf&b on RS
- ■ No stitch
- ☐ K on RS, P on WS

6/6 LC
2/2 LC
2/2 LC Inc
6/6 LC Dec
3/3 LC Inc
5/5 LC Dec
4/4 LC Inc
4/4 LC Dec
5/5 LC Inc
3/3 LC Dec

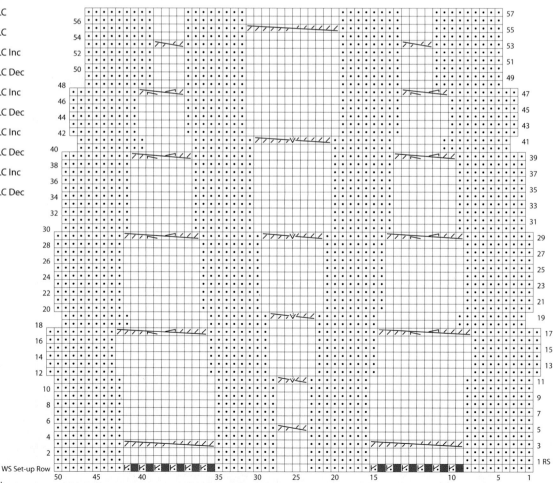

Rows 42, 44 and 46 K9, p6, k8, p12, k8, p6, k9.
Rows 43 and 45 P9, k6, p8, k12, p8, k6, p9.
Row 47 P9, 3/3 LC dec, p8, k12, p8, 3/3 LC dec, p9 (54 stitches).
Rows 48, 50 and 52 K9, p4, k8, p12, k8, p4, k9.

Rows 49 and 51 P9, k4, p8, k12, p8, k4, p9.
Row 53 P9, 2/2 LC, p8, k12, p8, 2/2 LC, p9.
Row 54 K9, p4, k8, p12, k8, p4, k9.
Row 55 P9, k4, p8, 6/6 LC, p8, k4, p9.
Row 56 K9, p4, k8, p12, k8, p4, k9.

Row 57 P9, k4, p8, k12, p8, k4, p9.
Bind off, working p2tog across the 12 cable stitches.

ANGLED CABLES AND RIBS page 135

BLOCK

Cast on 52 stitches.

Set-up row (WS) P3, *k2, p2; repeat from * to the last st, p1.

Rows 1, 5, 9, 13, 17, 21, 25, 29, 33, 37, 41, 45 and 49 P1, k2, *p2, k2; repeat from * to the last st, p1.

Row 2 and all WS rows P3, *k2, p2; repeat from * to the last st, p1.

Row 3 P1, RT, *p2, RT; repeat from * to the last st, p1.

Row 7 P1, [RT, p2] 11 times, k2, p2, RT, p1.

Row 11 P1, [RT, p2] 10 times, [k2, p2] twice, RT, p1.

Row 15 P1, [RT, p2] 9 times, [k2, p2] 3 times, RT, p1.

Row 19 P1, [RT, p2] 8 times, [k2, p2] 4 times, RT, p1.

Row 23 P1, [RT, p2] 7 times, [k2, p2] 5 times, RT, p1.

Row 27 P1, [RT, p2] 6 times, [k2, p2] 6 times, RT, p1.

Row 31 P1, [RT, p2] 5 times, [k2, p2] 7 times, RT, p1.

Row 35 P1, [RT, p2] 4 times, [k2, p2] 8 times, RT, p1.

Row 39 P1, [RT, p2] 3 times, [k2, p2] 9 times, RT, p1.

Row 43 P1, [RT, p2] 2 times, [k2, p2] 10 times, RT, p1.

Row 47 P1, RT, p2, [k2, p2] 11 times, RT, p1.

Rows 51 and 52 Repeat rows 3 and 4.

Rows 53–55 Repeat rows 1–3.

Bind off in pattern.

Stitch Key

☐ K on RS, P on WS

· P on RS, K on WS

⋈ RT

BOXED CABLES AND RIBS page 135

BLOCK

Cast on 46 stitches.

Set-up row (WS) P4, *k2, p4; repeat from * to end.

Row 1 (RS) K4, *p2, k4; repeat from * to end.

Row 2 P4, *k2, p4; repeat from * to end.

Rows 3–14 Repeat rows 1 and 2.

Row 15 [K4, p2] twice, [2/2 RC, p2] 3 times, 2/2 RC, [p2, k4] twice.

Rows 16 and 18 P4, *k2, p4; repeat from * to end.

Row 17 K4, *p2, k4; repeat from * to end.

Rows 19–42 Repeat rows 15–18.

Row 43 Repeat row 15.

Rows 44–57 Repeat rows 2 and 3.

Row 58 P4, [k2, p4] 7 times.

Bind off in pattern.

Stitch Key

☐ K on RS, P on WS

• P on RS, K on WS

⧓ 2/2 RC

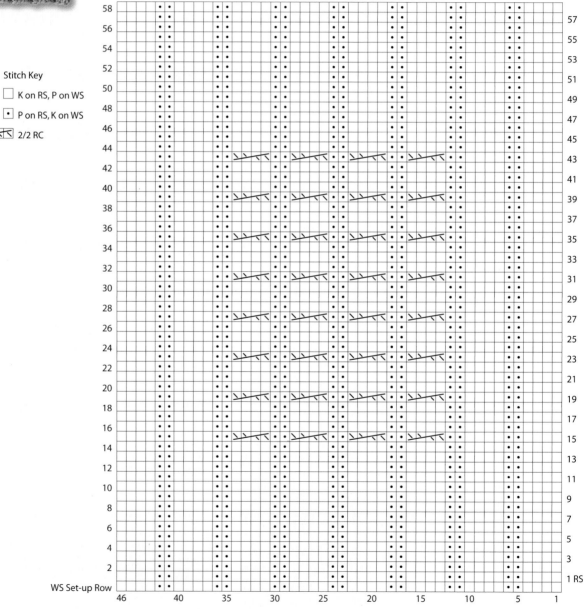

HOURGLASS page 136

BLOCK

Cast on 52 stitches.

Set-up row (WS) P3, *k2, p2; repeat from * to the last st, p1.

Row 1 P1, *k2, p2; repeat from * to the last 3 stitches, k2, p1.

Rows 2 and 4 P3, *k2, p2; repeat from * to the last st, p1.

Row 3 P1, *RT, p2; repeat from * to the last 3 stitches, RT, p1.

Rows 5–8 Repeat rows 1–4.

Row 9 P1, k2, p1, k4, p1, [k2, p2] 8 times, k2, p1, k4, p1, k2, p1.

Rows 10 and 12 P3, k1, p4, k1, p2, [k2, p2] 8 times, k1, p4, k1, p3.

Row 11 P1, RT, p1, k4, p1, [RT, p2] 8 times, RT, p1, k4, p1, RT, p1.

Row 13 P1, k2, p1, k8, p1, [k2, p2] 6 times, k2, p1, k8, p1, k2, p1.

Rows 14 and 16 P3, k1, p8, k1, [p2, k2] 6 times, p2, k1, p8, k1, p3.

Row 15 P1, RT, p1, k8, p1, [RT, k2] 6 times, RT, p1, k8, p1, RT, p1.

Row 17 P1, k2, p1, k12, p1, [k2, p2] 4 times, k2, p1, k12, p1, k2, p1.

Rows 18 and 20 P3, k1, p12, k1, [p2, k2] 4 times, p2, k1, p12, k1, p3.

Row 19 P1, RT, p1, k12, p1, [RT, p2] 4 times, RT, p1, k12, p1, RT, p1.

Row 21 P1, k2, p1, k16, p1, [k2, p2] 2 times, k2, p1, k16, p1, k2, p1.

Rows 22 and 24 P3, k1, p16, k1, [p2, k2] 2 times, p2, k1, p16, k1, p3.

Row 23 P1, RT, p1, k16, p1, [RT, p2] 2 times, RT, p1, k16, p1, RT, p1.

Row 25 P1, k2, p1, k20, p1, k2, p1, k20, p1, k2, p1.

Rows 26 and 28 P3, k1, p20, k1, p2, k1, p20, k1, p3.

Row 27 P1, RT, p1, k20, p1, RT, p1, k20, p1, RT, p1.

Rows 29–32 Repeat rows 25–28.

Rows 33–36 Repeat rows 21–24.

Rows 37–40 Repeat rows 17–20.

Rows 41–44 Repeat rows 13–16.

Rows 45–48 Repeat rows 9–12.

Rows 49–56 Repeat rows 1–8.

Row 57 Repeat row 1.

Bind off in pattern.

Stitch Key

☐ K on RS, P on WS

⊡ P on RS, K on WS

⋈ RT

WS Set-up Row

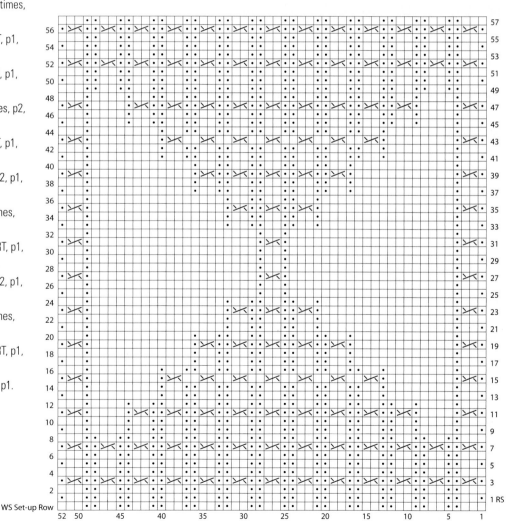

TREE BREEZE page 136

SPECIAL STITCHES

1/1 RC tbl Sl 1 st to cn and hold in back, k1 tbl, k1 tbl from cn.

1/1 LC tbl Sl 1 st to cn and hold in front, k1 tbl, k1 tbl from cn.

1/1 RPC tbl (RS & WS) Sl 1 st to cn and hold in back, k1 tbl, p1 tbl from cn.

1/1 LPC tbl (RS & WS) Sl 1 st to cn and hold in front, p1 tbl, k1 tbl from cn.

2/2 RPC tbl Sl 2 stitches to cn and hold in back, k2 tbl, p2 tbl from cn.

2/2 LPC tbl Sl 2 stitches to cn and hold in front, p2 tbl, k2 tbl from cn.

3/3 RC tbl Sl 3 stitches to cn and hold in back, k3 tbl, k3 tbl from cn.

BLOCK

Cast on 48 stitches.

Rows 1 and 3 (WS) Knit.

Row 2 Purl.

Row 4 (RS) P32, k1 tbl, p15.

Row 5 K16, 1/1 RPC tbl, p1 tbl, k29.

Row 6 P16, [1/1 LC tbl] twice, p4, k1 tbl, p3, k1 tbl, 1/1 RC tbl, p17.

Row 7 K19, 1/1 RPC tbl, k2, 1/1 RPC tbl, k1, p1 tbl, 1/1 LPC tbl, k19.

Row 8 P20, 1/1 LC tbl, p1, 1/1 RC tbl, p1, 1/1 RC tbl, p20.

Rows 9, 11, 13, 15, 17, 19, 21 and 23 K21, p6 tbl, k21.

Rows 10, 14, 16, 18 and 22 P21, k6 tbl, p21.

Rows 12 and 20 P21, 3/3 RC tbl, p21.

Row 24 P21, m1, k6 tbl, m1, p21.

Row 25 K21, p8 tbl, k21.

Row 26 P21, k1 tbl, m1, k6 tbl, m1, k1 tbl, p21.

Row 27 K21, p10 tbl, k21.

Row 28 P19, 2/2 RPC tbl, 3/3 RC tbl, 2/2 LPC tbl, p19.

Row 29 K19, p2 tbl, k2, p6 tbl, k2, p2 tbl, k19.

Row 30 P17, 2/2 RPC tbl, p2, m1, k6 tbl, m1, p2, 2/2 LPC tbl, p17.

Row 31 K17, p2 tbl, k4, p8 tbl, k4, p2 tbl, k17.

Row 32 P15, 2/2 RPC tbl, p4, k1 tbl, m1, k6 tbl, m1, k1 tbl, p4, 2/2 LC tbl, p15.

Row 33 K15, p2 tbl, k6, p10 tbl, k6, p2 tbl, k15.

Row 34 P13, 2/2 RPC tbl, p4, 2/2 RPC tbl, k6 tbl, 2/2 LPC tbl, p4, 2/2 LPC tbl, p13.

Row 35 K13, p2 tbl, k6, p2 tbl, k2, p6 tbl, k2, p2 tbl, k6, p2 tbl, k13.

Row 36 P13, k2 tbl, p4, 2/2 RPC tbl, p2, 3/3 RC tbl, p2, 2/2 LPC tbl, p4, k2 tbl, p13.

Row 37 K13, p2 tbl, k4, p2 tbl, k4, p6 tbl, k4, p2 tbl, k4, p2 tbl, k13.

Row 38 P12, 1/1 RPC tbl, k1 tbl, p2, 2/2 RPC tbl, p4, k6 tbl, p4, 2/2 LPC tbl, p2, k1 tbl, 1/1 LPC tbl, p12.

Row 39 K12, p1 tbl, k1, p1 tbl, k2, p2 tbl, k6, p6 tbl, k6, p2 tbl, k2, p1 tbl, k1, p1 tbl, k12.

Row 40 P11, 1/1 RPC tbl, p4, k2 tbl, p4, 2/2 RPC tbl, k2 tbl, 2/2 LPC tbl, p4, k2 tbl, p4, 1/1 LC tbl, p11.

Row 41 K7, k2tog, k2, p1 tbl, k5, p2 tbl, k4, p2 tbl, k2, p2 tbl, k2, p2 tbl, k4, p2 tbl, k5, p1 tbl, k2, k2tog, k7.

Row 42 P9, 1/1 RPC tbl, p4, 1/1 RPC tbl, k1 tbl, p2, 2/2 RPC tbl, p2, k2 tbl, p2, 2/2 LPC tbl, p2, k1 tbl, 1/1 LPC tbl, p4, 1/1 LPC tbl, p9.

Row 43 K9, p1 tbl, k5, p1 tbl, k1, p1 tbl, k2, [p2 tbl, k4] twice, p2 tbl, k2, p1 tbl, k1, p1 tbl, k5, p1 tbl, k9.

Row 44 P14, 1/1 RPC tbl, p4, [k2 tbl, p4] 3 times, 1/1 LPC tbl, p14.

Row 45 K7, k2tog, k5, p1 tbl, k5, [p2 tbl, k4] twice, p2 tbl, k5, p1 tbl, k5, k2tog, k7.

Row 46 P12, 1/1 RPC tbl, p4, 1/1 RPC tbl, k1 tbl, p4, k2 tbl, p4, k1 tbl, 1/1 LPC tbl, p4, 1/1 LPC tbl, p12.

Row 47 K12, p1 tbl, k5, p1 tbl, k1, p1 tbl, k4, p2 tbl, k4, p1 tbl, k1, p1 tbl, k5, p1 tbl, k12.

Row 48 P17, 1/1 RPC tbl, p5, 1/1 RPC tbl, 1/1 LPC tbl, p5, 1/1 LPC tbl, p17.

Row 49 K7, k2tog, k8, p1 tbl, k6, p1 tbl, k2, p1 tbl, k6, p1 tbl, k8, k2tog, k7.

Row 50 P15, 1/1 RPC tbl, p5, 1/1 RPC tbl, p2, 1/1 LPC tbl, p5, 1/1 LPC tbl, p15.

Row 51 K15, p1 tbl, k6, p1 tbl, k4, p1 tbl, k6, p1 tbl, k15.

Row 52 P21, 1/1 RPC tbl, p4, 1/1 LPC tbl, p21.

Row 53 K7, k2tog, k12, p1 tbl, k6, p1 tbl, k12, k2tog, k7.

Row 54 P20, k1 tbl, p6, k1 tbl, p20.

Rows 56 and 58 Knit.

Rows 55 and 57 Purl.

Bind off.

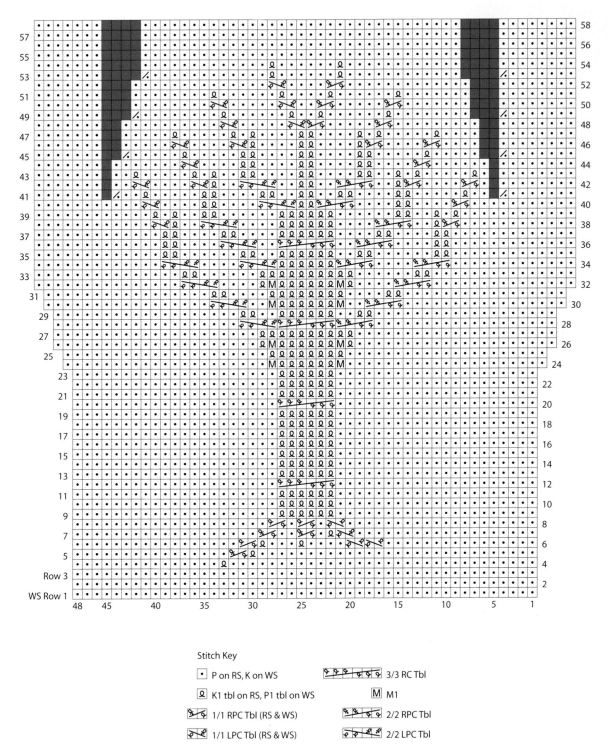

Stitch Key

⦁ P on RS, K on WS

Ω K1 tbl on RS, P1 tbl on WS

1/1 RPC Tbl (RS & WS)

1/1 LPC Tbl (RS & WS)

1/1 RC Tbl

1/1 LC Tbl

3/3 RC Tbl

M M1

2/2 RPC Tbl

2/2 LPC Tbl

P2tog on RS, K2tog on WS

No stitch

REVERSIBLE CABLES page 137

Reversible Cables (Front)

Reversible Cables (Back)

BLOCK

Cast on 48 stitches (a multiple of 11 stitches plus 4 more).

Rows 1 and 3 (RS) *[K1, p1] 5 times, k1; repeat from * to the last 4 stitches, [k1, p1] twice.

Rows 2 and 4 [P1, k1] twice, *[p1, k1] 3 times, p1, [p1, k1] twice; repeat from * to end.

Row 5 *[K1, p1] twice, 3/4 RKPC; repeat from * to the last 4 stitches, [k1, p1] twice.

Rows 6 and 8 Repeat row 2.

Rows 7 and 9 Repeat row 1.

Row 10 Repeat row 2.

Repeat rows 1–10 for pattern 5 more times

Bind off.

Stitch Key

☐ K on RS, P on WS

⊡ P on RS, K on WS

3/4 RKPC

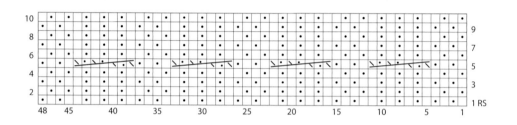

CROSSED CABLES page 138

BLOCK

Cast on 46 stitches.

Set-up row (WS) K6, p4, k26, p4, k6.

Row 1 P6, m1P, 2/2 LC, p2tog, p22, p2tog tbl, 2/2 RC, m1P, p6.

Row 2 K7, p4, k24, p4, k7.

Row 3 P7, m1P, k4, p2tog, p20, p2tog tbl, k4, m1P, p7.

Row 4 K8, p4, k22, p4, k8.

Row 5 P8, m1P, k4, p2tog, p18, p2tog tbl, k4, m1P, p8.

Row 6 K9, p4, k20, p4, k9.

Row 7 P9, m1P, 2/2 LC, p2tog, p16, p2tog tbl, 2/2 RC, m1P, p9.

Row 8 K10, p4, k18, p4, k10.

Row 9 P10, m1P, k4, p2tog, p14, p2tog tbl, k4, m1P, p10.

Row 10 K11, p4, k16, p4, k11.

Row 11 P11, m1P, k4, p2tog, p12, p2tog tbl, k4, m1P, p11.

Row 12 K12, p4, k14, p4, k12.

Row 13 P12, m1P, 2/2 LC, p2tog, p10, p2tog tbl, 2/2 RC, m1P, p12.

Row 14 K13, p4, k12, p4, k13.

Row 15 P13, m1P, k4, p2tog, p8, p2tog tbl, k4, m1P, p13.

Row 16 K14, p4, k10, p4, k14.

Row 17 P14, m1P, k4, p2tog, p6, p2tog tbl, k4, m1P, p14.

Row 18 K15, p4, k8, p4, k15.

Row 19 P15, m1P, 2/2 LC, p2tog, p4, p2tog tbl, 2/2 RC, m1P, p15.

Row 20 K16, p4, k6, p4, k16.

Row 21 P16, m1P, k4, p2tog, p2, p2tog tbl, k4, m1P, p16.

Row 22 K17, p4, k4, p4, k17.

Row 23 P17, m1P, k4, p2tog, p2tog tbl, k4, m1P, p17.

Row 24 K18, p4, k2, p4, k18.

Row 25 P18, m1P, 2/2 LC dec, 2/2 RC dec, m1P, p18.

Rows 26 and 28 K19, p8, k19.

Row 27 P19, k8, p19.

Row 29 P19, 4/4 LC, p19.

Rows 30 and 32 K19, p8, k19.

Row 31 P19, 2/2 RC, 2/2 LC, p19.

Row 33 P17, p2tog tbl, k4, m2P, k4, p2tog, p17.

Row 34 K18, p4, k2, p4, k18.

Row 35 P16, p2tog tbl, k4, m1P, p2, m1P, k4, p2tog, p16.

Row 36 K17, p4, k4, p4, k17.

Row 37 P15, p2tog tbl, 2/2 RC, m1P, p4, m1P, 2/2 LC, p2tog, p15.

Row 38 K16, p4, k6, p4, k16.

Row 39 P14, p2tog tbl, k4, m1P, p6, m1P, k4, p2tog, p14.

Row 40 K15, p4, k8, p4, k15.

Row 41 P13, p2tog tbl, k4, m1P, p8, m1P, k4, p2tog, p13.

Row 42 K14, p4, k10, p4, k14.

Row 43 P12, p2tog tbl, 2/2 RC, m1P, p10, m1P, 2/2 LC, p2tog, p12.

Row 44 K13, p4, k12, p4, k13.

Row 45 P11, p2tog tbl, k4, m1P, p12, m1P, k4, p2tog, p11.

Row 46 K12, p4, k14, p4, k12.

Row 47 P10, p2tog tbl, k4, m1P, p14, m1P, k4, p2tog, p10.

Row 48 K11, p4, k16, p4, k11.

Row 49 P9, p2tog tbl, 2/2 RC, m1P, p16, m1P, 2/2 LC, p2tog, p9.

Row 50 K10, p4, k18, p4, k10.

Row 51 P8, p2tog tbl, k4, m1P, p18, m1P, k4, p2tog, p8.

Row 52 K9, p4, k20, p4, k9.

Row 53 P7, p2tog tbl, k4, m1P, p20, m1P, k4, p2tog, p7.

Row 54 K8, p4, k22, p4, k8.

Row 55 P6, p2tog tbl, 2/2 RC, m1P, p22, m1P, 2/2 LC, p2tog, p6.

Row 56 K7, p4, k24, p4, k7.

Row 57 P5, p2tog tbl, k4, m1P, p24, m1P, k4, p2tog, p5.

Bind off in pattern.

Stitch Key

· P on RS, K on WS

☐ K on RS, P on WS

M M1P

2/2 LC

P2tog

P2tog tbl

2/2 LC Dec

2/2 RC Dec

4/4 LC

2/2 RC

2/2 LC

M2P

WS Set-up Row

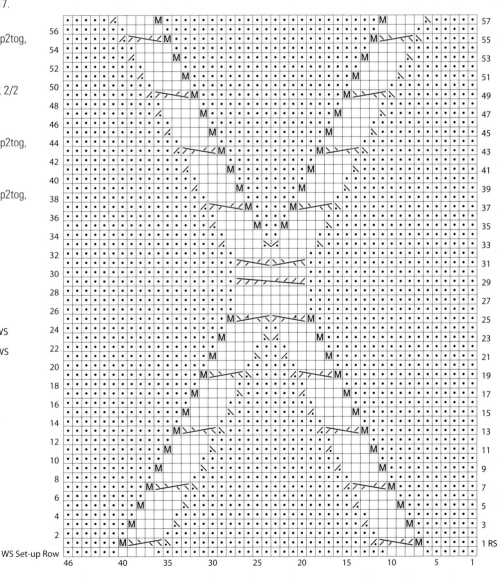

SPECIAL STITCH

SP2P Wyif slip 1 knitwise, p2tog, pass the slipped st over.

BLOCK

Cast on 45 stitches.

Set-up row (WS) P1, *k1, p1; repeat from * to end.

Row 1 (RS) P1, *k1, p1; repeat from * to end.

Rows 2–6 Repeat row 1.

Row 7 P1, [k1, p1] twice, p35, [p1, k1] twice, p1.

Row 8 P1, [k1, p1] twice, k35, [p1, k1] twice, p1.

Rows 9–13 Repeat rows 7 and 8 twice, then row 7 once more.

Row 14 P1, [k1, p1] twice, p7, k9, p3, k9, p7, [p1, k1] twice, p1.

Row 15 P1, [k1, p1] twice, k7, p4, (k1, yo, k1) into the next st, p4, k3, p9, k7, [p1, k1] twice, p1 (47 stitches).

Row 16 P1, [k1, p1] twice, p7, k9, p3, k4, p3, k4, p7, [p1, k1] twice, p1.

Row 17 P1, [k1, p1] twice, k7, p4, 3/1 LPC, p3, k3, p9, k7, [p1, k1] twice, p1.

Row 18 P1, [k1, p1] twice, p7, k9, p3, k3, p3, k5, p7, [p1, k1] twice, p1.

Row 19 P1, [k1, p1] twice, k7, p5, 3/1 LPC, p2, k3, p6, (k1, yo, k1) into the next st, p2, k7, [p1, k1] twice, p1.

Row 20 P1, [k1, p1] twice, p7, k2, p3, k6, p3, k2, p3, k6, p7, [p1, k1] twice, p1.

Row 21 P1, [k1, p1] twice, k7, p6, 3/1 LPC, p1, k3, p4, 3/2 RPC, p2, k7, [p1, k1] twice, p1.

Row 22 P1, [k1, p1] twice, p7, k4, p3, k4, p3, k1, p3, k7, p7, [p1, k1] twice, p1.

Row 23 P1, [k1, p1] twice, k7, p7, 3/1 LPC, k3, p2, 3/2 RPC, p4, k7, [p1, k1] twice, p1.

Row 24 P1, [k1, p1] twice, p7, k6, p3, k2, p6, k8, p7, [p1, k1] twice, p1.

Row 25 P1, [k1, p1] twice, k7, p8, 3/3 RC, 3/2 RPC, p6, k7, [p1, k1] twice, p1.

Row 26 P1, [k1, p1] twice, p7, k8, p9, k8, p7, [p1, k1] twice, p1.

Row 27 P1, [k1, p1] twice, k7, p8, k3, 3/3 LC, p8, k7, [p1, k1] twice, p1.

Row 28 P1, [k1, p1] twice, p7, k8, p9, k8, p7, [p1,

Stitch Key

☐ K on RS, P on WS

• P on RS, K on WS

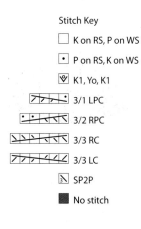 K1, Yo, K1

3/1 LPC

3/2 RPC

3/3 RC

3/3 LC

SP2P

■ No stitch

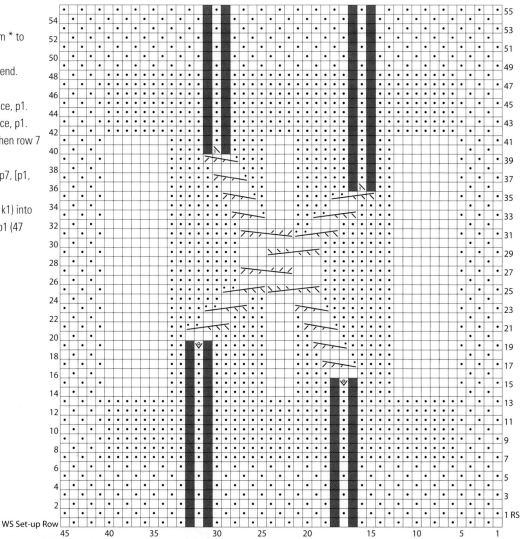

WS Set-up Row

k1] twice, p1.

Row 29 P1, [k1, p1] twice, k7, p8, 3/3 RC, k3, p8, k7, [p1, k1] twice, p1.

Row 30 P1, [k1, p1] twice, p7, k8, p9, k8, p7, [p1, k1] twice, p1.

Row 31 P1, [k1, p1] twice, k7, p6, 3/2 RPC, 3/3 LC, p8, k7, [p1, k1] twice, p1.

Row 32 P1, [k1, p1] twice, p7, k8, p6, k2, p3, k6, p7, [p1, k1] twice, p1.

Row 33 P1, [k1, p1] twice, k7, p4, 3/2 RPC, p2, k3, 3/1 LPC, p7, k7, [p1, k1] twice, p1.

Row 34 P1, [k1, p1] twice, p7, k7, p3, k1, p3, k4, p3, k4, p7, [p1, k1] twice, p1.

Row 35 P1, [k1, p1] twice, k7, p2, 3/2 RPC, p4, k3, p1, 3/1 LPC, p6, k7, [p1, k1] twice, p1.

Row 36 P1, [k1, p1] twice, p7, k6, p3, k2, p3, k6, SP2P, k2, p7, [p1, k1] twice, p1.

Row 37 P1, [k1, p1] twice, k7, p9, k3, p2, 3/1 LPC, p5, k7, [p1, k1] twice, p1.

Row 38 P1, [k1, p1] twice, p7, k5, p3, k3, p3, k9, p7, [p1, k1] twice, p1.

Row 39 P1, [k1, p1] twice, k7, p9, k3, p3, 3/1 LPC, p4, k7, [p1, k1] twice, p1.

Row 40 P1, [k1, p1] twice, p7, k4, SP2P, k4, p3, k9, p7, [p1, k1] twice, p1.

Row 41 P1, [k1, p1] twice, k7, p9, k3, p9, k7, [p1, k1] twice, p1.

Rows 42, 44, 46 and 48 Repeat row 8.

Rows 43, 45 and 47 Repeat row 7.

Rows 49–55 Repeat row 1.

Bind off in pattern.

CABLE VISION page 139

BLOCK

Cast on 45 stitches. K 1 row.

Row 1 (RS) K4, 2/1 LC, k5, 2/1 LC, k1, k2tog, yo, k9, yo, SKP, k1, 2/1 RC, k5, 2/1 RC, k4.

Row 2 and all WS rows K1, p43, k1.

Row 3 [K5, 2/1 LC] twice, k2, 2/2 LC, k1, 2/2 RC, k2, [2/1 RC, k5] twice.

Row 5 K1, [k5, 2/1 LC] twice, k3, 2/3 RC, k3, [2/1 RC, k5] twice, k1.

Row 7 K1, [k5, 2/1 RC] twice, k1, 2/2 RC, k1, 2/2 LC, k1, [2/1 LC, k5] twice, k1.

Row 9 [K5, 2/1 RC] twice, k2tog, yo, k9, yo, SKP, [2/1 LC, k5] twice.

Row 11 K4, 2/1 RC, k5, 2/1 RC, k2tog, yo, k1, 2/2 LC, k1, 2/2 RC, k1, yo, SKP, 2/1 LC, k5, 2/1 LC, k4.

Row 13 K3, 2/1 RC, k5, 2/1 RC, [k2tog, yo] twice, k2, 2/3 RC, k2, [yo, SKP] twice, 2/1 LC, k5, 2/1 LC, k3.

Row 15 K2, 2/1 RC, k5, 2/1 RC, [k2tog, yo] twice, k1, 2/2 RC, k1, 2/2 LC, k1, [yo, SKP] twice, 2/1 LC, k5, 2/1 LC, k2.

Row 17 K1, 2/1 RC, k5, 2/1 RC, [k2tog, yo] 3 times, k9, [yo, SKP] 3 times, 2/1 LC, k5, 2/1 LC, k1.

Row 19 K1, 2/1 LC, k5, 2/1 LC, k1, [k2tog, yo] twice, k1, 2/2 LC, k1, 2/2 RC, k1, [yo, ssk] twice, k1, 2/1 RC, k5, 2/1 RC, k1.

Row 21 K2, 2/1 LC, k5, 2/1 LC, k1, [k2tog, yo] twice, k2, 2/3 RC, k2, [yo, SKP] twice, k1, 2/1 RC, k5, 2/1 RC, k2.

Row 23 K3, 2/1 LC, k5, 2/1 LC, k1, k2tog, yo, k1, 2/2 RC, k1, 2/2 LC, k1, yo, SKP, k1, 2/1 RC, k5, 2/1 RC, k2, k1.

Row 24 Repeat row 2.

Repeat rows 1–24 for pattern once, then rows 1–10 once more.

Bind off purlwise.

Stitch Key

• P on RS, K on WS	◣ SSK
☐ K on RS, P on WS	⟋⟍ 2/1 RC
⟋⟍ 2/1 LC	⟋⟍ 2/2 LC
⟋ K2tog	⟍⟋ 2/2 RC

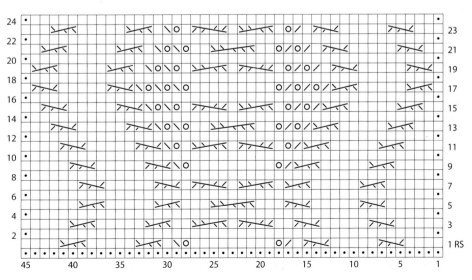

ROSEMARY SPRIGS page 139

BLOCK

Cast on 192 stitches (48 stitches each on 4 double-pointed needles).

Note Stitch counts are noted for each needle.

Rnd 1 *K1, p2tog, p2, k1, p37, k1, p2, p2tog; repeat from * to end (46 stitches).

Rnd 2 *K1, p3, k1, p37, k1, p3; repeat from * to end.

Rnd 3 *K1, p2tog, p1, k1, p37, k1, p1, p2tog; repeat from * to end.

Rnd 4 *[K1, p2] twice, k33, p2, k1, p2; repeat from * to end.

Rnd 5 *K1, p2tog, k1, p2, k33, p2, k1, p2tog; repeat from * to end.

Rnd 6 *K1, p1, k1, p2, k33, p2, k1, p1; repeat from * to end.

Rnd 7 *K1, k2tog, p2, k1, p31, k1, p2, ssk; repeat from * to end.

Rnd 8 *K2, p2, k1, p31, k1, p2, k1; repeat from * to end.

Rnd 9 *K1, p2tog, p1, k1, p31, k1, p1, p2tog; repeat from * to end.

Rnd 10 *[K1, p2] twice, k27, p2, k1, p2; repeat from * to end.

Rnd 11 *K1, p2tog, k1, p2, k27, p2, k1, p2tog; repeat from * to end (36 stitches).

Rnd 12 *K1, p1, k1, p2, k27, p2, k1, p1; repeat from * to end.

Rnd 13 *K1, k2tog, p2, k1, p25, k1, p2, ssk; repeat from * to end.

Rnd 14 *K2, p2, k1, p25, k1, p2, k1; repeat from * to end.

Rnd 15 *K1, p2tog, p1, k1, p25, k1, p1, p2tog; repeat from * to end.

Rnd 16 *[K1, p2] twice, k21, p2, k1, p2; repeat from * to end.

Rnd 17 *K1, p2tog, k1, p2, k21, p2, k1, p2tog; repeat from * to end.

Rnd 18 *K1, p1, k1, p2, k21, p2, k1, p1; repeat from * to end.

Rnd 19 *K1, k2tog, p2, k1, p19, k1, p2, ssk; repeat from * to end.

Rnd 20 *K2, p2, k1, p19, k1, p2, k1; repeat from * to end.

Rnd 21 *K1, p2tog, p1, k1, p19, k1, p1, p2tog; repeat from * to end (26 stitches).

Rnd 22 *[K1, p2] twice, k15, p2, k1, p2; repeat from * to end.

Rnd 23 *K1, p2tog, k1, p2, k15, p2, k1, p2tog; repeat from * to end.

Rnd 24 *K1, p1, k1, p2, k15, p2, k1, p1; repeat from * to end.

Rnd 25 *K1, k2tog, p2, k1, p13, k1, p2, (sl 1, k1, psso); repeat from * to end.

Rnd 26 *K2, p2, k1, p13, k1, p2, k1; repeat from * to end.

Rnd 27 *K1, p2tog, p1, k1, p13, k1, p1, p2tog; repeat from * to end.

Rnd 28 *[K1, p2] twice, k9, p2, k1, p2; repeat from * to end.

Rnd 29 *K1, p2tog, k1, p2, k9, p2, k1, p2tog; repeat from * to end.

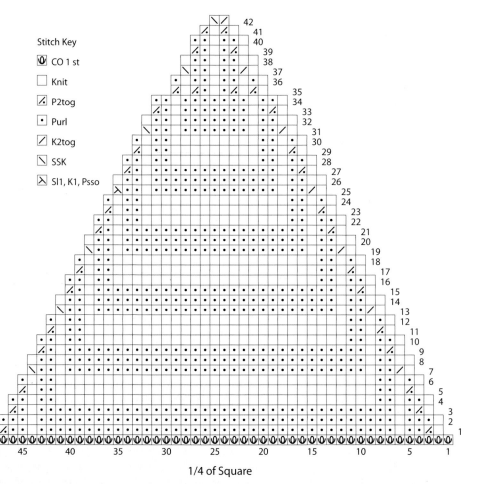

Stitch Key

⓪	CO 1 st
☐	Knit
⟋	P2tog
•	Purl
⟋	K2tog
⟍	SSK
⟋	Sl1, K1, Psso

1/4 of Square

Rnd 30 *K1, p1, k1, p2, k9, p2, k1, p1; repeat from * to end.

Rnd 31 *K1, k2tog, p2, k1, p7, k1, p2, ssk; repeat from * to end (16 stitches).

Rnd 32 *K2, p2, k1, p7, k1, p2, k1; repeat from * to end.

Rnd 33 *K1, p2tog, p1, k1, p7, k1, p1, p2tog; repeat from * to end (14 stitches).

Rnd 34 *K1, p2, k1, p7, k1, p2; repeat from * to end.

Rnd 35 *[K1, p2tog] twice, p1, k1, p1, p2tog, k1, p2tog; repeat from * to end (10 stitches).

Rnd 36: *K1, p1 [k1, p2] twice, k1, p1; repeat from * to end.

Rnd 37: *K1, k2tog, p2, k1, p2, ssk; repeat from * to end (8 stitches).

Rnd 38: *K2, [p2, k1] twice; repeat from * to end.

Rnd 39: *K1, p2tog, p1, k1, p1, p2tog; repeat from * to end (6 stitches).

Rnd 40: *[K1, p2] twice; repeat from * to end.

Rnd 41: *[K1, p2tog] twice (4 stitches); repeat from * to end.

Rnd 42: *K2tog, ssk; repeat from * to end (2 stitches).

Break off yarn and thread tail through remaining stitches.

THREE KINGS page 140

Colors MC and CC

BLOCK

Cast on 52 stitches with MC (a multiple of 16 stitches plus 4 more).

Row 1 (RS) P4, *k12, p4; repeat from * to end.

Row 2 K4, *p12, k4; repeat from * to end.

Rows 3–6 Repeat rows 1 and 2.

Row 7 P4, *6/6 RC, p4; repeat from * to end.

Row 8 Repeat row 2.

Row 9 P4 MC, *k4 MC, join CC and k4 CC, k4 MC, p4 MC; repeat from * to end.

Row 10 K4 MC, *p4 MC, p4 CC, p4 MC, k4 MC; repeat from * to end.

Rows 11–14 Repeat rows 9 and 10.

Row 15 P4 MC, *k3 MC, p1 MC, 2/2 RC with CC, p1 MC, k3 MC, p4 MC; repeat from * to end.

Row 16 K4 MC, *p3 MC, k1 MC, p4 CC, k1 MC, p3 MC, k4 MC; repeat from * to end.

Row 17 P4 MC, *k3 MC, p1 MC, k4 CC, p1 MC, k3 MC, p4 MC; repeat from * to end.

Row 18 Repeat row 16.

Rows 19–46 Repeat rows 15–18.

Row 47 Repeat row 15.

Row 48 Repeat row 10, fastening off CC in each repeat.

Rows 49 and 50 Repeat rows 1 and 2.

Row 51 Repeat row 7.

Row 52 Repeat row 8.

Rows 53–58 Repeat rows 1–6.

Bind off.

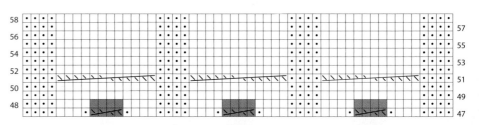

Rows 19–46: Repeat rows 15–18

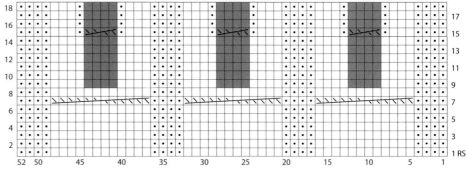

Stitch Key

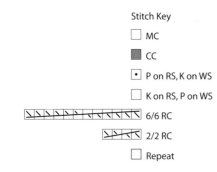

☐ MC

■ CC

• P on RS, K on WS

☐ K on RS, P on WS

6/6 RC

2/2 RC

☐ Repeat

CASSIE'S CABLE LADDER page 140

Stitch Key

- ⊡ P on RS, K on WS
- ☐ K on RS, P on WS
- ⧄⧅ 2/2 RC
- ⧄⧅ 2/2 LC
- ☐ Repeat

BLOCK

Cast on 46 stitches (a multiple of 22 stitches plus 2 more).

Set-up row (WS) K2, *p4, k2, p8, k2, p4, k2; repeat from * to end.

Row 1 (RS) P2, *k4, p12, k4, p2; repeat from * to end.

Row 2 K2, *p4, k12, p4, k2; repeat from * to end.

Row 3 P2, *k4, p2, k8, p2, k4, p2; repeat from * to end.

Rows 4, 6, 8 and 10 K2, *p4, k2, p8, k2, p4, k2; repeat from * to end.

Row 5 P2, *2/2 RC, p2, 2/2 RC, 2/2 LC, p2, 2/2 LC, p2; repeat from * to end.

Row 7 P2, *k4, p2, k8, p2, k4, p2; repeat from * to end.

Row 9 P2, *2/2 RC, p2, 2/2 LC, 2/2 RC, p2, 2/2 LC, p2; repeat from * to end.

Row 11 P2, *k4, p12, k4, p2; repeat from * to end.

Row 12 K2, *p4, k12, p4, k2; repeat from * to end.

Row 13 P2, *2/2 RC, p12, 2/2 LC, p2; repeat from * to end.

Repeat rows 2–13 for pattern 3 more times, then rows 2–4 once more.

Bind off in pattern.

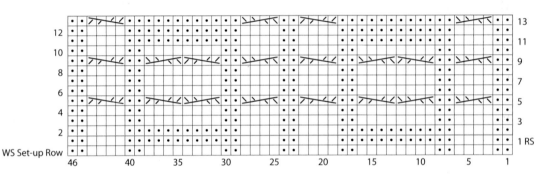

WS Set-up Row

PORTAL CABLE page 141

BLOCK

Cast on 51 stitches.

Rows 1, 5, 7, 11 and 13 (RS) Sl 1, [p4, k8] twice, p1, [k8, p4] twice, p1.

Rows 2, 4, 6, 8, 10, 12, 14, 16 and 18 Sl 1, [k4, p8] twice, k1, [p8, k4] twice, p1.

Rows 3 and 15 Sl 1, p4, 2/2 RC, 2/2 LC, p4, 4/4 RC, p1, 4/4 LC, p4, 2/2 RC, 2/2 LC, p5.

Row 9 Sl 1, p4, 2/2 RC, 2/2 LC, p4, k8, p1, k8, p4, 2/2 RC, 2/2 LC, p5.

Row 17 Sl 1, p4, k8, p4, k6, 1/1 RC, p1, 1/1 LC, k6, p4, k8, p5.

Row 19 Sl 1, p4, k8, p4, k5, 1/1 RC, p1, k1, p1, 1/1 LC, k5, p4, k8, p5.

Row 20 Sl 1, k4, p8, k4, p7, k1, p1, k1, p7, k4, p8, k4, p1.

Row 21 Sl 1, p4, 2/2 RC, 2/2 LC, p4, k4, 1/1 RC, [p1, k1] twice, p1, 1/1 LC, k4, p4, 2/2 RC, 2/2 LC, p5.

Row 22 Sl 1, k4, p8, k4, p6, [k1, p1] twice, k1, p6, k4, p8, k4, p1.

Row 23 Sl 1, p4, k8, p4, k3, 1/1 RC, [p1, k1] 3 times, p1, 1/1 LC, k3, p4, k8, p5.

Row 24 Sl 1, k4, p8, k4, p5, [k1, p1] 3 times, k1, p5, k4, p8, k4, p1.

Row 25 Sl 1, k12, 4/4 RPC, [p1, k1] 4 times, p1, 4/4 LPC, k12, p1.

Rows 26 and 30 Sl 1, p16, k4, [k1, p1] 4 times, k5, p17.

Row 27 Sl 1, k4, 2/2 RC, 2/2 LC, k4, p4, [k1, p1] 4 times, k1, p4, k4, 2/2 RC, 2/2 LC, k4, p1.

Rows 28 and 32 Sl 1, p16, k4, [p1, k1] 4 times, p1, k4, p17.

Row 29 Sl 1, k16, p4, [p1, k1] 4 times, p5, k16, p1.

Row 31 Sl 1, k16, p4, [k1, p1] 4 times, k1, p4, k16, p1.

Row 33 Sl 1, 4/4 RC, 4/4 LC, p4, [k1, p1] 4 times, p5, 4/4 RC, 4/4 LC, p1.

Rows 34 and 38 Sl 1, p16, k4, [k1, p1] 4 times, k5, p17.

Row 35 Sl 1, k16, p4, [k1, p1] 4 times, k1, p4, k16, p1.

Row 36 Sl 1, p16, k4, [p1, k1] 4 times, p1, k4, p17.

Row 37 Repeat row 29.

Row 39 Sl 1, k4, 2/2 RC, 2/2 LC, k4, p4, [k1, p1] 4 times, k1, p4, k4, 2/2 RC, 2/2 LC, k4, p1.

Row 40 Sl 1, p16, k4, [p1, k1] 4 times, p1, k4, p17.

Row 41 Sl 1, p4, k8, 4/4 LPC, [p1, k1] 4 times, p1, 4/4 RPC, k8, p5.

Row 42 Sl 1, k4, p8, k4, p4, [k1, p1] 4 times, k1, p4, k4, p8, k4, p1.

Row 43 Sl 1, p4, k8, p4, k3, 1/1 LC, [p1, k1] 3 times, p1, 1/1 RC, k3, p4, k8, p5.

Row 44 Sl 1, k4, p8, k4, p5, [k1, p1] 3 times, k1, p5, k4, p8, k4, p1.

Row 45 Sl 1, p4, 2/2 RC, 2/2 LC, p4, k4, 1/1 LC, [p1, k1] twice, p1, 1/1 RC, k4, p4, 2/2 RC, 2/2 LC, p5.

Row 46 Sl 1, k4, p8, k4, p6, [k1, p1] twice, k1, p6, k4, p8, k4, p1.

Row 47 Sl 1, p4, k8, p4, k5, 1/1 LC, p1, k1, p1, 1/1 RC, k5, p4, k8, p5.

Row 48 Sl 1, k4, p8, k4, p7, k1, p1, k1, p7, k4, p8, k4, p1.

Row 49 Sl 1, p4, k8, p4, k6, 1/1 LC, p1, 1/1 RC, k6, p4, k8, p5.

Rows 50, 52, 54, 56, 58, 60 and 62 Sl 1, [k4, p8] twice, k1, [p8, k4] twice, p1.

Rows 51 and 63 Sl 1, p4, 2/2 RC, 2/2 LC, p4, 4/4 LC, p1, 4/4 RC, p4, 2/2 RC, 2/2 LC, p5.

Rows 53, 55, 59 and 61 Sl 1, [p4, k8] twice, p1, [k8, p4] twice, p1.

Row 57 Sl 1, p4, 2/2 RC, 2/2 LC, p4, k8, p1, k8, p4, 2/2 RC, 2/2 LC, p5.

Row 64 Repeat row 50.

Bind off in pattern.

Stitch Key

- ☑ Sl 1 st
- · P on RS, K on WS
- ☐ K on RS, P on WS
- 2/2 RC
- 2/2 LC
- 4/4 RC
- 4/4 LC
- 1/1 RC
- 1/1 LC
- 4/4 RPC
- 4/4 LPC

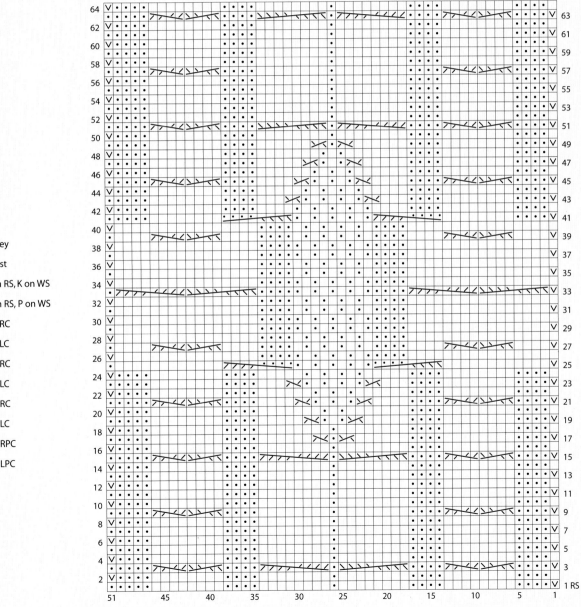

Row 8 [P1, k1] twice, [p8, K3/2/1, p8] twice, [p1, k1] twice.

Row 9 Repeat row 7.

Row 10 [P1, k1] twice, [p8, k3, p8] twice, [p1, k1] twice.

Rows 11–14 Repeat rows 7–10.

Row 15 [K1, p1] twice, k8, p3, k15, p5, k7, [k1, p1] twice.

Row 16 [P1, k1] twice, p7, k5, p15, K3/2/1, p8, [p1, k1] twice.

Row 17 [K1, p1] twice, k8, p3, k14, p7, k6, [k1, p1] twice.

Row 18 [P1, k1] twice, p6, k7, p14, k3, p8, [p1, k1] twice.

Row 19 [K1, p1] twice, k8, p3, k13, p9, k5, [k1, p1] twice.

Row 20 [P1, k1] twice, p5, k1, k2tog, [k1, yo] twice, k1, ssk, k1, p13, K3/2/1, p8, [p1, k1] twice.

Row 21 [K1, p1] twice, k8, p3, k12, p4, k1, p1, k1, p4, k4, [k1, p1] twice.

Row 22 [P1, k1] twice, p4, k1, k2tog, k1, yo, p1, k1, p1, yo, k1, ssk, k1, p12, k3, p8, [p1, k1] twice.

Row 23 [K1, p1] twice, k8, p3, k11, p4, k2, p1, k2, p4, k3, [k1, p1] twice.

SPECIAL STITCH

Make Bobble (MB) [K1, p1] twice in the next st, turn, p4, turn, k4, turn, [p2tog] twice, turn, k2tog.

BLOCK

Cast on 46 stitches.

Row 1 (WS) *K1, p1; repeat from * to end.

Row 2 *P1, k1; repeat from * to end..

Rows 3–6 Repeat rows 1 and 2 for Seed stitch.

Row 7 [K1, p1] twice, [k8, p3, k8] twice, [k1, p1] twice.

Bobble

Stitch Key

- · P on RS, K on WS
- ☐ K on RS, P on WS
- ⟍⟋ K3/2/1
- ⟋ K2tog on RS, P2tog on WS
- ■ No stitch
- Ⓞ Yo
- ⟍ SSK
- Ⓑ MB
- ⟋ P2tog on RS
- ⬇ [K1, P1] twice in 1 st

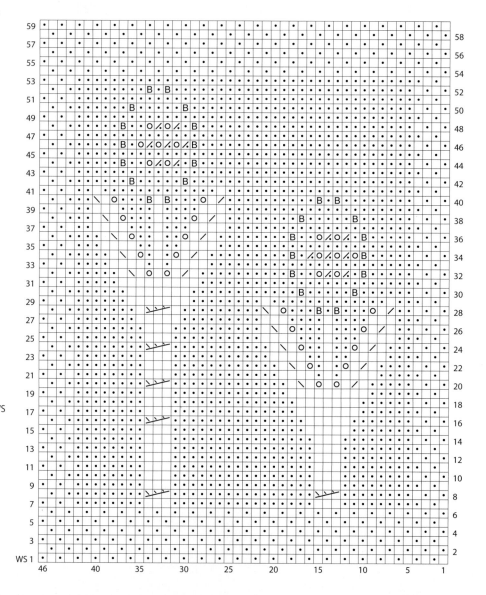

Row 24 [P1, k1] twice, p3, k1, k2tog, k1, yo, p2, k1, p2, yo, k1, ssk, k1, p11, K3/2/1, p8, [p1, k1] twice.

Row 25 [K1, p1] twice, k8, p3, k10, p4, k3, p1, k3, p4, k2, [k1, p1] twice.

Row 26 [P1, k1] twice, p2, k1, k2tog, k1, yo, p3, k1, p3, yo, k1, ssk, k1, p10, k3, p8, [p1, k1] twice.

Row 27 [K1, p1] twice, k7, p5, k9, p3, k4, p1, k4, p3, k2, [k1, p1] twice.

Row 28 [P1, k1] twice, p2, k2tog, k1, yo, p3, MB, p1, MB, p3, yo, k1, ssk, p9, k1, K3/2/1, k1, p7, [p1, k1] twice.

Row 29 [K1, p1] twice, k6, p7, k8, p1, k13, p1, k2, [k1, p1] twice.

Row 30 [P1, k1] twice, p6, MB, p5, MB, p12, k7, p6, [p1, k1] twice.

Row 31 [K1, p1] twice, k5, p9, k24, [k1, p1] twice.

Row 32 [P1, k1] twice, p5, MB, p1, [p2tog, yo] twice, p2, MB, p10, k1, k2tog, [k1, yo] twice, k1, ssk, k1, p5, [p1, k1] twice.

Row 33 [K1, p1] twice, k4, p4, k1, p1, k1, p4, k23, [k1, p1] twice.

Row 34 [P1, k1] twice, p5, MB, [p2tog, yo] 3 times, p1, MB, p9, k1, k2tog, k1, yo, p1, k1, p1, yo, k1, ssk, k1, p4, [p1, k1] twice.

Row 35 [K1, p1] twice, k3, p4, k2, p1, k2, p4, k22, [k1, p1] twice.

Row 36 [P1, k1] twice, p5, MB, p1, [p2tog, yo] twice, p2, MB, p8, k1, k2tog, k1, yo, p2, k1, p2, yo, k1, ssk, k1, p3, [p1, k1] twice.

Row 37 [K1, p1] twice, k2, p4, k3, p1, k3, p4, k21, [k1, p1] twice.

Row 38 [P1, k1] twice, p6, MB, p5, MB, p8, k1, k2tog, k1, yo, p3, k1, p3, yo, k1, ssk, k1, p2, [p1, k1] twice.

Row 39 [K1, p1] twice, k2, p3, k4, p1, k4, p3, k21, [k1, p1] twice.

Row 40 [P1, k1] twice, p8, MB, p1, MB, p10, k2tog, k1, yo, p3, MB, p1, MB, p3, yo, k1, ssk, p2, [p1, k1] twice.

Row 41 [K1, p1] twice, k2, p1, k13, p1, k21, [k1, p1] twice.

Row 42 [P1, k1] twice, p25, MB, p5, MB, p6, [p1, k1] twice.

Row 43 [K1, p1] twice, k38, [k1, p1] twice.

Row 44 [P1, k1] twice, p24, MB, p1, [p2tog, yo] twice, p2, MB, p5, [p1, k1] twice.

Row 45 Repeat row 43.

Row 46 [P1, k1] twice, p24, MB, [p2tog, yo] 3 times, p1, MB, p5, [p1, k1] twice.

Row 47 Repeat row 43.

Row 48 Repeat row 44.

Row 49 Repeat row 43.

Row 50 [P1, k1] twice, p25, MB, p5, MB, p6, [p1, k1] twice.

Row 51 Repeat row 43.

Row 52 [P1, k1] twice, p27, MB, p1, MB, p8, [p1, k1] twice.

Row 53 [K1, p1] twice, k38, [k1, p1] twice.

Rows 54–59 Work in Seed stitch.

Bind off.

CURVY CABLE page 142

BLOCK

Cast on 46 stitches (a multiple of 28 stitches plus 18 more).

Row 1 (RS) P6, k6, *p4, [k2, p4] 3 times, k6; repeat from * to the last 6 stitches, p6.

Row 2 K6, p6, *k4, p14, k4, p6; repeat from * to the last 6 stitches, k6.

Row 3 P4, 2/2 RPC, k2, *[2/2 LPC, p2] twice, k2, [p2, 2/2 RPC] twice, k2; repeat from * to the last 8 stitches, 2/2 LPC, p4.

Row 4 K4, *p10, k4; repeat from * to end.

Row 5 P2, 2/2 RPC, p2, k2, *[p2, 2/2 LPC] 2 times, k2, [2/2 RPC, p2] twice, k2; repeat from * to the last 8 stitches, p2, 2/2 LPC, p2.

Row 6 K2, p14, *k4, p6, k4, p14; repeat from * to the last 2 stitches, k2.

Row 7 P2, *[k2, p4] 3 times, k6, p4; repeat from * to the last 16 stitches, k2, [p4, k2] twice, p2.

Row 8 Repeat row 6.

Row 9 P2, 2/2 LPC, p2, k2, *[p2, 2/2 RPC] twice, k2, [2/2 LPC, p2] twice, k2; repeat from * to the last 8 stitches, p2, 2/2 RPC, p2.

Row 10 Repeat row 4.

Row 11 P4, 2/2 LPC, k2, *[2/2 RPC, p2] twice, k2, [p2, 2/2 LPC] twice, k2; repeat from * to last 8 stitches, 2/2/ RPC, p4.

Row 12 Repeat row 2.

Repeat rows 1–12 for pattern 4 more times.

Bind off.

Stitch Key

- ⦁ P on RS, K on WS
- ☐ K on RS, P on WS
- ⬚ 2/2 RPC
- ⬚ 2/2 LPC
- ☐ Repeat

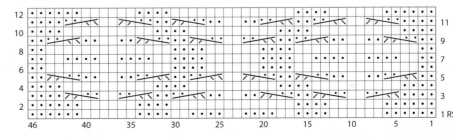

SPECIAL STITCH

W4 Sl 4 stitches to cn and wind the yarn counter-clockwise around the base of these stitches 4 times ending with the yarn in back, sl the 4 stitches onto the right-hand needle.

BLOCK

Cast on 46 stitches.

Set-up row (WS) K19, p8, k19.

Row 1 (RS) P19, k2, W4, k2, p19.

Row 2 K19, p8, k19.

Row 3 P17, 2/4 RPC, 2/4 LPC, p17.

Rows 4 and 6 K17, p4, k4, p4, k17.

Row 5 P17, k4, p4, k4, p17.

Row 7 P15, 2/4 RPC, p4, 2/4 LPC, p15.

Rows 8 and 10 K15, p4, k8, p4, k15.

Row 9 P15, k4, p8, k4, p15.

Row 11 P13, 2/4 RPC, p8, 2/4 LPC, p13.

Rows 12 and 14 K13, p4, k12, p4, k13.

Row 13 P13, k4, k12, k4, p13.

Row 15 P11, 2/4 RPC, p12, 2/4 LPC, p11.

Rows 16 and 18 K11, p4, k16, p4, k11.

Stitch Key

⊡ P on RS, K on WS

☐ K on RS, P on WS

W4

2/4 RPC

2/4 LPC

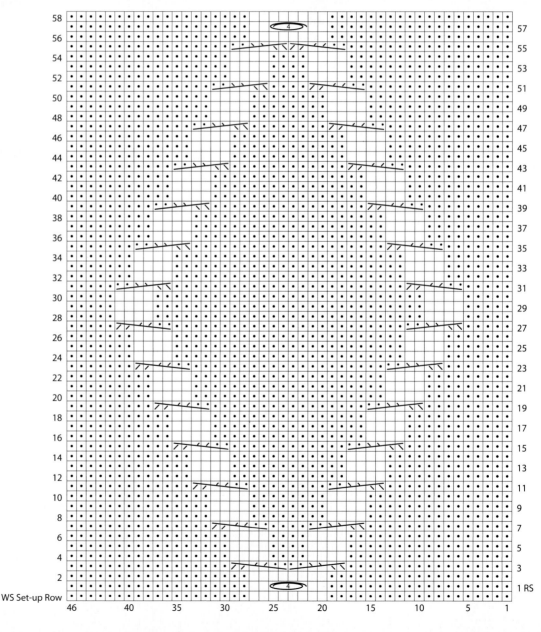

WS Set-up Row

Row 17 P11, k4, p16, k4, p11.
Row 19 P9, 2/4 RPC, p16, 2/4 LPC, p9.
Rows 20 and 22 K9, p4, p20, p4, k9.
Row 21 P9, k4, p20, k4, p9.
Row 23 P7, 2/4 RPC, p20, 2/4 LPC, p7.
Rows 24 and 26 K7, p4, k24, p4, k7.
Row 25 P7, k4, p24, k4, p7.
Row 27 P5, 2/4 RPC, p24, 2/4 LPC, p5.
Rows 28 and 30 K5, p4, p28, p4, k5.
Row 29 P5, k4, p28, k4, p5.
Row 31 P5, 2/4 LPC, p24, 2/4 RPC, p5.

Rows 32 and 34 K7, p4, k24, p4, k7.
Row 33 P7, k4, p24, k4, p7.
Row 35 P7, 2/4 LPC, p20, 2/4 RPC, p7.
Rows 36 and 38 K9, p4, k20, p4, k9.
Row 37 P9, k4, p20, k4, p9.
Row 39 P9, 2/4 LPC, p16, 2/4 RPC, p9.
Rows 40 and 42 K11, p4, k16, p4, k11.
Row 41 P11, k4, p16, k4, p11.
Row 43 P11, 2/4 LPC, p12, 2/4 RPC, p11.
Rows 44 and 46 K13, p4, k12, p4, k13.
Row 45 P13, k4, p12, k4, p13.

Row 47 P13, 2/4 LPC, p8, 2/4 RPC, p13.
Rows 48 and 50 K15, p4, k8, p4, k15.
Row 49 P15, k4, p8, k4, p15.
Row 51 P15, 2/4 LPC, p4, 2/4 RPC, p15.
Rows 52 and 54 K17, p4, k4, p4, k17.
Row 53 P17, k4, p4, k4, p17.
Row 55 P17, 2/4 LPC, 2/4 RPC, p17.
Row 56 K19, p8, k19.
Row 57 P19, k2, W4, k2, p19.
Row 58 Repeat row 56.
Bind off.

INTERLOCKED CABLES page 143

BLOCK

Square 1
Cast on 27 stitches (a multiple of 8 stitches plus 3 more).

Row 1 (RS) *P1, k1 tbl, p1, 1/1 RPC, k1, 1/1 LPC; repeat from * to the last 3 stitches, p1, k1 tbl, p1.

Row 2 K1, p1 tbl, k1, *p5, k1, p1 tbl, k1; repeat from * to end.

Row 3 *P1, k1 tbl, p1, 1/1 LPC, k1, 1/1 RPC; repeat from * to the last 3 stitches, p1, k1 tbl, p1.

Row 4 K1, p1 tbl, k1, *k1, p3, k2, p1 tbl, k1; repeat from * to end.

Row 5 *P1, k1 tbl, p2, K3/2/1, p1; repeat from * to the last 3 stitches, p1, k1 tbl, p1.

Row 6 K1, p1 tbl, k1, *k1, p3, k2, p1 tbl, k1; repeat from * to end.

Repeat rows 1–6 for pattern 3 more times, then rows 1–3 once more.
Bind off.

Square 2
With the right side facing, pick up and k27 stitches along the right side edge of square 1. K 1 WS row.
Starting with row 1, work the same as square 1.

Square 3
With the right side facing, pick up and k27 stitches along the left side edge of square 2.
K 1 WS row.
Starting with row 1, work the same as square 1.

Square 4
With the right side facing, pick up and k27 stitches along the left side edge of square 3.
K 1 WS row.
Starting with row 1, work the same as square 1.
Sew left side edge of square 4 to bound-off edge of square 1.

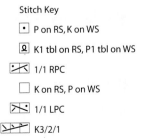

Stitch Key

· P on RS, K on WS

ℚ K1 tbl on RS, P1 tbl on WS

⟋ 1/1 RPC

☐ K on RS, P on WS

⟍ 1/1 LPC

K3/2/1

Row 28 K27, kf&b of the last st.
Row 29 K28, kf&b of the last st (30 stitches).
Row 30 K29, kf&b of the last st.
Row 31 K30, kf&b of the last st.
Row 32 P31, kf&b of the last st.
Row 33 K32, kf&b of the last st.
Row 34 K33, kf&b of the last st (35 stitches).
Row 35 K2, [yo, k2tog] 16 times, kf&b of the last st.
Row 36 K35, kf&b of the last st.
Row 37 K36, kf&b of the last st.

Row 38 P37, kf&b of the last st.
Row 39 K2, [MB, k4] 7 times, MB, pf&b of the last st (40 stitches).
Row 40 P39, pf&b of the last st.
Row 41 K40, kf&b of the last st.
Row 42 K41, kf&b of the last st.
Row 43 K2, [yo, k2tog] 20 times, kf&b of the last st.
Row 44 K43, kf&b of the last st (45 stitches).
Bind off.
Sew the 4 triangles together to make a square.

SPECIAL STITCH
Make Bobble (MB) (K1, p1, k1, p1, k1) all in the next st, turn, k5, turn, p5tog.

BLOCK
Triangle (make 4)
Cast on 1 st.
Row 1 (RS) Kf&b of st (2 stitches).
Row 2 K1, kf&b of the next st (3 stitches).
Row 3 K1, MB, kf&b of the next st (4 stitches).
Row 4 K3, kf&b of the next st (5 stitches).
Rows 5–13 K to last st, kf&b of the next st (14 stitches after row 13).
Row 14 P13, pf&b of the next st.
Row 15 K14, kf&b of the next st.
Row 16 P15, pf&b of the next st.
Row 17 [K2, p2] 4 times, kf&b of the next st.
Row 18 P2, [k2, p2] 3 times, k2, p1, kf&b of the next st.
Row 19 P1, [k2, p2] 4 times, k1, kf&b of the next st (20 stitches).
Row 20 K1 [p2, k2] 4 times, p2, kf&b of the next st.
Row 21 [P2, k2] 5 times, kf&b of the last st.
Row 22 P21, pf&b of the last st.
Row 23 K22, kf&b of the last st.
Row 24 P23, pf&b of the last st (25 stitches).
Row 25 K24, kf&b of the last st.
Row 26 K25, kf&b of the last st.
Row 27 K26, kf&b of the last st.

Triangle

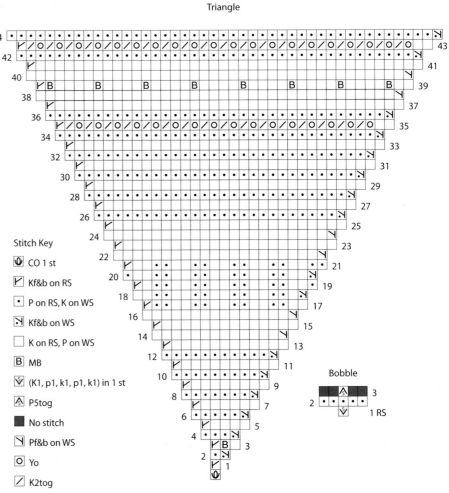

Stitch Key
- ⓊCO 1 st
- ↗ Kf&b on RS
- ⋅ P on RS, K on WS
- ↘ Kf&b on WS
- ☐ K on RS, P on WS
- Ⓑ MB
- ⓥ (K1, p1, k1, p1, k1) in 1 st
- ⊼ P5tog
- ■ No stitch
- ↘ Pf&b on WS
- ⊙ Yo
- ╱ K2tog

Bobble

SPECIAL STITCH

Make Bobble (MB) (K1, p1, k1, p1, k1) all in the next st, turn, k5, turn, p5tog.

BLOCK

Triangle (make 4)

Cast on 3 stitches.

Row 1 (RS) P1, yo, k1, yo, p1 (5 stitches).

Row 2 K2, p1, k2.

Row 3 [P1, yo] twice, k1, [yo, p1] twice (9 stitches).

Row 4 K3, p3, k3.

Row 5 P1, yo, p2, [k1, yo] twice, k1, p2, yo, p1 (13 stitches).

Row 6 K4, p5, k4.

Row 7 P1, yo, p3, k2, yo, k1, yo, k2, p3, yo, p1 (17 stitches).

Row 8 K5, p7, k5.

Row 9 P1, yo, p4, k3, yo, k1, yo, k3, p4, yo, p1 (21 stitches).

Row 10 K6, p9, k6.

Row 11 P1, yo, p5, k4, yo, k1, yo, k4, p5, yo, p1 (25 stitches).

Row 12 K7, p11, k7.

Row 13 P1, yo, p6, k5, yo, k1, yo, k5, p6, yo, p1 (29 stitches).

Row 14 K8, p13, k8.

Row 15 P1, yo, p7, k6, yo, k1, yo, k6, p7, yo, p1 (33 stitches).

Row 16 K9, p15, k9.

Row 17 P1, yo, p8, ssk, k11, k2tog, p8, yo, p1.

Row 18 and all even-numbered rows through row 42 Purl the p and yo stitches, knit the k stitches.

Row 19 P1, yo, p9, ssk, k9, k2tog, p9, yo, p1.

Row 21 P1, yo, p10, ssk, k7, k2tog, p10, yo, p1.

Row 23 P1, yo, p11, ssk, k5, k2tog, p11, yo, p1.

Row 25 P1, yo, p12, ssk, k3, k2tog, p12, yo, p1.

Row 27 P1, yo, p13, ssk, k1, k2tog, p13, yo, p1.

Row 29 P1, yo, p14, SK2P, p14, yo, p1.

Row 31 P1, yo, p31, yo, p1 (35 stitches).

Row 33 P1, [yo, k2tog] 16 times, [yo, p1] twice (37 stitches).

Row 35 P1, [yo, k2tog] 17 times, [yo, p1] twice (39 stitches).

Row 37 P1, [yo, k2tog] 18 times, [yo, p1] twice (41 stitches).

Row 39 P1, yo, p39, yo, p1 (43 stitches).

Row 41 P1, yo, p41, yo, p1 (45 stitches).

Row 43 P1, yo, p3, [MB, p5] 6 times, MB, p3, yo, p1 (47 stitches).

Bind off.

Sew the triangles together to make a square.

Bobble

Triangle

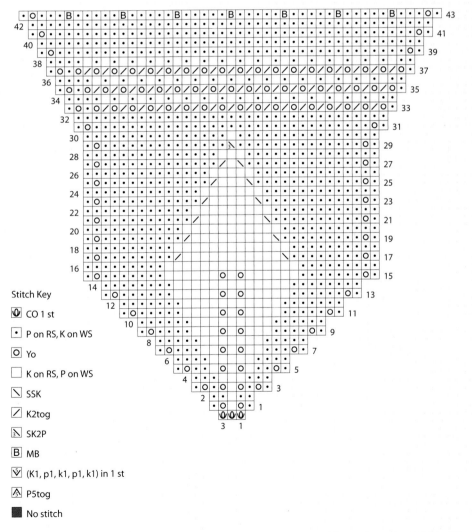

Stitch Key

Ѡ CO 1 st

· P on RS, K on WS

O Yo

☐ K on RS, P on WS

◣ SSK

◢ K2tog

◿ SK2P

B MB

Ɏ (K1, p1, k1, p1, k1) in 1 st

◮ P5tog

■ No stitch

BLOCK

Note Stitch counts are noted for each needle.

Cast on 8 stitches (2 stitches each on 4 double-pointed needles). K 1 rnd.

Rnd 1 *[Yo, k1] twice; repeat from * to end (4 stitches).

Rnd 2 and all even-numbered rnds through rnd 40 Knit.

Rnd 3 *Yo, k1, yo, ssk, yo, k1; repeat from * to end.

Rnd 5 *Yo, k2tog, yo, k1, yo, ssk, yo, k1; repeat from * to end.

Rnd 7 *Yo, k2, yo, p3tog, yo, k2, yo, k1; repeat from * to end.

Rnd 9 *Yo, k1, k2tog, yo, k3, yo, ssk, k1, yo, k1; repeat from * to end.

Rnd 11 *Yo, k3, yo, k1, p3tog, k1, yo, k3, yo, k1; repeat from * to end (14 stitches).

Rnd 13 *Yo, k2, k2tog, yo, k5, yo, ssk, k2, yo, k1; repeat from * to end.

Rnd 15 *Yo, k4, yo, k2, p3tog, k2, yo, k4, yo, k1; repeat from * to end.

Rnd 17 *Yo, k3, k2tog, yo, k7, yo, ssk, k3, yo, k1; repeat from * to end.

Rnd 19 *Yo, k5, yo, k3, p3tog, k3, yo, k5, yo, k1; repeat from * to end.

Rnd 21 *Yo, k4, k2tog, yo, k9, yo, ssk, k4, yo, k1; repeat from * to end (24 stitches).

Rnd 23 *Yo, k6, yo, k4, p3tog, k4, yo, k6, yo, k1; repeat from * to end.

Rnd 25 *Yo, k5, k2tog, yo, k11, yo, ssk, k5, yo, k1; repeat from * to end.

Rnd 27 *Yo, k7, yo, k5, p3tog, k5, yo, k7, yo, k1; repeat from * to end.

Rnd 29 *Yo, k6, k2tog, yo, k1, yo, ssk, k7, k2tog, yo, k1, yo, ssk, k6, yo, k1; repeat from * to end.

Rnd 31 *Yo, k6, k2tog, yo, k3, yo, ssk, k5, k2tog, yo, k3, yo, ssk, k6, yo, k1 (34 stitches); repeat from * to end.

Row 33 *[Yo, k1, yo, ssk, k3, k2tog, yo, k1, yo, SK2P] twice, yo, k1, yo, ssk, k3, k2tog, yo, k1, yo, k1; repeat from * to end.

Rnd 35 *Yo, k3, yo, [ssk, k1, k2tog, yo, k3, yo, ssk, k2, yo] twice, ssk, k1, k2tog, yo, k3, yo, k1; repeat from * to end.

Rnd 37 *[Yo, k1, yo, SK2P] 9 times, [yo, k1] twice; repeat from * to end.

Rnd 39 *Yo, k3, [yo, ssk, k2] 9 times, yo, k1; repeat from * to end.

Rnd 41 *[Yo, k1, yo, SK2P] 10 times, [yo, k1] twice; repeat from * to end (44 stitches).

Bind off knitwise.

FLOWER

Make a slip knot. *Using the cable cast-on, cast on 6 stitches, bind off 6 stitches; repeat from * 7 more times for a total of 8 petals.

Fasten off. Thread the tail through the stitches at the base of the petals to gather and sew flower to the center of the block.

Petal

Stitch Key

☐ Knit

⊙ Yo

◻ SSK

◻ K2tog

◻ P3tog

◻ SK2P

Ⓤ CO 1 st

⌒ BO

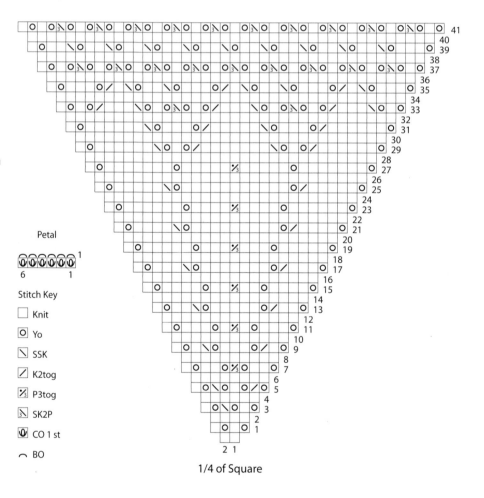

1/4 of Square

chapter 6

ECLECTIC STYLE

My goal for this chapter was to think outside the box—or in this case, the block! And it was, by far, the most fun chapter for me to create. I used textural stitches, cables, cords, appliqué, overlapping bobbles, balls, beads, and more to create these special blocks. I call it a block party.

I hope you'll all enjoy the uniqueness of the blocks and not think they are too difficult to make. Many can be made by novice knitters. Do not be intimidated by them . . . be inspired!

As with the other chapters, there are many ways you can use these blocks. They are certainly block designs that you won't see anywhere else! That really is the exciting part of designing for me—to go where no knitter has dared to go before ("beam me up, Scottie!"), and to encourage knitters to think outside the block.

Examples of projects made from the blocks in this chapter include the Academic Afghan (see page 216) and the Cool Ruffle Pod Bag (see page 220).

colored loopy

page 188

distressed seed stitch

page 188

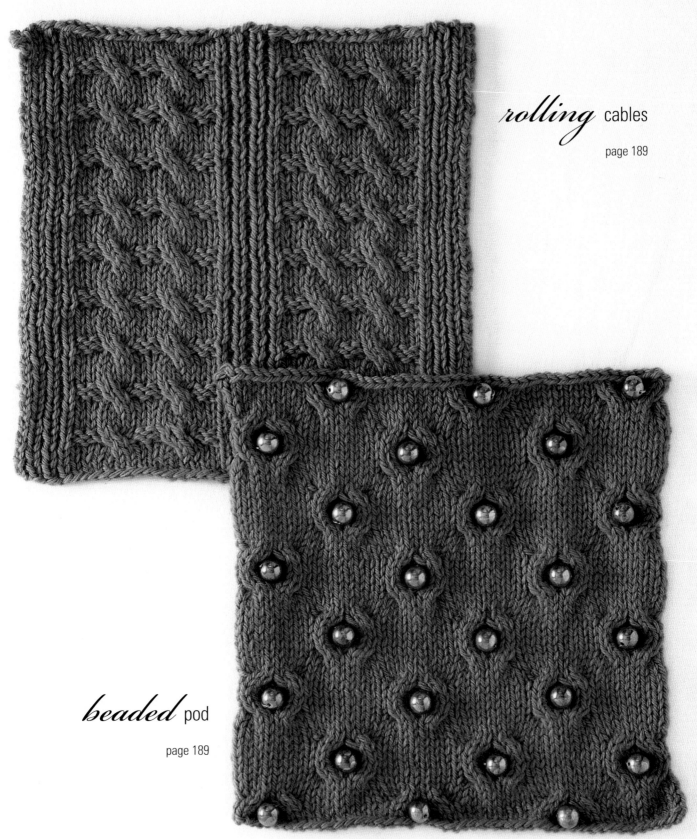

rolling cables

page 189

beaded pod

page 189

squared lamb's tail

page 191

cabled bell pull

page 190

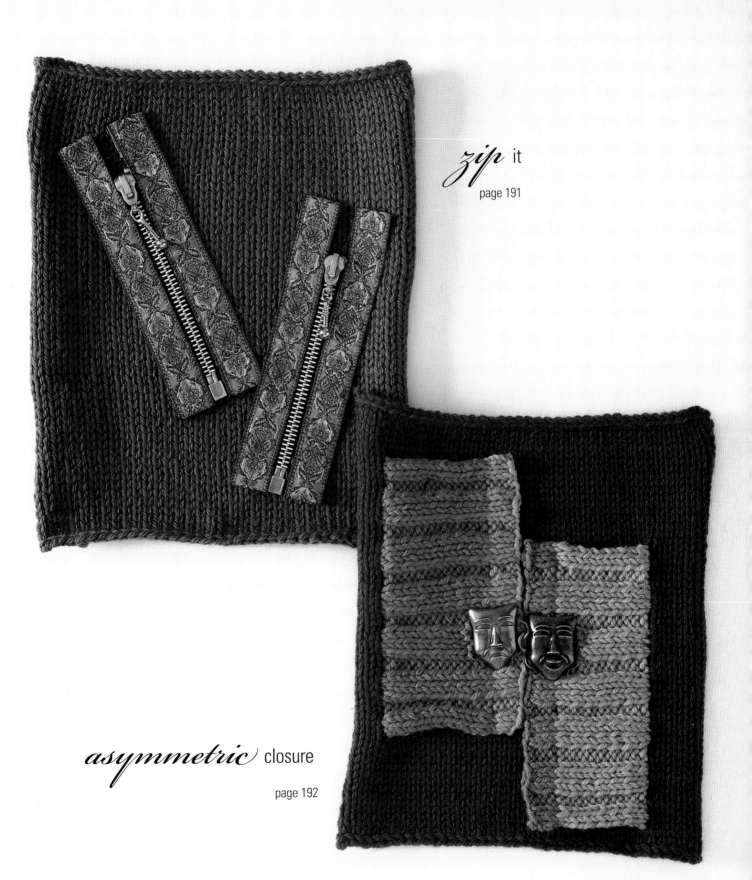

zip it

page 191

asymmetric closure

page 192

random rods (front)

page 193

random rods (back)

page 193

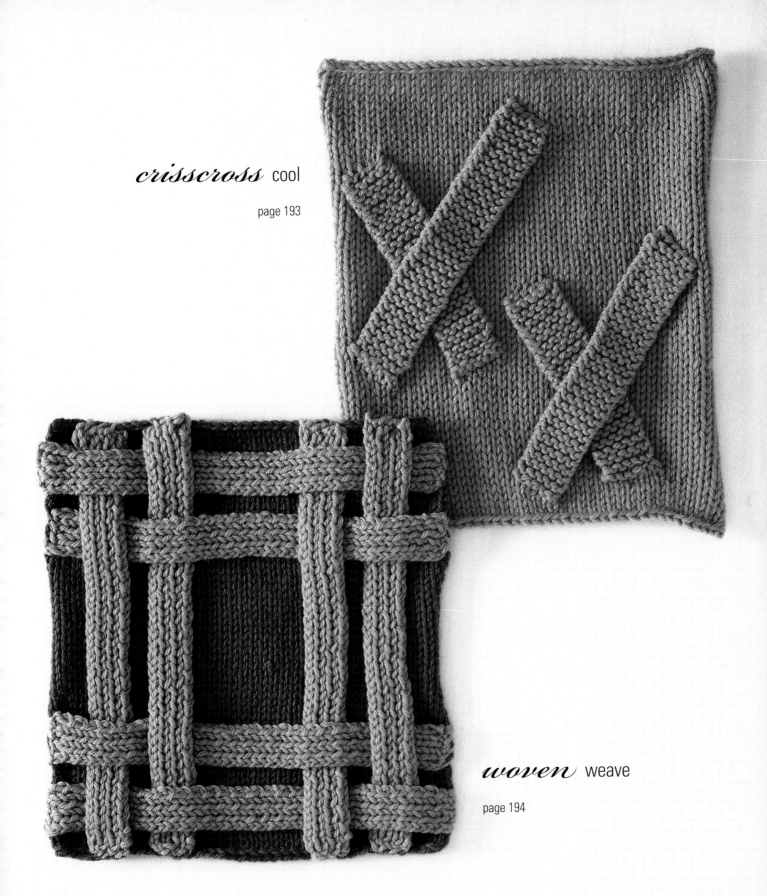

crisscross cool

page 193

woven weave

page 194

seed stitch
cookie twist

page 194

freedom flaps

page 195

windmill bobble

page 196

french braid

page 196

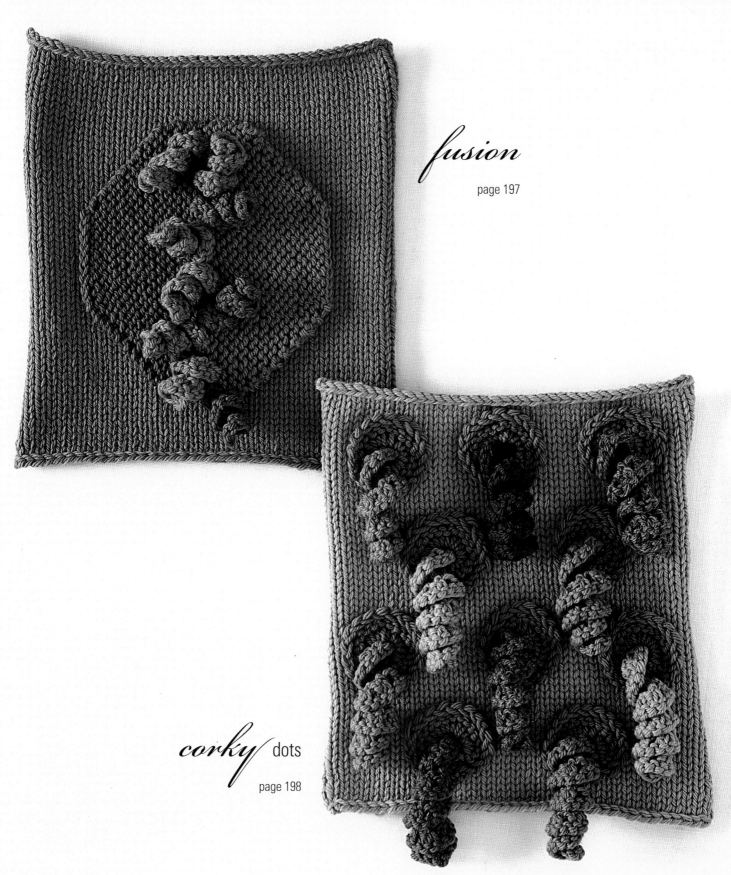

fusion

page 197

corky dots

page 198

ruffle and pod

page 198

layered ruffle

page 199

corkscrew cascade

page 201

cable tree

page 200

candy box

page 202

woven wicker

page 203

cathedral windows

page 204

synergy

page 205

reversible hourglass (front)

page 206

reversible hourglass (back)

page 206

COLORED LOOPY page 174

Colors A, B and C

BLOCK

With A, cast on 39 stitches (a multiple of 8 stitches plus 7).

Row 1 (RS) K1, p2, *k1, p7; repeat from * to the last 4 stitches, k1, p2, k1.

Rows 2 and 4 K3, *p1, k7; repeat from * to the last 4 stitches, p1, k3.

Rows 3 and 5 Repeat row 1.

Row 6 K3, *(k1, [yo, k1] 7 times) all in the same st (15 stitches), k7; repeat from * to the last 4 stitches, (k1, [yo, k1] 7 times) all in the same st, k3 (109 stitches).

Rows 7 and 9 K1, p to the last st, k1.

Row 8 Knit.

Row 10 K3, *k1, bind off the next 13 stitches, k8; repeat from *, ending last rep with k1, bind off the next 13 stitches k4 (44 stitches).

Row 11 K1, p2, *p2tog, p3, k1, p3, repeat from * to the last 5 stitches, p2tog, p2, k1 (39 stitches). Change to B.

Rows 12 and 14 With B, k7, *p1, k7; repeat from * to end.

Rows 13 and 15 K1, p6, *k 1, p7; repeat from * to the last 8 stitches, k1, p6, k1.

Row 16 K7, *(k1, [yo, k1] 7 times) all in the same st (15 stitches), k7; repeat from * to the end (95 stitches).

Rows 17 and 19 K1, purl to the last st, k1.

Row 18 Knit.

Row 20 *K8, bind off the next 13 stitches, k1; repeat from * to the last 7 stitches, k7 (43 stitches).

Row 21 K1, p2, k1, p3, *p2tog, p3, k1, p3; repeat from *, ending last rep with, p2tog, p3, k1, p2, k1 (39 stitches). Change to C.

Rows 22–31 Repeat rows 2–11. Change to B.

Rows 32–41 Repeat rows 12–21. Change to A.

Rows 42–51 Repeat rows 2–11. Bind off.

Stitch Key

☐ K on RS, P on WS
· P on RS, K on WS
O Yo
 (K1, [Yo, K1] 7 times) in 1 st
⌒ BO
╱ P2tog
☐ Repeat

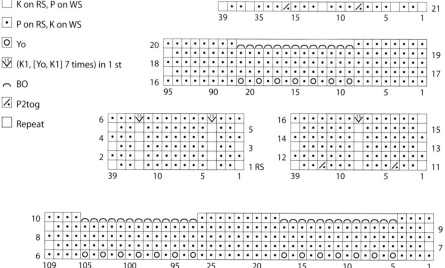

DISTRESSED SEED STITCH page 174

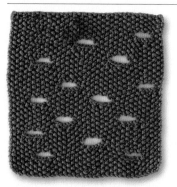

SLITS

(worked over 5 stitches)

Row 1 (RS) Bind off 5 stitches.

Row 2 Cast on 5 stitches over the bound-off stitches.

Repeat rows 1–2 for pattern.

Stitch Key

☐ K on RS, P on WS
· P on RS, K on WS
⌒ BO
Ⓤ CO 1 st

BLOCK

Cast on 41 stitches.

Row 1 K1, *p1, k1; repeat from * to end.

Repeat row 1 in Seed st until block length measures same as width, inserting slits randomly as pictured.

Slit

WS ⊙⊙⊙⊙⊙
⌒⌒⌒⌒⌒ RS
5   1

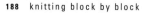

ROLLING CABLES page 175

ROLLING CABLES PATTERN

(a multiple of 21 stitches plus 7 more)

Set-up row (WS) *P1, [k1, p1] 3 times, p14; repeat from * to the last 7 stitches, p1, [k1, p1] 3 times.

Rows 1 and 3 (RS) *K1, [p1, k1] 3 times, k14; repeat from * to the last 7 stitches, k1, [p1, k1] 3 times.

Row 2 *P1, [k1, p1] 3 times, p14; repeat from * to the last 7 stitches, p1, [k1, p1] 3 times.

Row 4 *P1, [k1, p1] 3 times, k2, [p4, k2] twice; repeat from * to the last 7 stitches, p1, [k1, p1] 3 times.

Row 5 *K1, [p1, k1] 3 times, p2, *2/2 LC, p2; repeat from * to the last 7 stitches, k1, [p1, k1] 3 times.

Row 6 Repeat row 2.

Repeat rows 1–6 for pattern.

BLOCK

Cast on 49 stitches.

Work set-up row, rows 1–6 of Rolling Cables pattern 9 times, then repeat rows 1–2 once more.

Bind off.

.

Rolling Cables Pattern

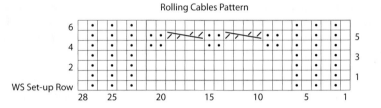

BEADED POD page 175

POD STITCH

(a multiple of 8 stitches)

Set-up row (WS) Purl.

Row 1 (RS) Knit.

Row 2 and all WS rows Purl.

Row 3 *K8, 2/2 LC, 2/2 RC; repeat from * to end.

Row 5 Knit.

Row 7 *2/2 RC, 2/2 LC, k8; repeat from * to end.

Row 9 Knit.

Row 11 *2/2 LC, 2/2 RC, k8; repeat from * to end.

Row 13 Knit.

Row 15 *K8, 2/2 RC, 2/2 LC; repeat from * to end.

Row 16 Purl.

Repeat rows 1–16 for pattern.

BLOCK

Cast on 48 stitches.

Work rows 1–16 of Pod st 3 times, then rows 1–8 once more.

Bind off.

FINISHING

Sew a bead to the center of each pod as pictured.

Pod Stitch

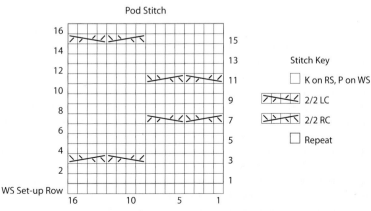

Note Pattern is worked from the top down.

BLOCK

Cast on 47 stitches (a multiple of 8 stitches plus 7 more).

Row 1 (WS) K7, *p1, k7; repeat from * to end.
Row 2 P7, *k in front, back and front again of next st, p7; repeat from * to end.
Row 3 and all WS rows through row 43 K7, *p3, k7; repeat from * to end.
Row 4 P7, *1/1 LC, k1, p7; repeat from * to end.
Row 6 P7, *k1, 1/1 RC, p7; repeat from * to end.
Rows 7–42 Repeat rows 3–6, nine more times.

Row 43 Work as for row 3.
Row 44 P7, *SK2P, p7; repeat from * to end.
Row 45 K7, *p1, k7; repeat from * to end.
Row 46 P7, *k1, p7; repeat from * to end.
Row 47 K7, *p1, k7; repeat from * to end.
Row 48 P7, *yo, k1, yo, p7; repeat from * to end.
Row 49 K7, *p2, p1 tbl, k7; repeat from * to end.
Row 50 P7, *yo, k3, yo, p7; repeat from * to end.
Row 51 K7, *p4, p1 tbl, k7; repeat from * to end.

Row 52 P7, *yo, k5, yo, p7; repeat from * to end.
Row 53 K7, *p6, p1 tbl, k7; repeat from * to end.
Row 54 P7, *yo, k7, yo, p7; repeat from * to end.
Row 55 K7, *p8, p1 tbl, k7; repeat from * to end.
Row 56 P7, *yo, k9, yo, p7; repeat from * to end.
Row 57 K7, *p10, p1 tbl, k7; repeat from * to end.
Row 58 P7, *yo, k11, yo, p7; repeat from * to end.
Row 59 K7, *p12, p1 tbl, k7; repeat from * to end.
Bind off in pattern.

Stitch Key

- ⋅ P on RS, K on WS
- ■ No stitch
- □ K on RS, P on WS
- □ Repeat
- ⱱ (K1, K1 tbl, K1) in 1 st
- ⤬ 1/1 LC
- ⤬ 1/1 RC
- O Yo
- ⋋ SK2P on RS
- ℞ K1 tbl
- ◹ P2tog tbl

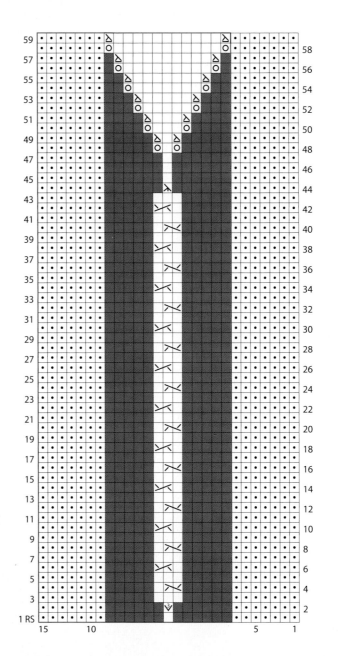

SQUARED LAMB'S TAIL page 176

LAMB'S TAIL PATTERN

(a multiple of 4 stitches plus 1 more)

Make Tail (MT) [K1 without taking st off needle, and place the st onto the left-hand needle beside the st just knit] 4 times (4 new stitches); bind off 4 stitches.

Rows 1 and 2 Knit.

Row 3 (RS) *K3, MT; repeat from * to the last st, k1.

Row 4 K1, *p1, k3; repeat from * to end.

Rows 5 and 6 Knit.

Row 7 K1, *MT, k3; repeat from * to end.

Row 8 *K3, p1; repeat from * to the last st, k1.

Repeat rows 1–8 for pattern.

BLOCK

Cast on 42 stitches.

First Half

Row 1 (RS) Work 21 stitches in Garter st, work 21 stitches in Lamb's Tail pattern.

Rows 2–36 Continue in patterns as established.

Second Half

Row 37 (RS) Work 21 stitches in Lamb's Tail pattern, work 21 stitches in Garter st.

Rows 38–72 Continue in patterns as established.

Rows 73 and 74 Knit.

Bind off.

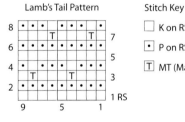

Lamb's Tail Pattern

Stitch Key

☐ K on RS, P on WS

• P on RS, K on WS

T MT (Make Tail)

ZIP IT page 177

BLOCK

Cast on 45 stitches.

Work in St st until block length measures same as width.

Bind off.

FINISHING

Cut ribbon 1" (2.5cm) longer than zipper length. Fold ½" (13mm) under each end and sew in place. Sew covered zippers to block as pictured.

Note Be creative—you can use lace, buttons, ribbon, or whatever you desire to embellish a block.

Stitch Key

☐ K on RS, P on WS

☐ Repeat

Block

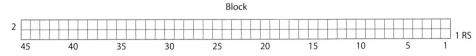

Colors A, B and C

BLOCK

With A, cast on 45 stitches.

Work in St st until block length measures same as width.

Bind off.

FIRST RIB CLOSURE

With B, cast on 39 stitches.

Row 1 (RS) K3, *p3, k3; repeat from * to end.

Row 2 P3, *k3, p3; repeat from * to end.

Rows 3–14 Repeat rows 1 and 2.

Change to C.

Rows 15–18 Repeat rows 1 and 2.

Bind off in pattern.

SECOND RIB CLOSURE

With C, cast on 39 stitches.

Row 1 (RS) K3, *p3, k3; repeat from * to end.

Row 2 P3, *k3, p3; repeat from * to end.

Rows 3–14 Repeat rows 1 and 2.

Change to B.

Rows 15–18 Repeat rows 1 and 2.

Bind off in pattern.

FINISHING

Sew each rib closure to block following the photo for placement. Sew clasp to closures; buttons can also be used.

Stitch Key

- ☐ A
- ☐ B
- ☐ C
- ☐ K on RS, P on WS
- ☐ Repeat
- ⊡ P on RS, K on WS

Block

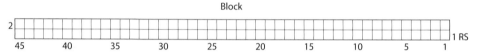

First Rib Closure

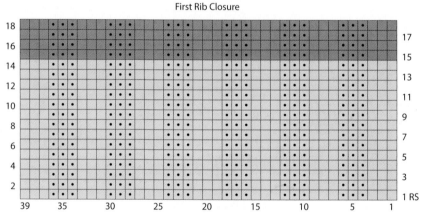

Second Rib Closure

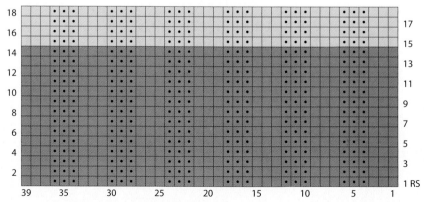

RANDOM RODS page 178

RODS
(over 2 stitches)

Row 1 Cast-on row (RS) P1, cast on 5 stitches onto the left-hand needle, p1 (7 stitches).

Row 2 K1, p5, k1.

Row 3 P1, k5, p1.

Repeat the last 2 rows for each set of rod stitches for approximately 2"–3" (5cm–7.5cm), ending with a WS row, then work as follows:

Row 5 Bind-off row (RS) K1, bind off the next 5 stitches (2 stitches).

Row 6 P2.

BLOCK
Cast on 45 stitches.

Work in St st for ½" (13mm), ending with a WS row. Work rods at random or follow photo while working background in St st until block length measures same as width.

Bind off.

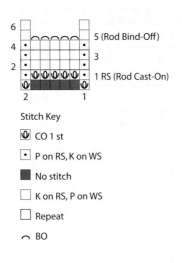

Stitch Key

- ⓪ CO 1 st
- · P on RS, K on WS
- ■ No stitch
- □ K on RS, P on WS
- □ Repeat
- ⌒ BO

Rods (Front)

Rods (Back)

CRISSCROSS COOL page 179

BLOCK
Cast on 45 stitches.

Work in St st until block length measures same as width.

Bind off.

RIGHT CRISSCROSS
Note Refer to the photo for placement.

Right Band

With the right side facing, pick up and k6 stitches at a 90-degree downward angle. Work in Garter st for 4" (10cm). Bind off.

Left Band
With the right side facing, starting approximately 1" (2.5cm) from the right leg, pick up and k6 stitches at a 90-degree upward angle. Work in Garter st for 5¼" (13.5cm). Bind off.

LEFT CRISSCROSS
Work same as Right Crisscross starting 3" (7.5cm) from the lower edge as pictured.

FINISHING
Cross the bands and sew the bound-off edges to the block.

WOVEN WEAVE page 179

Colors MC and CC

BLOCK
With MC, cast on 45 stitches.
Work in St st until block length measures same as width.
Bind off.

STRIPS (make 8)
With CC, cast on 7 stitches.
Work in k1, p1 rib for length/width of block.
Bind off.

FINISHING
Lay strips onto the block and weave them together at the corners following the photo for placement.
Sew the strips in place.

Stitch Key

☐ MC

☐ Repeat

▨ CC

⊡ P on RS, K on WS

☐ K on RS, P on WS

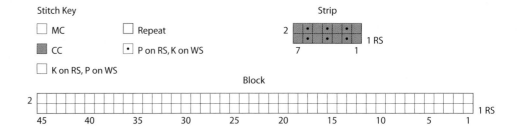

SEED STITCH COOKIE TWIST page 180

*With a second ball of yarn, slip the stitches from a holder onto a needle and work in Seed st for 3" (7.5cm) or to length needed to match block with a twist. Cut the yarn and place these stitches on a holder; repeat from * for each set of held stitches.
Next row (WS) Work 4 stitches in Seed st, *twist stitches on holder counterclockwise once, [work 1 st from the holder together with 1 st from the block] 9 times, work 4 stitches in Seed st; repeat from * to end.
Work 4 rows in Seed st.
Repeat from row 1 once more.
Bind off.

BLOCK
Cast on 43 stitches (a multiple of 13 stitches plus 4 more). Work 4 rows in Seed st.
Row 1 (RS) Work 4 stitches in Seed st, *slip the next 9 stitches to a holder, cast on 9 stitches, work 4 stitches in Seed st; repeat from * to end. Continue in Seed st for 3" (7.5cm). Leave stitches on the needle; do not cut the yarn.

Stitch Key

☐ K on RS, P on WS

⊡ P on RS, K on WS

☐ Sts on hold

Ⓤ CO 1 st

☐ Repeat

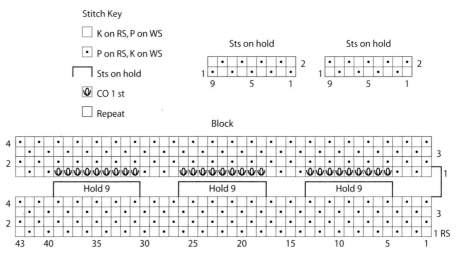

FREEDOM FLAPS page 180

Note Flaps can be left plain or the ends can folded up and stitched in place with a bobble or button ornament as pictured.

BLOCK

Cast on 39 stitches.

Work in Seed st for 1" (2.5 cm).

Flap Opening 1

Next row (RS) Work 14 stitches in Seed st, slip the next 7 stitches onto a holder, cast on 7 stitches, continue in Seed st to the end.

Work in Seed st for 1" (2.5cm) more.

Flap Opening 2

Next row (RS) Work 4 stitches in Seed st, slip the next 5 stitches onto a holder, cast on 5 stitches, continue in Seed st to the end.

Work in Seed st for 1" (2.5cm) more.

Flap Opening 3

Next row (RS) Work 28 stitches in Seed st, slip the next 7 stitches onto a holder, cast on 7 stitches, continue in Seed st to the end.

Work in Seed st for 2" (5cm) more.

Flap Opening 4

Next row (RS) Work 12 stitches in Seed st, slip the next 5 stitches onto a holder, cast on 5 stitches, continue in Seed st to the end.

Work in Seed st for 1" (2.5cm) more.

Flap Opening 5

Next row (RS) Work 20 stitches in Seed st, slip the next 7 stitches onto a holder, cast on 7 stitches, continue in Seed st to the end.

Work in Seed st for 1" (2.5cm) more.

Flap Opening 6

Next row (RS) Work 6 stitches in Seed st, slip the next 5 stitches onto a holder, cast on 5 stitches, continue in Seed st to the end.

Work in Seed st for 1" (2.5cm).

Flap Opening 7

Next row (RS) Work 32 stitches in Seed st, slip the next 5 stitches onto a holder, cast on 5 stitches, continue in Seed st to the end.

Work in Seed st until block measures 9" (23cm).

FLAPS

Slip the stitches from a holder onto a needle. Work in Seed st to the desired length.

Next row (RS) Work in Seed st, decreasing 1 st at each end of the row.

Next row (WS) Work even in Seed st.

Repeat the last 2 rows until 3 stitches remain.

K3tog.

Fasten off.

Repeat for each flap.

Stitch Key

☐	K on RS, P on WS
•	P on RS, K on WS
Ⓤ	CO 1 st
☐	Repeat
◣	SSK
◩	K2tog
◪	K3tog
☐	Sts on hold

7-st Flap

5-st Flap

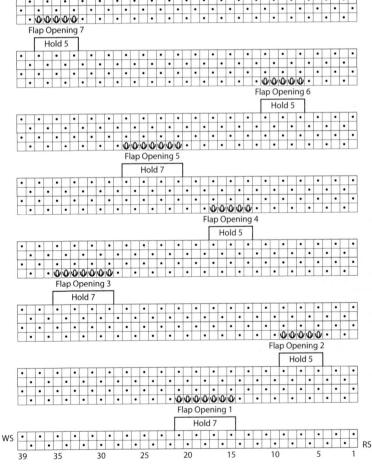

Block

Flap Opening 7
Hold 5

Flap Opening 6
Hold 5

Flap Opening 5
Hold 7

Flap Opening 4
Hold 5

Flap Opening 3
Hold 7

Flap Opening 2
Hold 5

Flap Opening 1
Hold 7

WINDMILL BOBBLE page 181

WINDMILL PATTERN

(a multiple of 20 stitches)

Row 1 (RS) *P1, k9, p9, k1; repeat from * to end.

Row 2 *P2, k8, p8, k2; repeat from * to end.

Row 3 *P3, k7, p7, k3; repeat from * to end.

Row 4 *P4, k6, p6, k4; repeat from * to end.

Row 5 *P5, k5; repeat from * to end.

Row 6 *P6, k4, p4, k6; repeat from * to end.

Row 7 *P7, k3, p3, k7; repeat from * to end.

Row 8 *P8, k2, p2, k8; repeat from * to end.

Row 9 *P9, k1, p1, k9; repeat from * to end.

Row 10 *P10, k10; repeat from * to end.

Row 11 *K10, p10; repeat from * to end.

Row 12 *K9, p1, k1, p9; repeat from * to end.

Row 13 *K8, p2, k2, p8; repeat from * to end.

Row 14 *K7, p3, k3, p7; repeat from * to end.

Row 15 *K6, p4, k4, p6; repeat from * to end.

Row 16 *K5, p5; repeat from * to end.

Row 17 *K4, p6, k6, p4; repeat from * to end.

Row 18 *K3, p7, k7, p3; repeat from * to end.

Row 19 *K2, p8, k8, p2; repeat from * to end.

Row 20 *K1, p9, k9, p1; repeat from * to end.

Row 21 Repeat row 10.

Row 22 Repeat row 11.

Repeat rows 1–22 for pattern.

BLOCK

Cast on 42 stitches.

Keeping the first and last stitches in St st, work rows 1–22 of Windmill pattern twice, then rows 1–10 once more.

Bind off.

BOBBLES (make 12)

Cast on 1 st. K into the front, back, front, back and front of the same st (5 stitches), turn; p5, turn; k5, turn; p5, turn; k2tog, k1, k2tog, turn; p3tog. Fasten off.

FINISHING

Tie a bobble to the center of each windmill as pictured. Hide the ends inside the bobbles.

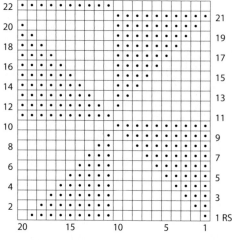

Windmill Pattern

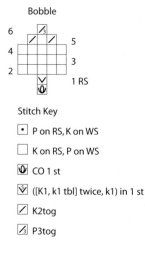

Bobble

Stitch Key

- ● P on RS, K on WS
- ☐ K on RS, P on WS
- CO 1 st
- ([K1, k1 tbl] twice, k1) in 1 st
- ⁄ K2tog
- ⁄ P3tog

FRENCH BRAID page 181

FRENCH BRAID PATTERN

(a multiple of 15 stitches plus 2 more)

Row 1 (RS) Knit.

Row 2 Purl.

Row 3 K1, 5/5 LC, *k5, 5/5 LC; repeat from * to the last 6 stitches, k6.

Rows 4, 6 and 8 Purl.

Rows 5 and 7 Knit.

Row 9 K6, 5/5 RC, *k5, 5/5 RC; repeat from * to the last st, k1.

Row 10 Purl.

Row 11 Knit.

Row 12 Purl.

Repeat rows 1–12 for pattern.

BLOCK

Cast on 62 stitches.

Work rows 1–12 of French Braid pattern 5 times, then repeat rows 1–6 once more.

Bind off.

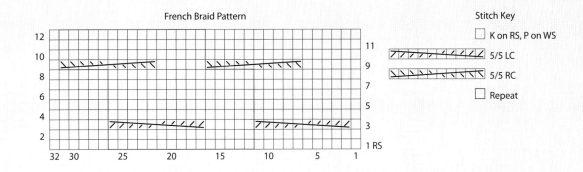

French Braid Pattern

Stitch Key

□ K on RS, P on WS

▱ 5/5 LC

▱ 5/5 RC

□ Repeat

FUSION page 182

Colors A, B, and C

BLOCK

With A, cast on 45 stitches.

Note Cast on over 2 needles for a loose cast on.

Work in St st until block length measures same as width.

Bind off.

HEXAGON

With B, cast on 12 stitches.

K 2 rows.

Inc row (RS) Kf&b of first st, k to the last st, kf&b of last st.

Repeat inc row every RS row until there are 26 stitches.

Work even in Garter st for 1½" (3.8cm), ending with a WS row. Change to C.

Work even in Garter st for 1½" (3.8cm), ending with a WS row.

Dec row (RS) Ssk, k to the last 2 stitches, k2tog.

Repeat dec row every RS row until there are 12 stitches.

K 2 rows.

Bind off.

CORKSCREWS (make 3 each in A, B and C)

With A, B or C, cast on 8 stitches.

Row 1 K into the front, back and front of each st (24 stitches).

Bind off purlwise.

Twist and twirl each tassel into a corkscrew.

FINISHING

Sew hexagon to center of block and attach corkscrews across the color change row as pictured.

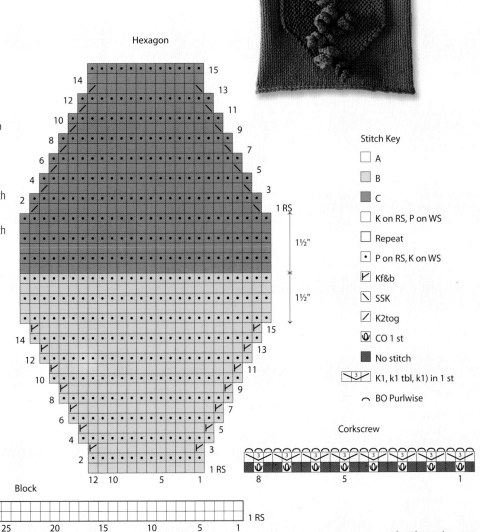

Hexagon

Stitch Key

□ A

▨ B

▨ C

□ K on RS, P on WS

□ Repeat

• P on RS, K on WS

▱ Kf&b

◺ SSK

◹ K2tog

Ⓞ CO 1 st

■ No stitch

▱ K1, k1 tbl, k1) in 1 st

⌒ BO Purlwise

Corkscrew

Block

CORKY DOTS page 182

Colors A, B, C, D, E

BLOCK

With A, cast on 45 stitches.
Work in St st until block length measures same as width.
Bind off.

DOTS (make 10)

With B, cast on 20 stitches loosely.
Note Cast on over 2 needles for a loose cast on.
Work 3 rows in Garter st.
Pass all the stitches, one at a time, over the first st and off the needle. Fasten off and sew ends together leaving a ½" (13mm) opening at the center.

CORKSCREW (make 2 each with A, B, C, D and E)

With C, cast on 20 stitches loosely.
Row 1 K into the front, back and front of each st (60 stitches).
Bind off purlwise.

FINISHING

Sew dots to the block following the photo for placement. Sew a corkscrew to the center of each dot.

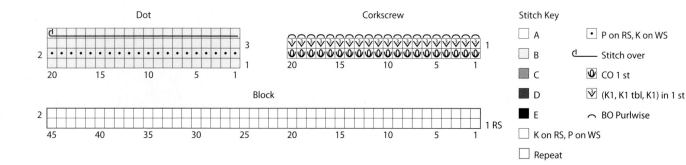

Dot

Corkscrew

Stitch Key

	A		• P on RS, K on WS
	B		Stitch over
	C		CO 1 st
	D		(K1, K1 tbl, K1) in 1 st
	E		BO Purlwise
	K on RS, P on WS		
	Repeat		

Block

RUFFLE AND POD page 183

Colors MC and CC

BLOCK

With MC, cast on 41 stitches.
Work in St st until block length measures same as width.
Bind off.

RUFFLES

With MC, cast on 120 stitches.
Work in St st for 2" (5cm), ending with a WS row.
K 1 row.
Bind off.

With MC, cast on 120 stitches.
Work in St st for 1½" (4cm), ending with a WS row.
K 1 row.
Bind off.

POD

With CC, cast on 11 stitches.
Row 1 (RS) Kf&b of each st (22 stitches).
Row 2 and all WS rows Purl.
Rows 3, 5, 7, 9 and 11 Knit.
Row 13 *K2tog; repeat from * to end (11 stitches).
Row 14 *P2tog; repeat from *, end p1 (6 stitches).
Pass all the stitches, one at a time, over the first st.

Fasten off.

Thread the bond-off tail through the bound-off stitches, gather and secure the end. Stuff with polyfil and sew the side seam. Thread the cast-on tail through the cast-on stitches and gather to close, then insert the tail through the center to the bind-off end to create a dimple and secure the end.

FINISHING

Sew the 1½" (4cm) ruffle to the center of the block following the photo for placement. Repeat for the 2" (5cm) ruffle. Sew the pod to the center as pictured.

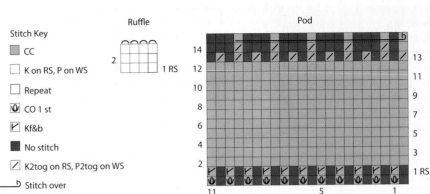

Stitch Key

- ▨ CC
- ☐ K on RS, P on WS
- ☐ Repeat
- ⓤ CO 1 st
- ⋀ Kf&b
- ◼ No stitch
- ╱ K2tog on RS, P2tog on WS
- ⎯ᵇ Stitch over

LAYERED RUFFLE page 183

Colors A (dark), B (medium) and C (light)

RUFFLE (make one each in A, B, and C)
Cast on 80 stitches.
K 2 rows.
Work in St st until the ruffle measures 2½" (6.5cm), ending with a WS row.
Next row (RS) *K2tog; repeat from * to end (40 stitches). Leave the stitches on a spare needle.

BLOCK
With A, cast on 40 stitches.
Work in St st for 2½" (6.5cm), ending with a RS row.

Joining row (WS) With the wrong sides facing and the ruffle needle behind the block needle, *purl 1 st from the ruffle together with 1 st from the block; repeat from * to end.
Continue in St st for 2¼" (5.5cm), ending with RS row.
Join the 2nd ruffle same as for the first.
Continue in St st for 2¼" (5.5cm), ending with RS row.
Join the 3rd ruffle same as for the first.
Bind off.

Stitch Key

◼ A (Dark)	☐ C (Light)	• P on RS, K on WS	╱ K2tog on RS, P2tog on WS
▨ B (Medium)	☐ K on RS, P on WS	☐ Repeat	◼ No stitch

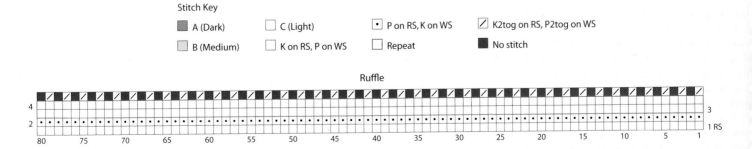

Colors MC and CC

2-COLOR SINGLE BOXED BOBBLE

(a multiple of 6 stitches plus 1 more)

Make Bobble (MB) With CC, k into the front, back, front and back of the same st (4 stitches), turn, k4, turn, p4, pass the 2nd, 3rd and 4th stitches, one at a time, over the first st.

Row 1 (RS) With MC, purl.

Rows 2, 4 and 6 With MC, purl.

Rows 3 and 7 With MC, p1, *k5, p1; repeat from * to end.

Row 5 *With MC, p1, k2; with CC, MB; with MC, k2; repeat from * to the last st, with MC, p1.

Rows 8 and 9 With MC, purl.

TWIST

(a multiple of 6 stitches plus 1 more)

SP2P Sl 1 knitwise, p2tog tbl, pass the slipped st over.

Row 1 (WS) P1, *p2, k1, p3; repeat from * to end.

Row 2 *K3, p1, k2; repeat from * to the last st, k1.

Row 3 P2tog, *p1, m1, k1, m1, p1, p3tog; repeat from * to the last 5 stitches, p1, m1, k1, m1, p1, p2tog.

Row 4 *K2, p3, k1; repeat from * to the last st, k1.

Row 5 P2tog, *m1, k3, m1, p3tog; repeat from * to the last 5 stitches, m1, k3, m1, p2tog.

Row 6 *K1, p5; repeat from * to the last st, k1.

Row 7 P1, *m1P, ssk, k1, k2tog, m1P, p1; repeat from * to end.

Row 8 *K2, p3, k1; repeat from * to the last st, k1.

Row 9 P1, *p1, m1P, SP2P, m1P, p2; repeat from * to end.

Row 10 *K3, p1, k2; repeat from * to the last st, k1.

Row 11 Purl.

BLOCK

With MC, cast on 43 stitches (a multiple of 6 stitches plus 1 more).

*Work rows 1–9 of 2-Color Single Boxed Bobble pattern, then work rows 1–11 of Twist pattern; repeat from * 2 more times.

Bind off.

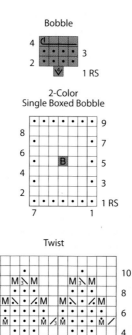

Bobble

2-Color
Single Boxed Bobble

Twist

Stitch Key

- ☐ MC
- ▨ CC
- • P on RS, K on WS
- ☐ K on RS, P on WS
- B MB
- ⱴ [K1, K1 tbl] twice in 1 st
- ⌐— Stitch over
- ◿ P2tog
- M M1P
- ◿ P3tog
- M̌ M1
- ◣ SSK
- ◢ K2tog
- ◣ SP2P

WOVEN WICKER page 185

Colors A, B and C

WICKER PATTERN

(a multiple of 8 stitches)

Set-up row (WS) P1, *k2, p2; repeat from * to the last 3 stitches, k2, p1.

Row 1 (RS) *K1, p1, 1/1 RPC, 1/1 LPC, p1, k1; repeat from * to end.

Row 2 *P1, k1, p1, k2, p1, k1, p1; repeat from * to end.

Row 3 *K1, 1/1 RPC, p2, 1/1 LPC, k1; repeat from * to end.

Row 4 P2, *k4, p4; repeat from * to the last 6 stitches, k4, p2.

Row 5 Knit.

Row 6 P1, *k2, p2; repeat from * to the last 3 stitches, k2, p1.

Row 7 *1/1 LPC, p1, k2, p1, 1/1 RPC; repeat from * to end.

Row 8 *K1, p1, k1, p2, k1, p1, k1; repeat from * to end.

Row 9 *P1, 1/1 LPC, k2, 1/1 RPC, p1; repeat from * to end.

Row 10 K2, *p4, k4; repeat from * to the last 6 stitches, p4, k2.

Row 11 Knit.

Row 12 Repeat row 6.

Repeat rows 1–12 for pattern.

BLOCK

With A, cast on 48 stitches.

Work set-up row, rows 1–12 of Wicker pattern twice, then rows 1–4 once more.

Change to B.

With B, work rows 5–12 once, then rows 1–12 twice more. Bind off.

CORD (make 3)

With double-pointed needles and C, cast on 3 stitches. Work in I-cord (see page 238) to fit across block. Bind off. Weave each cord in and out of pattern as pictured.

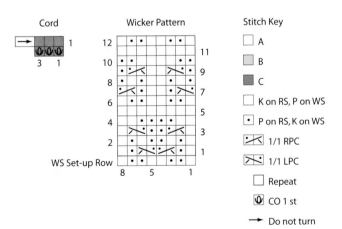

Cord

Wicker Pattern

Stitch Key

- ☐ A
- ☐ B
- ■ C
- ☐ K on RS, P on WS
- · P on RS, K on WS
- ⧄ 1/1 RPC
- ⧅ 1/1 LPC
- ☐ Repeat
- Ⓞ CO 1 st
- → Do not turn

SPECIAL STITCH

Make Bobble (MB) K in front, back, front and back of the next st (4 stitches), turn, k4, turn, pass the 2nd, 3rd and 4th stitches, one at a time, over the first st.

BLOCK

Cast on 43 stitches (a multiple of 10 stitches plus 3 more).

Row 1 (RS) K3, *p7, k3; repeat from * to end.

Row 2 P3, *k7, p3; repeat from * to end.

Rows 3–42 Repeat rows 1 and 2.

Row 43 K2, *yo, ssk, p5, k2tog, yo, k1; repeat from * to the last st, k1.

Row 44 P4, *k5, p5; repeat from * to the last 9 stitches, k5, p4.

Row 45 K3, *yo, ssk, p3, k2tog, yo, k3; repeat from * to end.

Row 46 P5, *k3, p7; repeat from * to the last 8 stitches, k3, p5.

Row 47 K2, *[yo, ssk] twice, p1, [k2tog, yo] twice, k1; repeat from * to the last st, k1.

Row 48 P6, *k1, p9; repeat from * to the last 7 stitches, k1, p6.

Row 49 K3, *yo, ssk, yo, SK2P, yo, k2tog, yo, k3; repeat from * to end.

Rows 50, 52 and 54 Purl.

Row 51 K4, *yo, ssk, k1, k2tog, yo, k5; repeat from * to the last 9 stitches, yo, ssk, k1, k2tog, yo, k4.

Row 53 K5, *yo, SK2P, yo, k7; repeat from * to the last 8 stitches, yo, SK2P, yo, k5.

Row 55 *K6, MB, k3; repeat from * to the last 3 stitches, k3.

Row 56 Purl.

Bind off.

Cathedral Windows Pattern

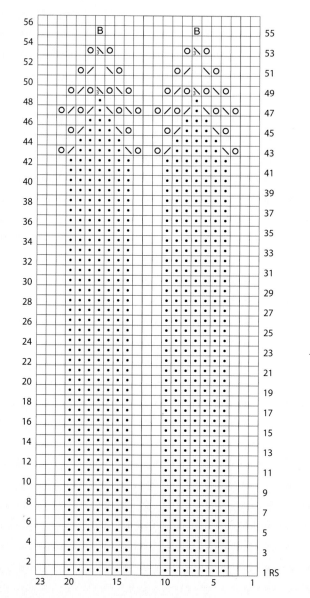

Bobble

Stitch Key

☐ K on RS, P on WS

• P on RS, K on WS

O Yo

╲ SSK

╱ K2tog

╲ SK2P

B MB

⬇ [K1, K1 tbl] twice in 1 st

⌐ Stitch over

SYNERGY page 186

Colors MC and CC

BLOCK

With MC, cast on 45 stitches.

Work in St st until block length measures same as width.

Bind off.

BALLS (make 8)

With CC, cast on 11 stitches.

Row 1 (RS) Kf&b of each st (22 stitches).

Row 2 and all WS rows Purl.

Rows 3, 5, 7 and 9 Knit.

Row 11 *K2tog; repeat from * to end (11 stitches).

Row 12 *P2tog; repeat from * to the last st, p1 (6 stitches).

Pass all the stitches, one at a time, over the first st. Fasten off.

Thread the cast-on tail through the cast-on stitches, gather and secure. Stuff with polyfil and sew side seam.

FINISHING

Tie balls to block as pictured. Thread a tapestry needle with two strands of CC. Make five long stitches from the center as pictured, pulling each stitch tightly and fasten off. Repeat for each ball.

Note Balls can be left plain, as shown in upper left corner.

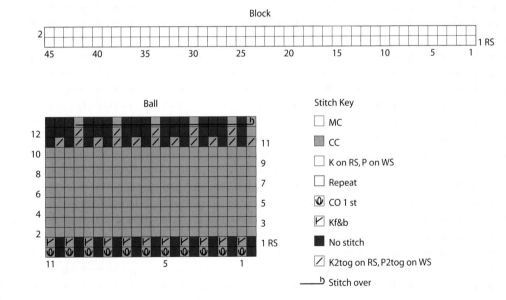

Block

Ball

Stitch Key

☐ MC

▨ CC

☐ K on RS, P on WS

☐ Repeat

Ⓥ CO 1 st

⊻ Kf&b

■ No stitch

◿ K2tog on RS, P2tog on WS

⌐ᵇ Stitch over

Reversible Hourglass (Front)

Reversible Hourglass (Back)

SPECIAL STITCHES

3/1 LPC SI 3 stitches to cn and hold in front, p1, k3 from cn.

3/1 RPC SI 1 st to cn and hold in back, k3, p1 from cn.

BLOCK

Cast on 43 stitches.

Row 1 (RS) *K1, [p1, k1] twice, p4, k6, p4; repeat from * to the last 5 stitches, k1, [p1, k1] twice.

Row 2 P1, [k1, p1] twice, *k4, p6, k4, p1, [k1, p1] twice; repeat from * to end.

Row 3 *K1, [p1, k1] twice, p3, 3/1 RPC, 3/1 LPC, p3; repeat from * to the last 5 stitches, k1, [p1, k1] twice.

Row 4 P1, [k1, p1] twice, *k3, p3, k2, p3, k3, p1, [k1, p1] twice; repeat from * to end.

Row 5 *K1, [p1, k1] twice, p2, 3/1 RPC, p2, 3/1 LPC, p2; repeat from * to the last 5 stitches, k1, [p1, k1] twice.

Row 6 P1, [k1,p1] twice, *k2, p3, k4, p3, k2, p1, [k1, p1]; repeat from * to end.

Row 7 *K1, [p1, k1] twice, p1, 3/1 RPC, p4, 3/1 LPC, p1; repeat from * to the last 5 stitches, k1, [p1, k1] twice.

Rows 8, 10 and 12 P1, [k1, p1] twice, *p4, k6, p4, [p1, k1] twice, p1; repeat from * to end.

Rows 9 and 11 *K1, [p1, k1] twice, k4, p6, k4; repeat from * to the last 5 stitches, k1, [p1, k1] twice.

Row 13 *K1, [p1, k1] twice, p1, 3/1 LPC, p4, 3/1 RPC, p1; repeat from * to the last 5 stitches, k1, [p1, k1] twice.

Row 14 Repeat row 6.

Row 15 *K1, [p1, k1] twice, p2, 3/1 LPC, p2, 3/1 RPC, p2; repeat from * to the last 5 stitches, k1, [p1, k1] twice.

Row 16 Repeat row 4.

Row 17 *K1, [p1, k1] twice, p3, 3/1 LPC, 3/1 RPC, p3; repeat from * to the last 5 stitches, k1, [p1, k1] twice.

Row 18 Repeat row 2.

Rows 19 and 20 Repeat rows 1 and 2.

Repeat rows 1–20 twice more, then repeat rows 1–2 once more.

Bind off.

Block

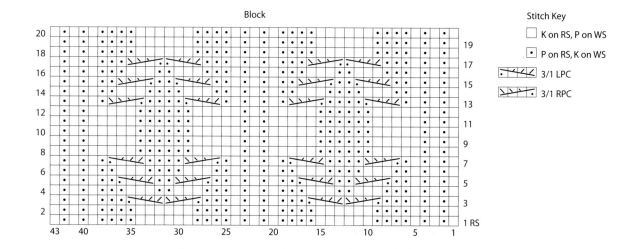

Stitch Key

☐ K on RS, P on WS

• P on RS, K on WS

3/1 LPC

3/1 RPC

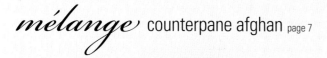

mélange counterpane afghan page 7

Made with 3 block designs—2 counterpanes and 1 Highland Fling block—this afghan will quickly become a classic "must-have."

Knitted Measurements
• Approx 44" x 70" (112cm x 178cm) point-to-point

Materials
• Cascade 220 Superwash (100% wool), each approximately 220 yards (201m) and 3.5oz (100g); 14 skeins of #870 Gold
• Size U.S. 7 (4.5mm) straight needles, size U.S. 6 (4mm) circular needle at least 36" (91cm) long
• Size U.S. 7 (4.5mm) double-pointed needles (set of 5)
• Stitch markers

Gauge
• 20 stitches and 26 rows = 4" (10cm) in St st on size U.S. 7 (4mm) straight needles
TAKE TIME TO CHECK GAUGE.

BLOCKS (make 31)
8 Highland Fling with Reverse St st background (see page 45)
8 Rosemary Sprigs (see page 160)
7 Regal Cable (see page 168)
8 Angled Squares (below)

Angled Square
With larger needles, cast on 45 stitches.
Row 1 (RS) P2tog, p to end.
Row 2 K to the last 2 stitches, k2tog.
Row 3 Purl.
Row 4 K to last 2 stitches, k2tog.
Repeat rows 1–4 until 3 stitches remain.
Next row (RS) P2tog, p1.
Next row K2tog.
Next row P1.
Fasten off.

FINISHING
Join the blocks following the diagram. The first and last rows of blocks begin and end with the Rosemary Sprigs blocks. The blocks with the round squiggles are the Highland Fling.

EDGING
Top and Bottom
With the right side facing and the circular needle, starting at the base of the first point, *pick up and k42 stitches along the first edge, pick up 1 st in the point, pick up 42 stitches along the second edge; repeat from * twice more (255 stitches).
Row 1 (WS) *K42, pm, p1, pm, k42; repeat from * to end.
Row 2 K2tog, k40 *m1, sm, k1, sm, m1, k41, k2tog and mark this stitch, k41; repeat from * once, m1, k1, m1, k40, k2tog.
Row 3 Knit.
Row 4 K2tog, k to the next marker, *m1, sm, k1, sm, m1, k to 1 st before the marked st, sk2p, k to the next marker; repeat from * once, m1, sm, k1, sm, m1, k to the last 2 stitches, k2tog.
Repeat the last 2 rows 4 times more.
Bind off. Repeat on the opposite end.

SIDES
With the right side facing, pick up and k214 stitches along the side edge, excluding the top and bottom edgings. Work 12 rows in Garter st. Bind off.

Sew the edging seams together.

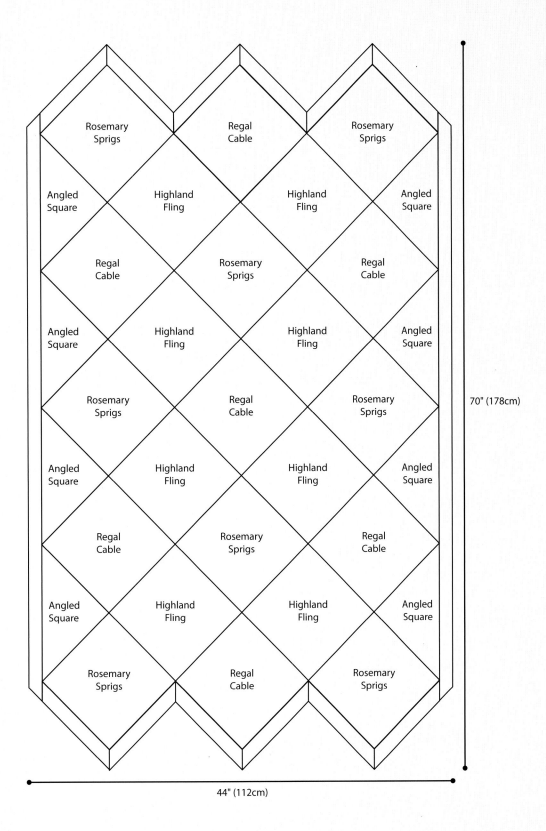

Rosemary Sprigs · Regal Cable · Rosemary Sprigs

Angled Square · Highland Fling · Highland Fling · Angled Square

Regal Cable · Rosemary Sprigs · Regal Cable

Angled Square · Highland Fling · Highland Fling · Angled Square

Rosemary Sprigs · Regal Cable · Rosemary Sprigs

Angled Square · Highland Fling · Highland Fling · Angled Square

Regal Cable · Rosemary Sprigs · Regal Cable

Angled Square · Highland Fling · Highland Fling · Angled Square

Rosemary Sprigs · Regal Cable · Rosemary Sprigs

70" (178cm)

44" (112cm)

winter solstice hooded scarf page 8

The Fair Isle-style blocks and a reindeer motif block make this a classic piece. It can be trimmed with cord if you want to go sans fur.

SANQUHAR BLOCK WITH POCKET (make 2)

Pocket lining With C and straight needles, cast on 27 stitches. Work 27 rows in St st and place these stitches on hold.

BLOCK

With C and straight needles, cast on 49 stitches.

Rows 1–11 With A and C, work Sanquhar chart (see page 81).

Rows 12–20 With C and D, work chart.

Rows 21–28 With A and C, work chart.

Row 29 Work 38 stitches of chart and place the last 27 stitches just worked on hold; with the right side facing, slip the 27 pocket lining stitches onto the right-hand needle; complete the row.

Rows 30–38 With C and D, work chart.

Rows 39–45 With A and C, work chart. Bind off with C.

FINISHING

Sew the blocks together following the diagram for placement. From top to bottom, blocks are Sanquhar, Buck, Birds and Flowers, Sanquhar with pockets. Sew pocket lining to WS.

HOOD

Sew the top and back seams of the top two blocks.

CORD EDGING

With A and double-pointed needles, cast on 5 stitches. Work in I-cord (see page 238) for approximately 170" (432cm). Sew the cord along the front and back edges and ends, making a twist at each of the 4 corners. Trim the entire front edge with fur.

POCKETS

Slip the 27 pocket stitches onto a straight needle so they are ready to work a right-side row. With A, k 1 row, then work in k1, p1 rib for 1¼" (3cm). Bind off in rib. Tack down the sides of the rib and trim the pocket opening with fur.

TRIM (optional)

Sew fur along front edge, ends, and top of pockets.

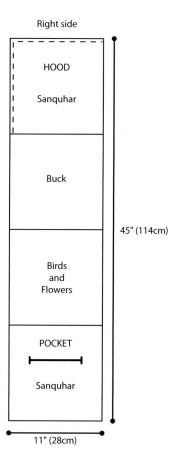

Knitted Measurements

- Approx 11" x 45" (28 cm x 114cm)

Materials

- Cascade Pastaza (50% llama/ 50% wool), each approximately 132 yards (121m) and 3.5oz (100g); 4 skeins of #064 Gray (A), 3 skeins of #309 Red (B), 1 skein of #006 Light Gray (C)
- Fur Yarn by Paula Lishman (100% fur), each approximately 3 yards (15g), 1 skein of Graphite Fox Fur (optional)
- Size U.S. 8 (5mm) straight needles
- Size U.S. 7 (4.5mm) double-pointed needles
- Stitch holders

Gauge

- 20 stitches and 20 rows = 4" (10cm) in Fair Isle pattern on size U.S. 8 (5mm) needles
TAKE TIME TO CHECK GAUGE.

BLOCKS

2 Buck (see page 84)
4 Sanquhar (see page 81; 2 with pockets)
2 Birds and Flowers (see page 83)

scarfosaurus page 9

There's nothing cooler than a dinosaur, except maybe a dinosaur skeleton. Here, the dino block is combined with two-color stripe blocks. This is just one example of the fun you can have with blocks by mixing and matching them.

BLOCKS (make 6)
Make 3 T-Rex blocks (see page 74) in MC using CC, green and blue for duplicate stitch and 3 Horizontal Stripes blocks (see page 27).

FINISHING
Sew the 6 blocks together following the diagram. All the horizontal stripe blocks are sideways (so they'll look vertical on the diagram), alternating stripes at the top with the T-Rex blocks.

Cut the lining fabric 1" (2.5cm) wider and longer than the scarf. Fold a ½" (1.25cm) hem to the wrong side of the fabric and press. Place the lining and scarf together with wrong sides together and whipstitch all around.

FRINGE (make 2)
With CC, place a slip knot onto the needle. Using the knitted on cast-on, *cast on 10 stitches, bind off 10 stitches, slip the remaining stitch to the left-hand needle; repeat from * 26 times more. Fringe will twist while knitting. Untwist and steam lightly. Sew to ends of scarf. Press scarf lightly.

Knitted Measurements
• Approx 9" x 60" (23cm x 152cm) without fringe

Materials
• Cascade 220 (100% wool), each approximately 220 yards (201m) and 3.5oz (100g); 2 skeins #8011 Light Gray (MC), 1 skein of #8400 Dark Gray (CC)
• Small amount of green and blue or desired colors
• Size U.S. 7 (4.5mm) straight needles
• Tapestry needle
• 12" x 60" (30.5cm x 152cm) corresponding fabric for lining
• Sewing needle and matching thread

Gauge
• 20 stitches and 26 rows = 4" (10cm) in St st on size U.S. 7 (4.5mm) needles
TAKE TIME TO CHECK GAUGE.

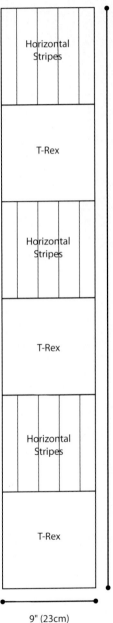

Horizontal Stripes

T-Rex

Horizontal Stripes

T-Rex

Horizontal Stripes

T-Rex

60" (152cm)

9" (23cm)

fairy leaves shrug duo page 10

Made with Fairy Leaves Blocks by alternating them bottom-up and sideways, this easy piece takes on a more complex, lovely look. It can be worn as a shrug or a shawl with a cool button or a ribbon tie.

BLOCKS
With size U.S. 7 (8, 9)/4.5 (5, 5.5)mm needles, make 10 Fairy Leaves blocks (see page 124).

Front
Sew 5 blocks together following the diagram at right.

Shoulder Edge
With size U.S. 7 (8, 9)/4.5 (5, 5.5)mm circular needle and the right side facing, pick up and k235 stitches across the length of all 5 blocks.
Work 10 rows in Garter st (5 ridges). Place the stitches on hold.

Button Band Edge
With size U.S. 7 (8, 9)/4.5 (5, 5.5)mm circular needle, and the opposite right side facing, pick up and k235 stitches across the length of all 5 blocks.
K 4 rows.
Buttonhole row (WS) K3, *bind off 2 stitches, k14; repeat from * 4 times more, k to end.
Next row K to the first bound-off space, *cast on 2 stitches, k15; repeat from * 4 times more, k to end.
K 4 rows.
Bind off.

BACK
Sew 5 blocks together following the diagram and work the shoulder edge same as the front.

Button Band Edge
With size U.S. 7 (8, 9)/4.5 (5, 5.5)mm circular needle, and the right side facing,

pick up and k235 stitches across the length of all 5 blocks.
K 4 rows.
Buttonhole row (WS) K162, bind off 2 stitches, *k14, bind off 2 stitches; repeat from * 3 times more, k to end.
Next row K to the first bound-off space, *cast on 2 stitches, k15; repeat from * 4 times more, k to end.
K 4 rows.
Bind off.

FINISHING
Join shoulder edges using the 3-needle bind-off (see page 236).
Weave in ends.

RIBBON CASING (at each cuff)
Cut a length of ribbon to fit the width of the shrug (approximately 21" [53cm]). With the wrong side facing, sew both edges of the ribbon across the center seams of the end blocks to form a casing (see diagram). Repeat on the other side.

RIBBON TIES
Cut two 26" (66cm) lengths of ribbon. *Attach a small safety pin to the end of one ribbon and thread through the casing, exiting at the shoulder seam. Tack down the outer end of the ribbon to secure. Repeat from * for the other side and for the other cuff. Draw the ribbons together to gather, tie at the center of the cuff, and cut to the desired length.

Sew buttons along the edges to correspond with the buttonholes.

Size
Small (Medium, Large)

Knitted Measurements
- 17½ (19½, 21½)" x 46 (48, 50)" (44.5 [49.5, 54.5]cm x 117 [122, 127]cm)

Materials
- Tilli Tomas Disco Lights (100% silk), each approximately 225 yards (206m) and 3.5oz (100g); 3 (4, 4) skeins of #249 Parchment
- Size U.S. 7 (4.5mm) for Small; size U.S. 8 (5mm) for Medium; U.S. size 9 (5.5mm) for Large straight and circular needles

- Ten ⅞" (2cm) buttons (JHB #70794 Melbourne Beige)
- 3 yards corresponding color ½" (13mm) wide ribbon

Gauge
- 20 stitches and 24 rows = 4" (10cm) in St st on size U.S. 7 (4.5mm) needles for Small
- 18 stitches and 22 rows = 4" (10cm) in St st on size U.S. 8 (5mm) needles for Medium
- 16 stitches and 20 rows = 4" (10cm) in St st on size U.S. 9 (5.5mm) needles for Large
TAKE TIME TO CHECK GAUGE.

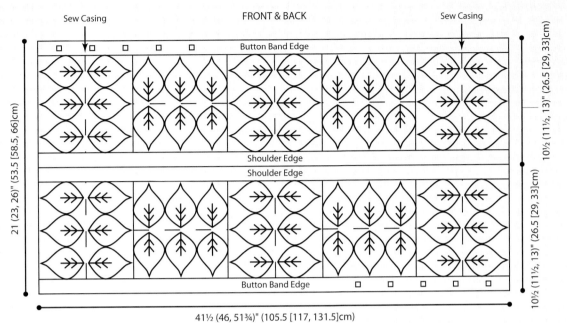

Sew Casing · FRONT & BACK · Sew Casing

Button Band Edge

Shoulder Edge

Shoulder Edge

Button Band Edge

21 (23, 26)" (53.5 [58.5, 66]cm)

10½ (11½, 13)" (26.5 [29, 33]cm)

10½ (11½, 13)" (26.5 [29, 33]cm)

41½ (46, 51¾)" (105.5 [117, 131.5]cm)

I've chosen several of my favorite blocks for this chic shawl-sweater. You can make it my way, or design with your favorite blocks to make a showstopping personal statement.

BLOCKS (make 24)

Make 2 each of the following blocks, to measure 8½" x 8½" (21.5cm x 21.5cm) each:

Topsy Turvy Cable (see page 150)
Curvy Cables (see page 165)
Portal Cables (see page 162)
Winding Road (see page 51)
Cable Leaf Trio (see page 47)
Embossed Rose (see page 128)
Diamond Back (see page 166)
Vintage Keys (see page 76)
Mock Tartan Plaid (see page 83)
Cable Vision (see page 159)

And make 1 each of the following:
Comedy/Tragedy (see page 80)
Horizontal Stripes (see page 27)

K3, P3 RIB

Row 1 (WS) P3, *k3, p3; repeat from * to end.
Row 2 *K3, p3; repeat from * to the last 3 stitches, k3.
Repeat rows 1 and 2 for pattern.

FRONTS AND BACK

Sew the blocks together following the front and back diagrams for placement.

Lower Front Edges

With the right side facing and A, pick up and k81 stitches across the lower front edge. Work in k3, p3 rib for ¾" (2cm), beginning and ending with a WS row. Change to B.
K1 row.
Work row 1 of rib.

Bind off in pattern. Repeat on the other front.

Lower Back Edge

With the right side facing and A, pick up and k165 stitches across the lower back edge.
Work same as the lower front edges.

Right Front Edge

With the right side facing and A, starting at the lower edge of the ribbing, pick up and k129 stitches along the right front edge.
Work in k3, p3 rib for ¾" (2cm), beginning and ending with a WS row. Change to B.
K 1 row.
Work row 1 of rib.
Bind off in pattern.

Left Front Edge

Work the same as the right front edge, starting at the upper edge and including the ribbing.

Sew the shoulder seams, easing the two center front blocks and front edges to fit across the two center back blocks.

Side Edges

With the right side facing and A, pick up and k255 stitches along one side edge, including the lower edge ribbings.
Work the same as the lower front edges. Repeat on the opposite side.

Size
One size

Knitted Measurements
- Shawl 26" (66cm) long x 36" (91cm) wide
- Sleeve 8" (20.5cm) rolled

Materials
- Berroco Ultra Alpaca (50% Super Fine Alpaca/50% Peruvian Wool), each approximately 215 yards (197m) and 3.5oz (100g); 10 skeins of #6214 Wheat (A), 1 skein of #6204 Brown (B), 1 skein of #6208 Linen (C)
- Size U.S. 7 (4.5mm) straight needles, size U.S. 7 (4.5mm) circular needle
- Size 6 (4mm) double-pointed needles
- 3 clasps (Nicky Epstein by JHB #4041 Comedy/Tragedy)

Gauge
- 20 stitches and 26 rows = 4" (10cm) in St st on size U.S. 7 (4.5mm) needles
TAKE TIME TO CHECK GAUGE.

SLEEVES

Measure and mark the center 12" (30.5cm) at each side edge.

With the right side facing and A, pick up and k61 stitches between the markers along the side edge (along the block edge and under the ribbing).

Work 3 rows in St st.

Dec row (RS) K1, k2tog, k to the last 3 stitches, ssk, k1.

Continue in St st, working dec row every 4th row until 47 stitches remain. Work even until sleeve measures 9" (23cm) or desired length. Bind off. Repeat on the opposite side.

FINISHING

Sew sleeve seams, reversing the seam for 1½" (4cm) at the bottom edge to accommodate the rolled edge. Sew the clasps to the front opening following the photo for placement.

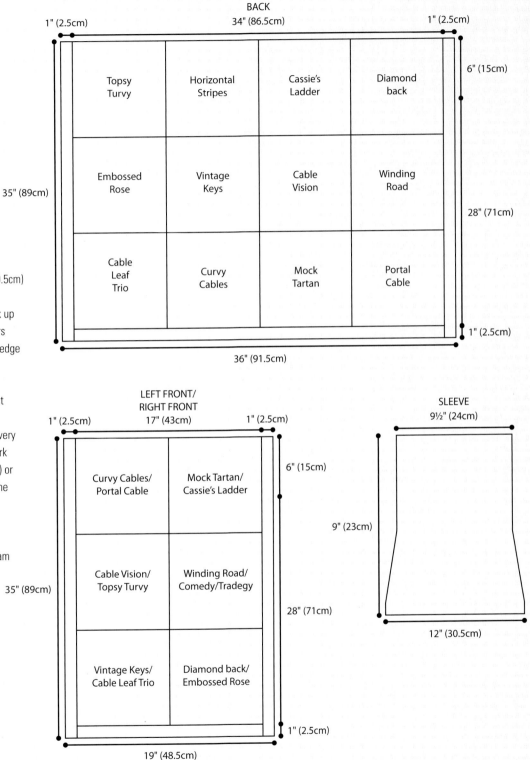

BACK
34" (86.5cm)
1" (2.5cm)   1" (2.5cm)
6" (15cm)

| Topsy Turvy | Horizontal Stripes | Cassie's Ladder | Diamond back |

35" (89cm)

| Embossed Rose | Vintage Keys | Cable Vision | Winding Road |

28" (71cm)

| Cable Leaf Trio | Curvy Cables | Mock Tartan | Portal Cable |

1" (2.5cm)
36" (91.5cm)

LEFT FRONT/
RIGHT FRONT
1" (2.5cm)   17" (43cm)   1" (2.5cm)
6" (15cm)

Curvy Cables/ Portal Cable	Mock Tartan/ Cassie's Ladder
Cable Vision/ Topsy Turvy	Winding Road/ Comedy/Tradegy
Vintage Keys/ Cable Leaf Trio	Diamond back/ Embossed Rose

35" (89cm)

28" (71cm)

1" (2.5cm)
19" (48.5cm)

SLEEVE
9½" (24cm)

9" (23cm)

12" (30.5cm)

academic afghan page 12

A daring combination of basic blocks and creative blocks makes this afghan an experience that will have everyone thinking outside the block!

BLOCKS (make 35)

Make 17 of the St st block (page 26) in A
Make one each of the following:
Random Rods (page 193) in D
Candy Box (page 202) in C and B
Fusion (page 197) in B, D and E
Colored Loopy (page 188) in C, D and E
Seed Stitch Cookie Twist (page 194) in B
Highland Fling (page 45) in C
Corkscrew Cascade (page 201) in C, D and F
Cable Tree (page 200) in B and E
Ruffle and Pod (page 198) in B and E
Beaded Pod (page 189) in D
Corky Dots (page 198) in A, B, C, D, E and F
Woven Wicker (page 203) in A, B and E
Woven Weave (page 194) in C and E
Crisscross Cool (page 193) in C
Windmill Bobble (page 196) in D
Reversible Hourglass (page 206) in D
Squared Lamb's Tail (page 191) in D
Synergy (page 205) in C and D

FINISHING

Join blocks together following the diagram.

MITERED EDGING

Top and Bottom

With the right side facing and A, pick up and k195 stitches along the top or bottom edge.

Row 1 (WS) *K3, p3; repeat from * to the last 3 stitches, k3.

Row 2 Cast on 1 st, *p3, k3; repeat from * to the last 3 stitches, p3, cast on 1 st (197 stitches).

Row 3 P1, *k3, p3; repeat from * to the last 4 stitches, k3, p1.
Change to B.

Row 4 Cast on 1 st, k to end, cast on 1 st (199 stitches).

Row 5 P2, *k3, p3; repeat from * to the last 5 stitches, k3, p2.

Row 6 Cast on 1 st, k2, *p3, k3; repeat from * to the last 5 stitches, p3, k2, cast on 1 st (201 stitches).

Row 7 P3, *k3, p3; repeat from * to end.
Change to A.

Row 8 Cast on 1 st, k to end, cast on 1 st (203 stitches).

Row 9 P4, *k3, p3; repeat from * to the last st, p1.
Bind off in pattern.
Repeat on the opposite edge.

SIDES

With the right side facing and A, pick up and k279 stitches along one side edge. Work rows 1–9 with color changes same as top and bottom edges above (287 stitches). Repeat on the opposite side edge.

Sew all mitered corner seams. Steam lightly.

Knitted Measurements

- Approx 44" x 65" (112cm x 165cm)

Materials

- Cascade 220 Superwash (100% wool), each approximately 220 yards (201m) and 3.5oz (100g); 6 skeins of #8408A Dark Taupe (A), 2 skeins #8229 Medium Teal (B), 2 skeins #8407 Light Taupe (C), 2 skeins #8234 Light Olive (D), 1 skein #9428 Dark Olive (E), 1 skein #9429 Forest (F)
- Size U.S. 7 (4.5mm) straight needles
- Size U.S. 6 (4.25mm) double-pointed needles

Gauge

- 20 stitches and 26 rows = 4" (10cm) in St st on size U.S. 7 (4.5mm) needles
TAKE TIME TO CHECK GAUGE.

Note Follow photo (see page 12) and placement diagram (opposite) for colors and block placement.

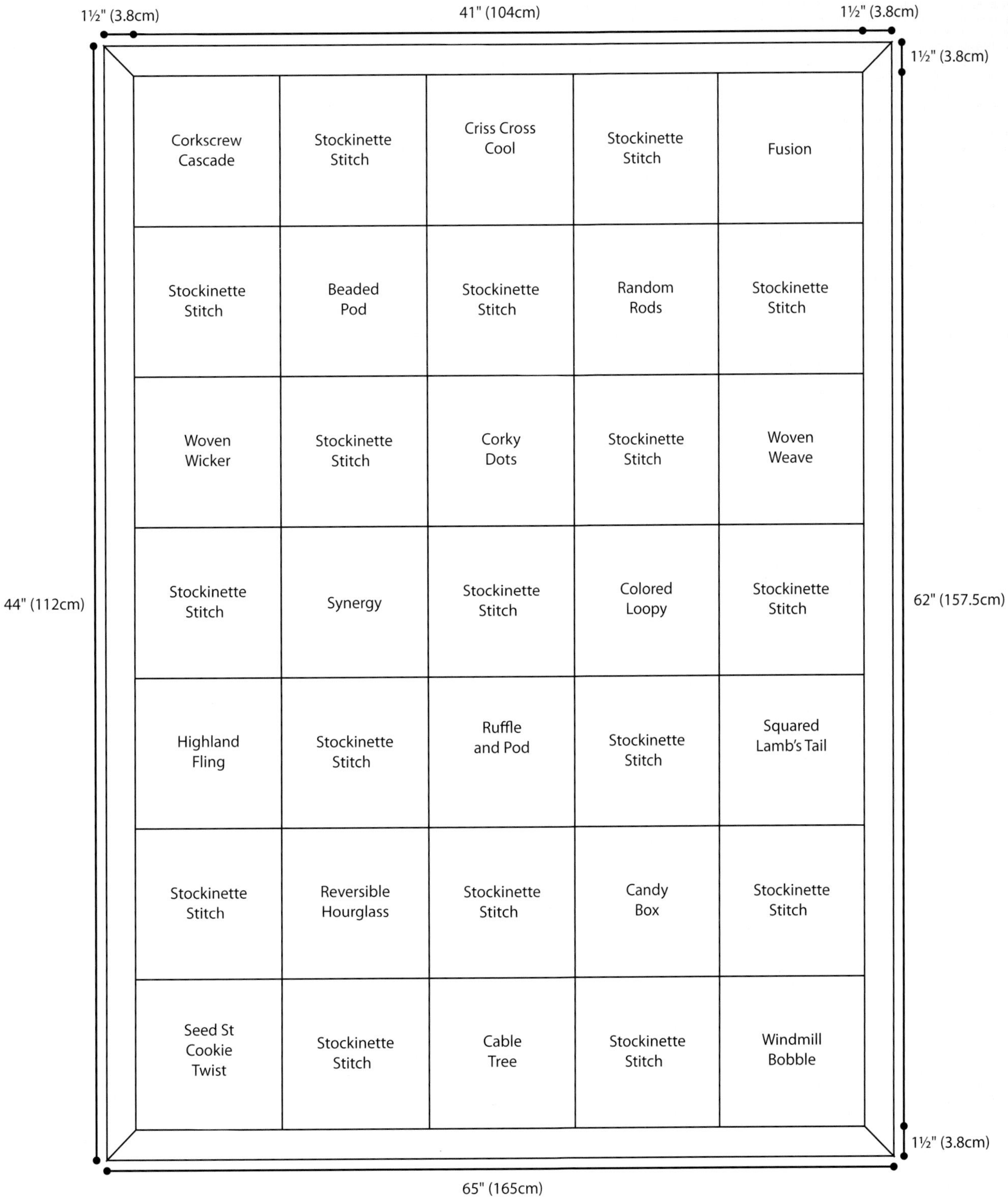

Corkscrew Cascade	Stockinette Stitch	Criss Cross Cool	Stockinette Stitch	Fusion
Stockinette Stitch	Beaded Pod	Stockinette Stitch	Random Rods	Stockinette Stitch
Woven Wicker	Stockinette Stitch	Corky Dots	Stockinette Stitch	Woven Weave
Stockinette Stitch	Synergy	Stockinette Stitch	Colored Loopy	Stockinette Stitch
Highland Fling	Stockinette Stitch	Ruffle and Pod	Stockinette Stitch	Squared Lamb's Tail
Stockinette Stitch	Reversible Hourglass	Stockinette Stitch	Candy Box	Stockinette Stitch
Seed St Cookie Twist	Stockinette Stitch	Cable Tree	Stockinette Stitch	Windmill Bobble

1½" (3.8cm)   41" (104cm)   1½" (3.8cm)

1½" (3.8cm)

44" (112cm)   62" (157.5cm)

1½" (3.8cm)

65" (165cm)

très chic pullover page 13

One bold block repeated, plus a bottom rib, make this design easy to create with any of the blocks in the book. I use a bulky cashmere here, but any yarn that gives you the right gauge will work well.

Size
Medium/Large

Knitted Measurements
• 15" (38cm) long x 30" (76cm) circumference at lower edge

Materials
• Jade Sapphire Mongolian Cashmere (100% cashmere), each approximately 60 yards (55m) and 2oz (55g); 12 skeins of #51 Lupine
• Size U.S. 11 (8mm) straight needles

Gauge
• 16 stitches = 4" (10cm) in pattern st on size U.S. 11 (8mm) needles
TAKE TIME TO CHECK GAUGE.

BLOCKS
Make 6 X's blocks (see page 168).

ASSEMBLY
Front and Back
Sew 3 blocks together for the front and back following the diagram. The diagram shows that the center square is worked side-to-side, and the 2 side squares are worked up-and-down.
Sew the top edges of the front and back together, leaving the center 10½" (26.5cm) free for the neck opening.

Front and Back Rib
With the right side facing, pick up and k62 stitches evenly across the lower edge of the center square. Work in k1, p1 rib for 3" (7.5cm). Bind off in pattern. Repeat on the other side.

Finishing
Sew the bottom edges of the side blocks together to form the sleeves. Sew the sides of the front and back ribs together.

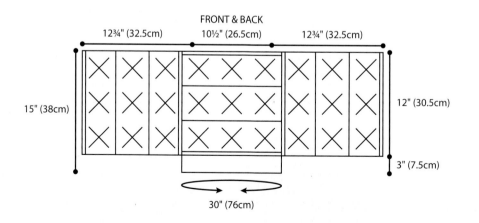

FRONT & BACK

12¾" (32.5cm)   10½" (26.5cm)   12¾" (32.5cm)

15" (38cm)   12" (30.5cm)   3" (7.5cm)

30" (76cm)

empire cropped vest page 14

Expect the unexpected—the bottom gathering of blocks gives the illusion that the bottom is knit in one piece, rather than sewn together from 8 blocks.

BLOCKS

With size U.S. 8 (9)/5 (5.5)mm needles, make 4 Rolling Cable blocks (see page 189), and 8 Cathedral Window blocks (see page 204).

Note To lengthen the Vest, add length to each of the Rolling Cable blocks. More yarn may be required.

ASSEMBLY

Sew 2 Rolling Cable blocks together side-by-side to form the upper back and one for each front. Sew 4 Cathedral Window blocks together side-by-side for the lower back and 2 together for each lower front.

Working each lower piece separately, thread a tapestry needle and weave yarn through the cast-on edge, gathering to fit across the cast-on edge of the upper pieces. Sew the upper and lower pieces together.

Sew the shoulder seams from armhole to neck edge, leaving the 7-stitch rib sections free for the neck opening. Sew the side seams along the Cathedral Window blocks only.

BELT (make 2)

With size U.S. 8 (9)/5 (5.5)mm needles, cast on 7 stitches. Work in k1, p1 rib for 25" (63.5cm). Bind off.

Sew one end of each section of belt to the center front and tack down at the side seams. Tie the belt in back and sew the clasp at center front.

FINISHING

Weave in ends.

Sizes

Small (Medium/Large)

Finished Measurements

- Bust Approximately 36 (38)" (91 [96.5]cm)
- Length Approximately 18 (19)" (45.5 [48.5]cm)

Materials

- Stacy Charles Zara Plus (100% Extrafine Merino wool), each approximately 77 yards (70m) and 1¾oz (50g); 17 (18) skeins of #23 Light Pink
- Size U.S. 8 (5mm) for Small; size U.S. 9 (5.5mm) for Medium/Large

- One clasp (Nicky Epstein by JHB Lily Clasp)
- Tapestry needle

Gauge

- 18 stitches and 26 rows = 4" (10cm) in St st on size U.S. 8 (5mm) needles for Small
- 16 stitches and 24 rows = 4" (10cm) in St st on size U.S. 9 (5.5mm) needles for Medium/Large

TAKE TIME TO CHECK GAUGE.

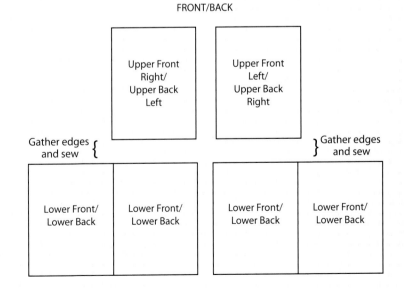

FRONT/BACK

cool ruffle pod bag page 15

Composed of 2 Ruffle and Pod blocks at the front and 2 basic Stockinette stitch blocks at the back, this charming bag is an easy update for your wardrobe.

Knitted Measurements
• Approx 11" x 18" (28cm x 45.5cm)

Materials
• Louet River Stone (100% wool), each approximately 193 yards (176.5m) and 3.5oz (100g); 4 skeins of #2284 Foxy Fuchsia (MC), 1 skein of #2224 Black (CC)
• Size U.S. 8 (5mm) straight needles
• ¼ yard (23cm) black satin or your choice of lining fabric (optional)
• One 13" (33cm) double purse handle (Leisure Arts Exclusively You #28306 Black)

Gauge
• 20 stitches and 26 rows = 4" (10cm) in St st on size U.S. 8 (4mm) needles
TAKE TIME TO CHECK GAUGE.

BACK
With MC, make 2 St st blocks (see page 26). Leave the stitches on the needle.
Connecting row (RS) With CC, k44 across the first block, k the last st together with the first st of the 2nd block, k44 across the 2nd block.
Work in Garter st for 1½" (3.8cm) (12 rows).
Bind off.

FRONT
With MC, make 2 Ruffle and Pod blocks (see page 198). Leave the stitches on the needle.
Complete the front same as for the back.

LINING (optional)
Line bag if desired.

FINISHING
Sew side, center and bottom seams. Make a 3" (7.5cm) inverted pleat at the top of each side seam and attach the handles at the side seams.

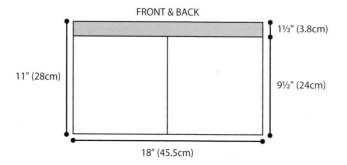

FRONT & BACK

1½" (3.8cm)

11" (28cm)

9½" (24cm)

18" (45.5cm)

snowflake splendor hat page 16

This simple style can be the basis for a lot of beautiful block hats. Here, the seam is in the front, but wearing the seams on the side of the hat would also work.

BLOCKS (make 2)
With size U.S. 8 (9)/5 (5.5mm) straight needles, make two Snowflake blocks (see page 81).

FINISHING
With CC and a crochet hook, work a row of slip st around the side and top edges leaving bottom edge open.

CORD TIES
With CC and double-pointed needles, cast on 4 stitches. Work in I-cord (see page 238) for 4" (10cm).
Change to MC and work in I-cord for 18" (45.5cm) more. Bind off.
Make 3 knots at the MC end of each cord. Sew the CC end of each cord to the center of each block.
Note The centers of the blocks form the sides of the hat.

Tack the top corners of the hat together.

TOP BALL
With MC, cast on 8 stitches leaving a long tail for seaming.
Row 1 (RS) Kf&b of every st (16 stitches).
Row 2 and all WS rows Purl.
Rows 3, 5, 7 and 9 Knit.
Row 11 *K2tog; repeat from * to end (8 stitches).
Pass all the stitches, one at a time, over the first st. Fasten off. Thread the cast-on tail through the cast-on stitches, gather and secure. Stuff with polyfil, sew the side seam and attach the ball to the top of the hat.

Sizes
Adult size Small/Medium (Large)

Knitted Measurement
• Approximately 20" (51cm) (21" [53.5cm]) diameter

Materials
• Cascade Pastaza (50% llama/ 50% wool), each approximately 132 yards (121m) and 3.5oz (100g); 1 skein #309 Red (MC), 1 skein #064 Gray (CC)
• Size U.S. 8 (5mm) straight needles for Small/Medium; size U.S. 9 (5.5mm) for Large size
• Size U.S. 7 (4.5mm) double-pointed needles for Small/ Medium; size U.S. 8 (5mm) for Large size
• Size G/6 (4.25mm) crochet hook
• Polyfil stuffing

Gauge
• 20 stitches and 20 rows = 4" (10cm) in Fair Isle pattern on size U.S. 8 (5mm) needles
• 18 stitches and 18 rows = 4" (10cm) in Fair Isle pattern on size U.S. 9 (5mm) needles
TAKE TIME TO CHECK GAUGE.

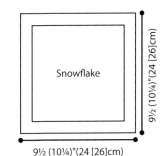

Snowflake

9½ (10¼)"(24 [26]cm)

9½ (10¼)"(24 [26]cm)

Top Ball

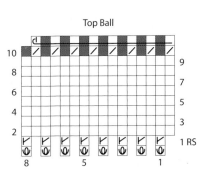

Stitch Key

Ⓞ	CO 1 st
☐	K on RS, P on WS
Ⅴ	Kf&b
╱	K2tog
■	No stitch
d—	Pass all sts, one at a time over first st

one-block toys

Could anything be more creatively rewarding and fun than making a great toy from just one block? I think not! These pieces are charming, and your friends will not believe they came from a single block!

HERE KITTY

Knitted Measurements
- Block 10" x 10" (25.5cm x 25.5cm)

Materials
- Lion Brand Vanna's Choice (100% premium acrylic), each approximately 170 yards (155m) and 3.5oz (100g); 1 skein of #306 Tangerine Mist
- Small amounts of pink and white yarn for embroidery
- Size U.S. 8 (5mm) straight needles
- Size U.S. 7 (4.5mm) double-pointed needles
- Tapestry needle
- 2 beads for eyes
- ½ yd (.5m) ¼" (6mm) ribbon for neck bow
- Small ball of yarn (optional)
- Polyfil stuffing

Gauge
- 18 stitches and 24 rows = 4" (10cm) in St st on size U.S. 8 (5mm) needles

TAKE TIME TO CHECK GAUGE.

BLOCK
Make one St st block (see page 26).

CONSTRUCTION
Follow the diagram for construction. Gather and stuff the head, sew the leg seams, stuff the body and legs, and sew the tummy seam closed.

EARS (make 2)
Cast on 7 stitches.

Rows 1–4 Knit.

Rows 5 and 7 Ssk, k to the last 2 stitches, k2tog.

Row 6 Knit.

Row 8 S2KP.

Fasten off.

TAIL
With double-pointed needles, cast on 4 stitches. Work in I-cord (see page 238) for 6½" (16.5cm). Bind off.

FINISHING
Following the photo for placement, sew the ears to the head, embroider the face and sew on eyes. Bend the back legs toward the front and stitch in place. Sew on the tail. Tie the ribbon around the neck. Place a small ball of yarn between the front legs (optional).

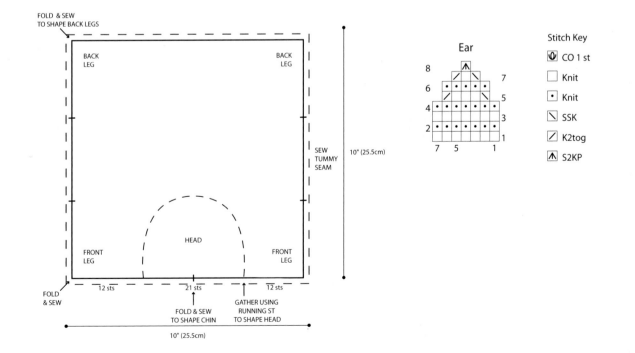

Knitted Measurements

• Block 10" x 10" (25.5cm x 25.5cm)

Materials

• Lion Brand Vanna's Choice (100% premium acrylic), each approximately 170 yards (155m) and 3.5oz (100g); 1 skein of #158 Mustard (MC), 1 skein of #135 Rust (CC)
• Small amounts of black and brown yarn for embroidery
• Size U.S. 8 (5mm) straight needles
• Size U.S. 7 (4.5mm) double-pointed needles
• Tapestry needle
• 2 beads for eyes
• Polyfil stuffing

Gauge

• 18 stitches and 24 rows = 4" (10cm) in St st on size U.S. 8 (5mm) needles
TAKE TIME TO CHECK GAUGE.

BLOCK

With MC, make one St st block (see page 26).

CONSTRUCTION

Follow the diagram for construction. Gather and stuff the head, sew the leg seams, stuff the body and legs, and sew the tummy seam closed.

OUTER MANE

With CC, cast on 24 stitches.
Next row (WS) K1, *insert the right-hand needle into the next st knitwise, wind yarn over the right-hand needle and the first and second fingers of your left hand 3 times, then over the right-hand needle point once more, draw all 4 loops through the st and slip them onto the left-hand needle, insert the right-hand needle through the back of these 4 loops and the original st and k them together tbl, k1; repeat from * to the last st, k1.
Bind off.

INNER MANE

With CC, cast on 12 stitches. Work the same as the Outer Mane.

EARS (make 2)

Cast on 7 stitches.
Rows 1–4 Knit.
Rows 5 and 7 Ssk, k to the last 2 stitches, k2tog.
Row 6 Knit.
Row 8 S2KP.
Fasten off.

TAIL

With double-pointed needles, cast on 3 stitches. Work in I-cord (see page TK) for 5½" (14cm). Bind off. With CC, add fringe to one end of the tail.

FINISHING

Following the photo for placement, sew the ears to the head, embroider the face and sew on eyes. Sew the inner mane in front of ears and the outer mane behind the ears around the head. Bend the back legs toward the front and stitch in place. Sew on the tail.

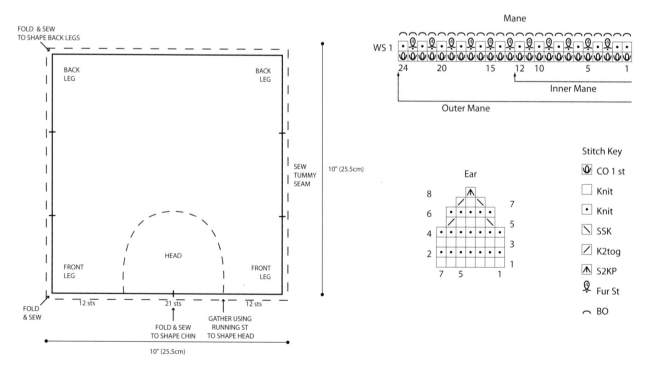

Knitted Measurements
• Block 10" x 10" (25.5cm x 25.5cm)

Materials
• Lion Brand Lion Wool (100% wool), each approximately 155 yards (142m) and 3oz (85g); 1 skein of #132 Lemongrass
• Small amount gold for mouth
• Size U.S. 8 (5mm) straight needles
• Tapestry needle
• 2 beads for eyes
• Polyfil stuffing

Gauge
• 18 stitches and 24 rows = 4" (10cm) in St st on size U.S. 8 (5mm) needles
TAKE TIME TO CHECK GAUGE.

BLOCK
Make a Fiddle Fern block, omitting the loops and stems (see page 48).

CONSTRUCTION
Follow the diagram for construction. Gather the head and stuff, then sew the chin seam. Gather the body, sew the leg seams, stuff the body and legs, and sew the tummy seam closed.

SHELL EDGING
Cast on 60 stitches. Work 4 rows in St st.
Next row (RS) *K6 and rotate the left-hand needle counterclockwise 360 degrees; repeat from * to end.
Bind off.
Sew the edging around the edge of the turtle shell.

TAIL
Cast on 7 stitches.
Row 1 Bind off 2 stitches, k to end (5 stitches).
Row 2 Purl.
Row 3 Bind off 2 stitches, k to end (3 stitches).
Row 4 Purl.
Bind off.
Sew the tail to the back end of the turtle under the edging. Sew on beads for the eyes. Embroider the mouth using Stem st.

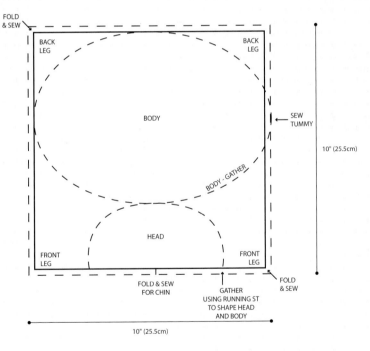

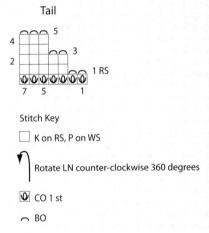

Tail

Stitch Key
☐ K on RS, P on WS

⤾ Rotate LN counter-clockwise 360 degrees

Ⓦ CO 1 st

⌒ BO

Shell Edging

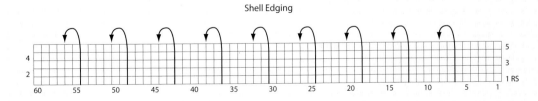

crossed cable cuffs

tree-x tote bag

CROSSED CABLE CUFFS

These crisscross cable mitts are just one example of the stylish pieces you can make by simply sewing a seam and leaving a thumb hole on your favorite block.

Size
One size

Knitted Measurements
• 8" x 8" (20.5cm x 20.5cm)

Materials
• Lion Brand Cashmere (100% cashmere), each approximately 82 yards (75m) and .88oz (25g); 2 balls #173 Sprout
• Size U.S. 6 (4.25mm) straight needles
• Size U.S. 5 (3.75mm) double-pointed needles

Gauge
• 24 stitches and 30 rows = 4" (10cm) in pattern on size U.S.
6 (4.25mm) needles
TAKE TIME TO CHECK GAUGE.

5-ST CABLE CORD (over 5 stitches)
1/2 LC Sl 1 st to cn and hold in front, k2, k1 from cn.
Rows 1–5 Knit, do not turn, slide the stitches to the other end of the needle.
Row 6 K1, 1/2 LC, k1, do not turn, slide the stitches to the other end of the needle.
Repeat rows 1–6 for desired length.

CUFFS (make 2)
With larger needles, cast on 45 stitches.
Work in k1, p1 ribbing for ½" (13mm).
Work 8 rows in St st.
Follow block starting at row 7.
Next row (RS) K6, *k5 and thread a length of waste yarn through the front of these 5 stitches (leaving them on the needle), k2*; repeat from * once more, k7; repeat from * to * twice more, k6.
Work 41 rows in St st, ending with a WS row.

CROSSED CABLE CORDS
With the right side facing and double-pointed needles, *pick up a set of 5 marked stitches and work in 5-st cable cord to match the length of St st (approx 10 cables), ending with a WS row. Cut the yarn and place the stitches on hold. Repeat from * for each set of marked stitches.

Cross the cords following the photo for placement and place the 20 cord stitches in order onto a spare needle. Arrange both needles with the right sides facing and the cord needle in front of the St st needle ready to work a RS row.
Next row (RS) K6 St stitches, *[k 1 st from the cord needle together with 1 st from the St st needle] 5 times, k2 St stitches*; repeat from * to * once more, k7; repeat from * to * twice, k4 St stitches.
Work 7 rows in St st.
Work in k1, p1 ribbing for ½" (13mm).
Bind off.
Note Cable cords can worked separately and tacked in place (optional).

FINISHING
Sew the side seam, leaving a 1¾" (4.5cm) thumb opening 1" (2.5cm) from the end.

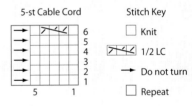

5-st Cable Cord	Stitch Key
	□ Knit
	⟋⟍ 1/2 LC
	→ Do not turn
	□ Repeat

TREE-X TOTE BAG

I have used only 2 blocks—the Tree Breeze block and an X block in a bulky yarn—to create this tote. You can choose any two blocks you like for your bag!

Knitted Measurements
• Approx 13½" (34.5cm) x 13½" (34.5cm)

Materials
• Lion Brand Alpine Wool (77% wool/50% acrylic/8% rayon), 3oz (93yds); 3 skeins of #223 Oatmeal
• Size U.S. 11 (8mm) straight needles
• 1 pair 13" (33cm) purse handles in black (Leisure Arts Exclusively You Croc Handle)
• ½ yd corresponding lining fabric (optional)

Gauge
• 14 stitches and 20 rows = 4" (10cm) in St st on size U.S. 11 (8mm) needles
TAKE TIME TO CHECK GAUGE

TREE BLOCK
Cast on 48 stitches.
Work 58 rows of Tree Breeze block (See page 136, Ch3 #10).
Hem
Row 59 Purl for the turning ridge.
Rows 60 and 62 Knit.
Rows 61 and 63 Purl.
Bind off knitwise.

X BLOCK
Cast on 46 stitches.
Work 58 rows of Crossed Cables block (See page 50, Ch3 #8).
Hem
Work rows 59-63 of Tree block.
Bind off knitwise.

FINISHING
With the right sides together, sew the side and bottom seams. Fold the hem to the wrong side and sew in place. Line bag if desired. Sew the handles 2" (5cm) from the top and sides following the photo for placement.

edgings

1

2

3

5

4

6

1 BOBBLE CORD

SPECIAL STITCH

Make Bobble (MB) K in front, back, front and back all in 1 stitch (4 stitches), turn, p4, turn, k4, turn, p4. With left-hand needle lift 2nd, 3rd and 4th stitches over the first stitch (1 stitch).

I-CORD

With double-pointed needles, cast on 5 stitches. Do not turn, slide the stitches to the other end of the needle.

Rows 1–5 K5, do not turn, slide the stitches to the other end of the needle.

Row 6 K2, MB, k2, do not turn, slide the stitchs to the other end of the needle.

Repeat rows 1–6 for desired length.

Bind off.

Sew I-cord around block.

2 CORD TWIST

I-CORD

With double-pointed needles, cast on 5 stitches. Do not turn, slide stitches to the other end of the needle.

Row 1 K5, do not turn, slide stitches to the other end of the needle.

Repeat row 1 for desired length.

Bind off.

Sew cord around block creating a 1" (2.5cm) loop in each corner.

3 COLOR BLOCK GARTER STITCH

Color Block Sequence A, B, C and D

Worked in the Intarsia method using short lengths of yarn for each color block and twisting colors on WS when changing colors to prevent holes.

With A and right side facing, pick up stitches evenly around piece making sure to have a multiple of 5 stitches on each side and an additional 1 stitch in each corner.

Row 1 (WS) *K5 in each color in sequence to the next corner stitch, with next color, m1, p1, m1; repeat from * around block.

Row 2 (RS) Maintaining color sequence k to the next corner stitch, k1; repeat from * around block.

Row 3 (WS) Maintaining color sequence k to the next corner stitch, m1, p1, m1; repeat from * around block.

Repeat rows 2 and 3 until 4 sts have been increased on each side of the corner stitch.

Bind off.

4 STRIPED GARTER STITCH

Colors MC and CC

With right side facing and CC, pick up stitches evenly around piece making sure to pick up 1 stitch in each corner.

Row 1 (WS) K to the corner stitch, p1; repeat from * around block.

Row 2 (RS) *K to the corner stitch, m1, k1, m1; repeat from * around block.

Rows 3–5 Repeat rows 1, 2, and 1.

Change to MC.

Repeat rows 2–5 alternating 4 rows each of CC and MC until 6 stitches have been increased on each side of the corner stitch.

Bind off.

5 SEED STITCH MITER

With right side facing, pick up stitches around piece making sure to have an odd number on each side and an additional 1 stitch in each corner.

Row 1 (WS) P1, *k1, p1; repeat from * to the next corner stitch, m1, p1, m1; repeat from * around block.

Row 2 *K1, p1; repeat from * to the next corner stitch, k1, p1; repeat from * around block.

Row 3 Work in Seed st to the next corner stitch, m1, k1, m1; repeat from * around.

Row 4 Work in Seed st to the next corner stitch, m1, p1, m1; repeat from * around.

Repeat rows 3 and 4 until 6 stitches have been increased on each side of the corner stitch.

Bind off.

6 3X3 MITERED RIB

With right side facing, pick up stitches evenly around piece making sure to have a multiple of 6 stitches plus 3 more on each side and an additional 1 stitch in each corner.

Row 1 (WS) K3, *p3, k3; repeat from * to next corner stitch, m1, p1, m1; repeat from * around block.

Row 2 (RS) Work in established rib to next corner stitch, k1; repeat from * around block.

Row 3 (WS) Work in established rib to next corner stitch, m1, p1, m1; repeat from * around.

Repeat rows 2 and 3 until 6 sts have been increased on each side of the corner stitch.

Bind off.

joinings

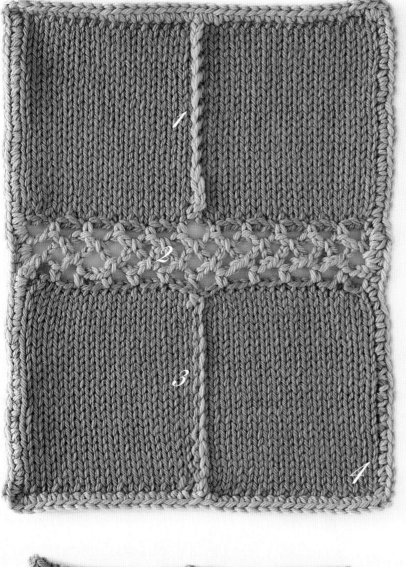

1 Single Crochet (Ridge Connect)
Place 2 blocks with wrong sides together, attach yarn to the right corner, *single crochet through both blocks picking up one loop of the stitch on each side; repeat from * to end.

2 Chain Loops (shown as horizontal seam)
Attach yarn to a corner of the first block, *chain 3, skip 2 stitches, single crochet in the next stitch; repeat from *, end chain 3, skip 2 stitches, slip stitch in the last stitch. Cut yarn.
Repeat for each block.

To connect blocks, attach yarn to the 2nd chain of beginning chain-3 of first block, chain 3, drop loop from hook, insert hook through first chain-3 space of 2nd block and back into dropped loop, chain 3, drop loop from hook, insert hook through next chain-3 space of first block. Continue until each chain-3 loop on first block is connected to each chain-3 loop of 2nd block, work slip stitch in end of block.

3 Slip Stitch (Flat Connect)
Place 2 blocks with wrong sides together, attach yarn to the right corner, *slip stitch through both blocks picking up one loop of the stitch on each side; repeat from * to end.

4 Single Crochet Edge for Sewing Seam
Attach yarn to the right corner, single crochet evenly across, taking care to keep edge from puckering and work 3 single crochet in each corner. Slip stitch to the first single crochet.

5 Cross Stitch
Work the first half same as the Slanted Whipstitch (below) ending with the needle on the right side of the work. Moving from right to left, *insert the needle 2 stitches over and 2 rows down. Repeat from * to work the other half of the Cross Stitch.

6 Slanted Whipstitch
Beginning with the threaded needle on the wrong side, bring the needle from the wrong side to the right side through the center of a knit stitch. Moving from left to right, *insert the needle 2 stitches over and 2 rows down. Bring the needle back out through the center of the stitch 2 stitches up. Repeat from *.

Mix-and-Match Blocks

Copy and cut these blocks, and then place them into the assembly diagrams to make your own creations!

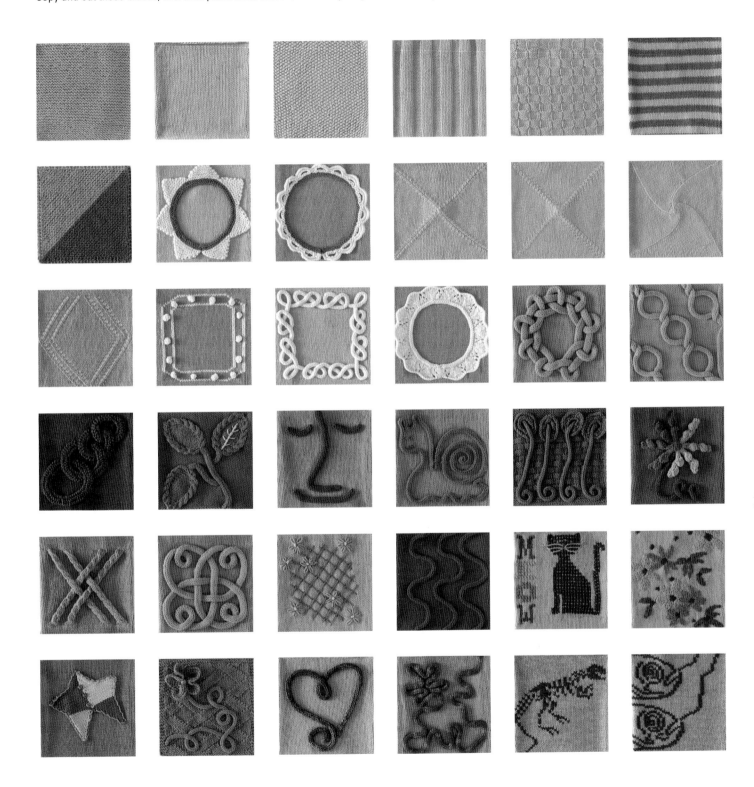

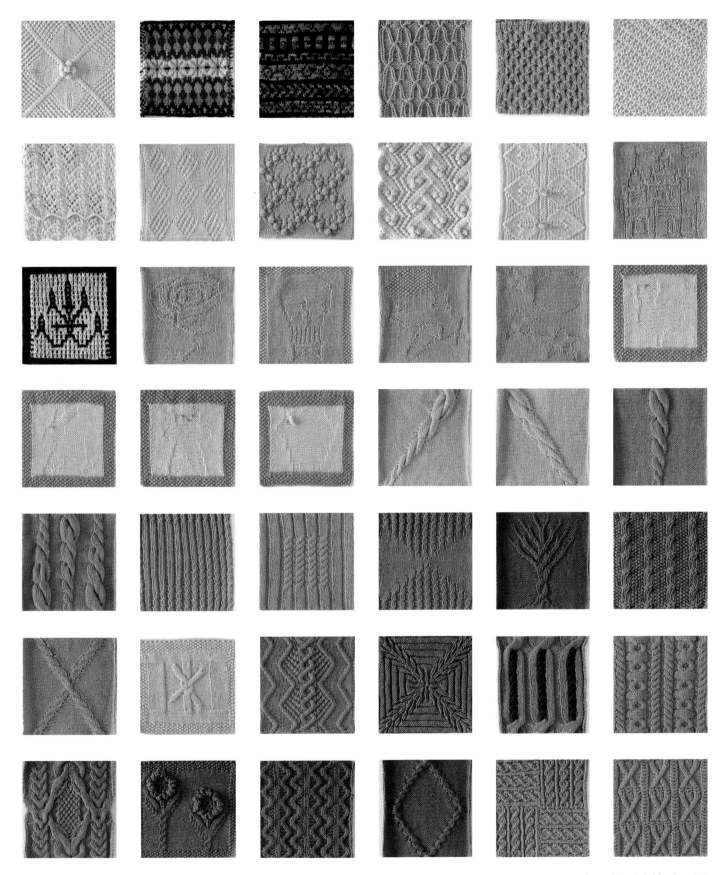

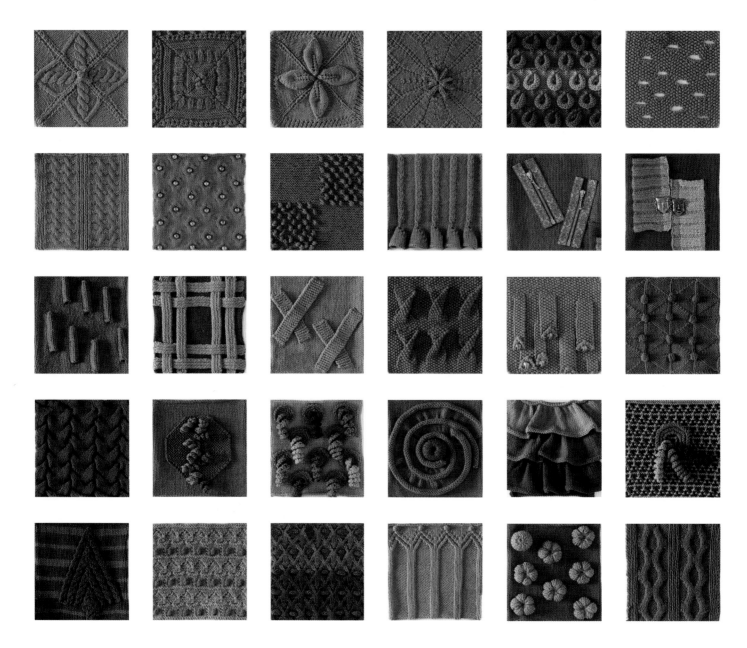

Abbreviations and Techniques

General Abbreviations

CC	contrasting color
cn	cable needle
dec	decrease
Garter st	k on RS, k on WS
inc	increase
k	knit
k2tog	knit 2 together
kf&b	knit in front and back

m1 (make 1)	with the left-hand needle, lift the horizontal strand between last st and next st, k through the back loop of this strand.
MB	make bobble
MC	main color
p	purl
p2tog	purl 2 together
pf&b	purl in front and back
pm	place marker

Reverse St st	p on RS, k on WS
rnd(s)	round(s)
RS	right side
S2KP	sl 2 stitches as if to k2tog, k1, pass the slipped stitches over the k1.
SKP	sl 1 st knitwise, k1, pass the slipped st over the k1.
SK2P	sl 1 st knitwise, k2tog, pass the slipped st over the k2tog.
S2PP	[Sl 1 st knitwise] twice, p1, pass the slipped stitches over the p1.
SP2P	sl 1 st knitwise, p2tog tbl, pass the slipped st over the p2tog.
sl	slip purlwise unless otherwise noted.
ssk	[sl 1 st knitwise] twice, insert the left-hand needle into the fronts of these 2 stitches from left to right, k2tog tbl.
ssp	[sl 1 st knitwise] twice, slip these 2 stitches back to the left-hand needle and p2tog tbl.
St st	Stockinette stitch; k on RS, p on WS
st(s)	stitch(es)
tbl	through back loop
tog	together
WS	wrong side
wyib	with yarn in back
wyif	with yarn in front
yo	yarn over

Cable Abbreviations

1/1 RC Sl 1 st to cn and hold in back, k1, k1 from cn.

1/1 LC Sl 1 st to cn and hold in front, k1, k1, from cn.

1/1 RPC Sl 1 st to cn and hold in back, k1, p1 from cn.

1/1 LPC Sl 1 st to cn and hold in front, p1, k1 from cn.

2/1 RC Sl 1 st to cn and hold in back, k2, k1 from cn.

2/1 LC Sl 2 stitches to cn and hold in front, k1, k2 from cn.

2/1 RPC Sl 1 st to cn and hold in back, k2, p1 from cn.

2/1 LPC Sl 2 stitches to cn and hold in front, p1, k2 from cn.

2/2 LC Sl 2 stitches to cn and hold in front, k2, k2 from cn.

2/2 RC Sl 2 stitches to cn and hold in back, k2, k2 from cn.

2/2 RPC Sl 2 stitches to cn and hold in back, k2, p2 from cn.

2/2 LPC Sl 2 stitches to cn and hold in front, p2, k2 from cn.

2/2 LC inc Sl 2 stitches to cn and hold in front, k2, M2, k2 from cn.

2/2 LC dec Sl 2 stitches to cn and hold in front, (k1, k2tog), k2 from cn.

2/2 RC dec Sl 3 stitches to cn and hold in back, k2, (k2tog, k1) from cn.

2/3 RC Sl 3 stitches to cn and hold in back, k2, sl 1 st from cn to left-hand needle, k1, k2 from cn.

2/4 RPC Sl 4 stitches to cn and hold in back, k2, (k2, p2) from cn.

2/4 LPC Sl 2 stitches to cn and hold in front, (p2, k2), k2 from cn.

3/1 LPC Sl 3 stitches to cn and hold in front, p1, k3 from cn.

3/2 RPC Sl 2 stitches to cn and hold in back, k3, p2 from cn.

3/3 LC Sl 3 stitches to cn and hold in front, k3, k3 from cn.

3/3 RC Sl 3 stitches to cn and hold in back, k3, k3 from cn.

3/3 LC dec Sl 3 stitches to cn and hold in front, (k1, k2tog), (ssk, k1) from cn.

3/3 LC inc Sl 3 stitches to cn and hold in front, k3, m1, M2, k3 from cn.

3/4 RKPC Sl 4 stitches to cn and hold in back, (k1, p1, k1), [p1, k1] twice from cn.

4/4 LC Sl 4 stitches to cn and hold in front, k4, k4 from cn.

4/4 RC Sl 4 stitches to cn and hold in back, k4, k4 from cn.

4/4 LPC Sl 4 stitches to cn and hold in front, p4, k4 from cn.

4/4 RPC Sl 4 stitches to cn and hold in back, k4, p4 from cn.

4/4 LC dec Sl 4 stitches to cn and hold in front, (k2, k2tog), (ssk, k2) from cn.

4/4 LC inc Sl 4 stitches to cn and hold in front, k4, M2, k4 from cn.

5/5 LC Sl 5 stitches to cn and hold in front, k5, k5 from cn.

5/5 RC Sl 5 stitches to cn and hold in back, k5, k5 from cn.

5/5 LC dec Sl 5 stitches to cn and hold in front, (k3, k2tog), (ssk, k3) from cn.

5/5 LC inc Sl 5 stitches to cn and hold in front, k5, M2, k5 from cn.

6/6 LC Sl 6 stitches to cn and hold in front, k6, k6 from cn.

6/6 RC Sl 6 stitches to cn and hold in back, k6, k6 from cn.

6/6 LC dec Sl 6 stitches to cn and hold in front, (k4, k2tog), (ssk, k4) from cn.

K3/2/1 K 3rd st on left-hand needle, then 2nd, then 1st, drop all 3 stitches from needle.

m1P (make 1 purlwise) Insert left-hand needle under the horizontal strand between last st and next st, p through back loop of this strand.

M2 (make 2) Insert left-hand needle under the horizontal strand between last st and next st, k in front and back loop of this strand.

LT K the 2nd st from the back leaving both stitches on the needle, then k the first st and drop both stitches.

RT K the 2nd st from the front leaving both stitches on the needle, then k the first st and drop both stitches.

Techniques

KNITTING

3-Needle Bind-off

Step 1: With the right side of the two pieces facing each other, and the needles parallel, insert a third needle knitwise into the first stitch of each needle, wrap the yarn around the needle as if to knit, as shown. Knit these two stitches together and slip them off the needles.

Step 2: Knit the next two stitches together in the same way as in Step 1.

Step 3: Slip the first stitch on the third needle over the second stitch and off the needle.

Repeat steps 2 and 3 across the row until all the stitches are bound off.

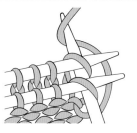

Knitted Cast-on

Place a slipknot on the left needle if there are no established stitches. With the right needle, knit into the first stitch (or slipknot) on left needle (A) and place the new stitch onto the left needle (B). With the right needle, knit into the last stitch made on the left needle and place the new stitch onto the left needle. Repeat Step 2 for desired number of stitches to cast on (C).

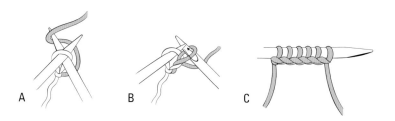

CROCHET

Single Crochet

Step 1: Keeping working yarn behind the work, insert the crochet hook into the second chain from the hook (A).

Step 2: Yarn over (wrap the yarn around the hook into the hook opening). Pull the hook and yarn on hook through the loop (B). Now there are two loops on the hook.

Step 3: Bring yarn over the hook again, and draw hook and yarn through both loops (C).

Step 4: Only one loop remains on the hook (D). This completes the single crochet stitch.

Chain stitch

Make a slip knot and slip over the crochet hook. Wrap the yarn around the hook and pull through the loop (A). You have made one chain (B). Make subsequent chains by wrapping the yarn around the hook and pulling through each loop (C).

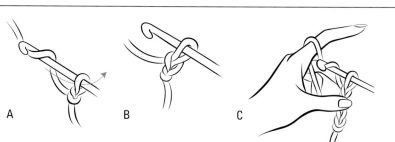

Slip stitch

Insert the hook into a chain or other stitch, wrap the yarn around the hook, and then draw the yarn through both the stitch and the loop already on the hook.

EMBROIDERY

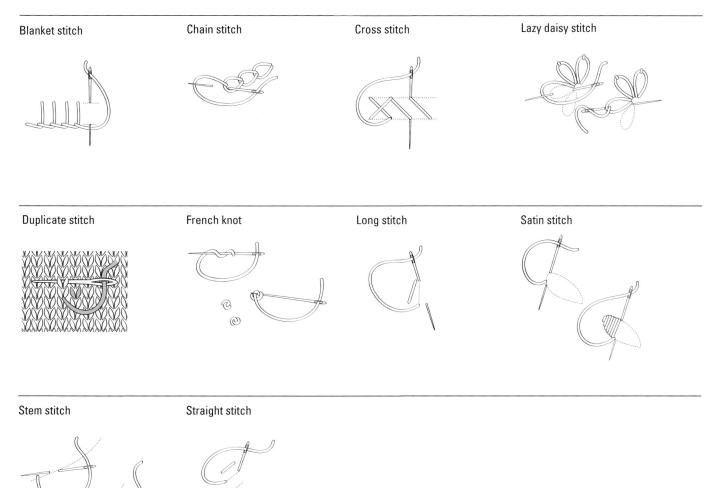

Blanket stitch

Chain stitch

Cross stitch

Lazy daisy stitch

Duplicate stitch

French knot

Long stitch

Satin stitch

Stem stitch

Straight stitch

Abbreviations and Techniques

MAKE BOBBLE

Make five stitches in one stitch as follows: [knit the stitch in the front loop and then knit in the back loop without slipping it from the left needle] twice, knit in the front loop once more. Slip the stitch from the left needle.

Turn the work and purl these five stitches, turn Then work and knit five. Do this twice.

With the left needle, pull the second, third, fourth and fifth stitches, one at a time over the first stitch and off the needle. One stitch remains and one bobble has been made.

COLOR STRANDING/FAIR ISLE

Stranding one-handed:

On the knit side, drop the working yarn. Bring the new color (now the working yarn) over the top of the dropped yarn and work to the next color change.

Drop the working yarn. Bring the new color under the dropped yarn and work to the next color change. Repeat these two steps.

On the purl side, drop the working yarn. Bring the new color (now the working yarn) over the top of the dropped yarn and work to the next color change.

Drop the working yarn. Bring the new color under the dropped yarn and work to the next color change. Repeat these two steps.

Stranding two-handed:

On the knit side, hold the working yarn in your right hand and the non-working yarn in your left hand. Bring the working yarn over the top of the yarn in your left hand and knit with the right hand to the next color change.

The yarn in your right hand is now the non-working yarn, the yarn in your left hand is the working yarn. Bring the working yarn under the non-working yarn and knit with the left hand needle to the next color change. Repeat these two steps.

On the purl side, hold the working yarn in your right hand and the non-working yarn in your left hand. Bring the working yarn over the top of the yarn in your left hand and purl with the right hand to the next color change.

The yarn in your right hand is now the non-working yarn, the yarn in your left hand is the working yarn. Bring the working yarn under the non-working yarn and purl with the left hand needle to the next color change. Repeat these two steps.

CIRCULAR KNITTING ON DOUBLE-POINTED NEEDLES

Cast on required number of stitches on the first needle, plus one extra. Slip extra stitch to next needle as shown. Continue in this way, casting on the required number of stitches on the needles (or cast on all stitches onto one needle, then divide them evenly over the other needles).

Arrange needles with cast-on edge facing center of triangle or square, make sure not to twist the stitches.

Place a stitch marker after the last cast-on stitch. With the free needle, knit the first cast-on stitch, pull the yarn tightly. Continue knitting rounds, slipping the marker before beginning each round.

I-CORD

Using two double-pointed needles, cast on three to five stitches.

*Knit one row on RS. Without turning the work, slip the stitches to the right end of needle to work the next row on the RS. Repeat from * until desired length. Bind off.

INTARSIA

On the knit side, drop the old color. Pick up the new color from under the old color and knit to the next color change.

On the purl side, drop the old color. Pick up the new color from under the old color and put to the next color change.
Repeat these two steps.

Resources

Berroco, Inc.
14 Elmdale Road
P.O. Box 367
Uxbridge, MA 01569
(508) 278-2527
www.berroco.com

Cascade Yarns
1224 Andover Park East
Tukwila, WA 98188
www.cascadeyarns.com

Jade Sapphire Exotic Fibres
(866) 857-3897
www.jadesapphire.com

JHB
1955 South Quince Street
Denver, CO 80231
(800) 525-9007
www.buttons.com

Leisure Arts
www.leisurearts.com

Lion Brand Yarn
34 West 15th Street
New York, NY 10011
www.lionbrand.com

Louet North America
808 Commerce Park Drive
Ogdensburg, NY 13669
In Canada:
R.R. 4
Prescott, Ontario K0E 1T0
Canada
www.louet.com

Tilli Tomas
(617) 524-3330
www.tillitomas.com

Charities to Knit For

The following organizations, charities, and foundations love blocks and block projects. Make sure you contact them in advance and ask what items they need, and if they have any special requirements.

Afghans for Afghans
c/o AFSC Collection Center
65 Ninth Street
San Francisco, CA 94103
www.afghansforafghans.org

Binky Patrol
c/o Carolyn Berndt
19065 Ridgeview Road
Villa Park, CA 92861
(503) 214-8346

Blankets for Canada Society
210A – 12 'A' St No, Suite 217
Lethbridge, Alberta
Canada, T1H 2J1
(403) 329-6586
www.blankets4canada.ca

Heartmade Blessings
13 Hawthorne Drive
Durham NC 27712
www.heartmadeblessings.org

Head Huggers
1006 Auckland Way
Chester, MD 21619
(410) 643-5767
www.headhuggers.org

Helping Hands Foundation, Inc.
1100-H Brandywine Boulevard
Zanesville, OH 43701-7303
(740) 452-4541
www.needleartsmentoring.com

Hilton Head Heroes
27 Rusty Rail Lane
Hilton Head Island, SC
   29926-2560
www.hhheroes.com

Knit-a-Square
Soweto Comfort Club
Private Bag X900
Bryanston 2021
South Africa
www.knit-a-square.com

Knit for the Cure
Susan G. Komen for the Cure
1000 East Walnut Street
Suite 123
Pasadena, CA 91106-2426

Project Linus
Project Linus National
   Headquarters
P.O. Box 5621
Bloomington, IL 61702-5621
(309) 664-7814
www.projectlinus.org

Snuggles Project
Hugs for Homeless Animals
P.O. Box 320245
Franklin, WI 53132-6031
(888) 483-8180
www.snugglesproject.org

Warm Up America!
Craft Yarn Council of America
469 Hospital Drive, 2nd Floor,
   Suite E
Gastonia, NC 28054
(704) 824-7838
www.warmupamerica.org

Acknowledgments

Many thanks to:

The Potter Craft staff, including my supportive editor Betty Wong, art director extraordinaire Chi Ling Moy, senior development editor Erica Smith, and the entire staff who have worked so hard to make this book a blockbuster.

Rose Callahan, whose eye for beautiful fashion photography is unsurpassed. Heather Weston for the amazing block photography.

My blockbuster knitters: Eileen Curry, Nancy Henderson, Dianne Weitzul, Claire Brenner, Jo Brandon, Sue Colistra, Mary Taylor, Eva Wilken, Esther Weinstock, Ana Joaquina Montalvo de Morales, Lucia Simon de Casis, Renay Leone, and Heris Stenzel.

My intrepid instruction writers: Nancy Henderson, Rita Greenfeder, Eve Ng. Jeannie Chin and Frances Soohoo for the charts and illustrations.

Jean Dunbabin at Cascade Yarns for her lovely yarns and to all the other generous yarn companies listed in the resource pages.

My special "blockhead" friends: Emily Brenner, Jo Brandon, Jenni Stone, Samantha Dornfeld, Chris Kitch, David Farrow, Leigh Merryfield, Keely Brandon, and to Allison Korleski for her friendship and support.

My father Benjamin Quinones, who perked my interest in blocks at an early age, and my mother Carmela, who bought me tinker toys and wooden blocks.

And finally thanks to my husband Howard, the biggest blockhead of all.

About the Author

Beloved knitwear designer **Nicky Epstein** is the bestselling author of numerous books, including *Knitting on Top of the World*, *Knitting on the Edge*, and *Knitting a Kiss in Every Stitch*. Her designs have also been featured in *Vogue Knitting* magazine and many other knitting publications, on television, and at art exhibitions. She currently resides in New York City and travels extensively, teaching and lecturing.

Index Note: Page numbers in italics indicate photos.